942

HOARE. Sir R.C.

H22 743 161 3

(THOMPSON,
M.W. (ED.)

The Journeys of
Sir Richard

Please renew/return this item by the last date shown.

So that your telephone call is charged at local rate,
please call the numbers as set out below:

	From Area codes 01923 or 0208:	From the rest of Herts:
Renewals:	01923 471373	01438 737373
Enquiries:	01923 471333	01438 737333
Minicom:	01923 471599	01438 737599

L32b

D1610284

The Journeys of
Sir Richard Colt Hoare

through Wales and England 1793–1810

Portraits by S. Woodforde in 1795 of Colt Hoare (aged 37) and his son, Henry (aged 11).

The Journeys of Sir Richard Colt Hoare

through Wales and England 1793–1810

Extracted from the Journals and edited
with an Introduction by

M. W. Thompson

ALAN SUTTON
1983

Alan Sutton Publishing Limited
17a Brunswick Road
Gloucester GL1 1HG

First published 1983

ISBN 0-86299-049-1

Typesetting and origination by
Alan Sutton Publishing Limited.
Photoset Garamond 10/11.
Printed in Great Britain

These ancient buildings may be called the guides and landmarks of history. They animate the artist's picture and often induce the tourist to trace their origin, their architecture, their history; by them he by degrees gains a daily knowledge of his country. Independent of the amusement and resources it affords the love of drawing has many essential advantages. The Man of Taste, gifted with a picturesque eye, views every object with a double pleasure: every tint, every shadow, in short every object in nature affords employment to his mind. Nothing remains to him unobserved for even in the dullest of countries something may be learnt by the steady observance of nature.

Colt Hoare, 1800.

PREFACE

Having catalogued the papers of General Pitt-Rivers at Salisbury and written his biography it was perhaps inevitable that I should be attracted by the volumes of journals of a much earlier antiquary, Sir Richard Colt Hoare, which after the sale of the Stourhead Library found their way to the Cardiff City Library. An added attraction was that Sir Richard's travels took him not only to Wales but to England into the Midlands and North as far as Durham, coinciding roughly with the area in which I had been concerned for many years with the preservation of ancient monuments. Sir Richard took the same roads, visited the same monuments, the same towns and even the same inns as I visited 160-80 years later!

I would have shrunk from such a daunting task as transcription of this large body of material had I not received encouragement from Colt Hoare's biographer, Mr Kenneth Woodbridge, with whom I passed a pleasant day at Bath. He had been over this ground himself and was able to lend me notes that proved of great value.

At an early stage it became clear, firstly, that a great deal of the journals was not suitable for publication. For example the 'ardor for monumental antiquities' of Hoare meant that increasing numbers of pages were devoted to tomb descriptions which one would not seek to inflict on the modern reader. The descriptions of scenery could be of intolerable length. Secondly it was evident that the topographical value of the journals was much less than supposed; usually more information is available in contemporary or slightly later published sources. I decided therefore drastically to limit the scale of the project by in effect reducing it to extracts covering the whole period. The discovery that the folio volumes were a later precis of the original record was a further complicating factor. Although the work still has topographical value its chief interest is biographical, in an area not covered by Woodbridge, the powerful influence of the cult of the picturesque on an individual, the starting point for the great Wiltshire projects. At a time when many others, like Turner and Wordsworth, were subject to the same influences there is a social aspect to this study. Hoare did much to promote the cult of Giraldus, one of his most permanent influences on the Welsh scene. I hope therefore that this shortened version of the journals will be of interest to the general reader as well as the historian and antiquary.

No work of this kind can be undertaken without the assistance of others. I am deeply grateful to the South Glamorgan County Council for allowing use of the manuscripts, and to their County Librarian, Mr G.A.C. Dart, for advice on problems connected with them. His staff have cheerfully produced the volumes the many scores of times they were needed. I have referred to the invaluable help from Colt Hoare's biographer, Mr Kenneth Woodbridge. Mr D. Moore, Keeper of Prints at the National Library of Wales in Aberystwyth has helped by listing Hoare's drawings in the collections under his charge. Mr P.H. Humphries has assisted with photo-

graphy. Lastly I must not omit the publishers without whose bold willing-
ness to undertake such a non-commercial project all my labours would have
come to nought.

M.W. Thompson
Cardiff, 1982.

CONTENTS

LIST OF ILLUSTRATIONS WITH ACKNOWLEDGEMENT

Apart from the frontispiece, which is a photograph of the Stourhead portrait reproduced by courtesy of the National Trust all the drawings reproduced in this book are the work of Colt Hoare himself, and even the map in figure 4 has been taken from his work of 1806. Grateful acknowledgement is made to the National Library of Wales for permission to use the original pen-and-ink drawings (Nos. 1, 3, 5, 6, 7, 12, 13, 15, 25, 26, 27, 28, 29, 30, 32, 33, 34, 38, 39, 40) and to South Glamorgan County Council for the use of pencil drawings (Nos. 11, 16, 17, 18, 23, 37). The other figures reproduce the contemporary prints of Hoare's drawings either in Coxe 1801 (Nos. 2, 19, 20, 21) or in Hoare, 1806 (Nos. 4, 8, 9, 10, 14, 22, 24, 31, 35, 36). Where the date of the original drawing is known it has been put in brackets.

INTRODUCTION

'Sir Richard's house, Stourhead, is shewn with the exception of his library to which no persons are admitted but through particular recommendation'.[1] So the Bishop of Salisbury warned the diarist Farington when he gave him a letter of introduction to Colt Hoare in September, 1809. According to his modern biographer this library 'was Colt Hoare's most significant contribution to the culture of his time'.[2] The building itself, erected by Hoare as one of a pair of new wings to the earlier house, together with the beautiful wooden fittings (shelves, desk, steps, stands etc) commissioned from Chippendale, still survive in the care of the National Trust and are on public view, but the books it contained have, alas, been largely dispersed. Fortunately we know of its contents from a catalogue compiled just after Hoare's death,[3] and from the Sotheby's sales catalogues of 1883 and 1887.[4]

Sir Richard had already given a Classical book collection to the British Museum during his lifetime but the Stourhead library ranged not only over the Classics but far beyond into history, topography, numismatics, natural history, grammars, dictionaries (particularly of Welsh, Gaelic and Breton) and so on. It was the topographical collection that was the remarkable feature, probably being as near comprehensive for the British Isles as it was possible to achieve at that time. It was a library of printed books, the exceptions being his own voluminous journals, notes and drawings, or drawings commissioned by him. In the section on the General Topography of Wales were two sets of autograph journals of tours in England, Wales and Ireland,[5] five in folio and six in quarto in their original leather bindings. In the Sotheby's catalogues of 1883 and 1887 these two sets re-appear respectively as lots 780 and 928, and 585 and 642.

There can be no reasonable doubt but that these correspond to the two sets of Hoare manuscripts (MS.3.127 and MS.4.302) in the Cardiff City Library, now South Glamorgan County Library. The Library in 1887 had bought 'a few manuscripts, several prints and a collection of drawings of great local interest, made at the end of the last century by Sir Richard Colt Hoare, Bart.',[6] but there seems reasons to doubt that these included these two sets.[7] However they have certainly been there since the inter-war period.

The quarto volumes are as described in the last century but the folio volumes have undergone major change since 1887. First a small folio (MS.4.302. 6/6), a neatly written version of the 1793 journal (probably not by Hoare), has been added. Secondly the volumes are in modern binding, the pages with blackened edges having been remounted in a major repair after a fire. In the rebinding the original chronological order, as set out in 1840, has been lost, a source of confusion ever since.

Comparison of the folio volumes with the quarto volumes leaves no doubt that both were written by Sir Richard himself but the quartos were written during the journeys, on the road, while the folios are condensed versions written some years later, re-arranged in chronological order and omitting the 1806 journal for Ireland (already published in 1807), no doubt with the intention of publication. Hoare did this with some of the Italian journals of even earlier date.[8] Although the texts of the quarto volumes were written on the road, and so have a decided immediacy about them, the bindings were put on later, presumably starting in 1801 with volume I, which no doubt accounts for them being out of chronological order.

Because they were written at the time of the event I have chosen to use the quarto volumes except for the small piece in 1808 where there is only a record in the folio volumes. They have been drastically reduced by omission to perhaps a third or quarter of the original. Hoare used the facing back of each page as a place for later notes if required: when I have included the note it has been in square brackets in the text. Interpolations by the editor are in italics in square brackets. The punctuation, paragraphs and capitals are modern but I have tried to retain variations in spelling. Abbreviations have often been expanded.

Hundreds of drawings by Hoare survive both from his Italian and British journeys. In the case of Wales he published over a hundred in the translation of Giraldus and the works by Coxe and Fenton. I have selected some pen-and-ink drawings from the large collection in the National Library at Aberystwyth together with a few pencil sketches from Cardiff to illustrate this book, and also some reproductions of those already published.

The Man

Sir Richard Colt Hoare (1758-1838) has, together with his grandfather, Henry Hoare (1705-1785), been the subject of a detailed and admirable biography by Mr K. Woodbridge,[9] so that it is unnecessary for me to do more than draw attention to the salient points of his life.

The family wealth derived from a merchant bank in the City (which still exists) founded in the 17th century. The house at Stourhead, Wiltshire, had been erected by Henry Hoare (1677-1725) and the famous lake and temples established by his son. He chose as successor to the property the grandson of his younger brother, Richard Colt Hoare, who inherited Stourhead through his mother's side and his baronetcy (he was second baronet) through his father, a nephew of Henry Hoare. Colt Hoare's wife Hester bore him a son, Henry, but after her death in 1785 he went to the Continent 'to alleviate his mind by travel'. Apart from a brief return to England he spent almost six years on the Continent, mainly in Italy, finally returning in 1791 when 'continental war put a stop to these projects'.[10]

Thereafter he took up permanent residence at Stourhead, building the flanking wings for his picture gallery and his library. As a kind of substitute for Continental travel he spent a long period in most summers between 1793 and 1813 on tours of Wales. The records of these journeys are the subject of this book. The latter part of his life was devoted to antiquarian researches:

first with William Cunnington on excavating barrows in Wiltshire, publishing the results in the two volumes of the *Ancient History of Wiltshire* (1812–19), and then on the parish histories of the county in the *History of Modern Wiltshire* (1822–44, completed after his death). The two works, together with the library already mentioned and his translation from Latin of the *Itinerary* of Archbishop Baldwin and *Description* of Wales by Giraldus Cambrensis (used in subsequent popular editions and so known to tens of thousands of readers) are his claims to fame.

The author of our diaries then was a mature man aged between 35 and 52, and a widower with a young son (born 1784) who sometimes accompanied him on his journeys. He made drawings and indeed conceived of himself as primarily an artist in 1793, although during the period of the journals antiquarian interests became paramount as we shall see. He was an extremely methodical, serious-minded and industrious man with financial resources that allowed him freedom to travel and execute the major schemes of scholarship to which he turned his mind.

The Background to the Journal

Sir Richard reveals (p. 55) that he had made previous visits to Wales without keeping a journal, presumably before his long sojourn on the Continent. He kept a meticulous record of the latter, and apart from what he published himself a mass of unpublished journals survive in the Wiltshire County Record Office. At the beginning of the published journal of his vist to Ireland in 1806 he gave a clue as to his reason for keeping it: '. . . let me endeavor to impress on the minds of the younger part of my readers the great utility of keeping a Journal. It is even useful at home to note down daily occurrences, but infinitely more so abroad; it assists the mind in recollecting passed scenes and improves it by describing them; and by causing observation it enforces instruction.'[11]

The journal is then an impersonal and serious work; there is no question of an intimate diary like that of Dorothy Wordsworth or Parson Woodforde. It begins as abruptly with the journey as it ends equally abruptly with its conclusion. Normally conversations are not mentioned and sometimes we do not even know if Sir Richard had a travelling companion with him! Impressions made by what was seen, particularly scenery and landscape and antiquities, were the main concern.

The tradition of recording a journey is a very old one going back to Leland and William of Worcester; Daniel Defoe's Tour in the early 18th century became very popular. The 'tourists' of the later 18th century were particularly prone to recording their experiences in journals. Hoare was well experienced in journal writing from his younger days in Italy, but in Wales there are some half dozen works that particularly influenced both his journeys and the journals recording them.

Sir Richard quotes from Thomas Gray's brief 'Journal in the Lakes' when he visited Gordale Scar, which clearly prompted him to go there.[12] The unusual setting out of the 1800 journal starting each day with an account of the weather probably owes something to Gray, although his was not, I think, a major influence.

William Gilpin had made his brief visit to the River Wye and South Wales in 1770 and published his 'Observations . . . relative chiefly to Picturesque Beauty' in 1782.[13] He followed it up with similar works on other areas and his *Essays on the Picturesque* were published in 1792,[14] the year before Hoare's journals start. Both men sketched and we may suppose that Gilpin's influence on Hoare was considerable, although he never mentioned Gilpin's name. We must return to this theme later.

Thomas Pennant (1726-98) was a scientist, a naturalist, of European repute and unlike the others with whom we are concerned, except Fenton, was a native Welshman from near Holywell in Flintshire. He was a much keener observer than Hoare, both of nature and antiquities. He published in 1772 his *Tour of Scotland in 1769*, which received high praise from Dr Johnson leading to a quarrel with Bishop Price.[15] Another tour in 1772 covered the Hebrides, with illustrations by Moses Griffiths 'an untaught genius, drawn from the most remote and obscure parts of North Wales'. Pennant subsequently made tours of some English counties and London, but out concern here is his *Tour of Wales*, published in two volumes in 1778 and 1784[16] which had a second edition in his lifetime (like Gilpin Pennant was succesful commercially). It started from his home but characteristically for a North Welshman he did not feel able to cover South Wales. The work is frequently quoted by Hoare when he was in North Wales although it can hardly have influenced his decision to go to South Wales in 1793. He himself regarded it as a model for is own work on Giraldus.[17]

Probably the most important influence was Henry Penruddocke Wyndham (1736-1819), a fellow Wiltshireman and, although of an older generation, a personal friend. Wyndham was variously Mayor of Salisbury, Sheriff and Member of Parliament for Wiltshire. Like Hoare he had been to Italy, as far south as Sicily, and in 1774 and 1777 to Wales. His *Tour through Monmouthshire and Wales* was published in 1781. Like Sir Richard he used Giraldus as a guide and his tour, following a clockwise direction around Wales resembled that of Archbishop Baldwin. His advice and library had been available to Coxe for the Monmouthshire Tour and no doubt for Hoare also, whose own library perhaps owed something to this example.[18] Wyndham's book was described by Hoare as 'the first tour I recollect to have seen that merits either credit or attention'.[19]

Two medieval writers on Wales, used both by Wyndham and Hoare and first published by David Powel in 1584 and 1585, deserve notice here. 'The History of Cambria' had four sources: an original chronicle by Caradoc of Llancarfan up to 1156, its continuation at Strata Florida and Aberconwy abbeys up to 1270, both translated into English with a continuation by Humphrey Llwyd, and finally additions by Powel himself.[20] New editions continued to appear from 1584 onwards, and the 1774 edition, no doubt that used by Hoare, had a figure of the Chief Druid with long beard, holding mistletoe and a book in one hand, and a staff in the other, on the title page, a fair indication of the associations aroused by the subject.

Giraldus de Barri or the Welshman, the prolific writer of the late 12th and early thirteenth centuries, the unsuccessful seeker of the see of St Davids, is a dominating figure in Welsh history. Powel had seen the topographical interest of his account of the journey through Wales in 1188 by Archbishop Baldwin seeking recruits for the third crusade, and had published it together with the Description of Wales by same author in 1585. It was of course in Latin. Hoare had no doubt learnt of its value as a guidebook from Wyndham and he was using it in 1793. It became almost an obsession, and after publishing a revised Latin edition of Powel in 1804 (including the second book of the Description, *De Illaudabalibus Walliae*, omitted by Powel!) he published the large two-volume English translation in 1806 to which we must shortly return.

On the Road

As we might expect from such a methodical man as Sir Richard he prepared himself thoroughly for the journey. The catalogue of his library itemises four small volumes, dated 1793, of material on castles and abbies in north and south Wales 'extracted from various authors', evidently a preparation for the first journey.[21] He was clearly well-supplied with maps and guide-books on the journey. Moreover as he was normally accompanied by a local guide, usually the landlord of the inn, he tended to be exceptionally well-informed about objects encountered *en route*.

Sir Richard did not journey on foot like George Borrow, or on horseback like Leland, or by public transport like the Wordsworths, but in his own vehicle, a chaise, either hired or his own. For day excursions from the inn or short journeys he rode. The advantages of a chaise were the same as with a modern motor car: ample luggage could be carried and the vehicle provided shelter from the rain, an important consideration in Wales. A driver was required and Sir Richard always had a servant with him, while the horse or horses had to be changed at post houses. A full travelling day fell into three parts: early rise to breakfast on the road, say three hours; up to dinner at three o'clock, say four hours; and another three hours before reaching the inn for tea. Dinner in the early afternoon instead of evening broke up the day differently to what would be case today. The turnpike roads made fairly swift travel possible and the speeds and distances covered were comparable to those of a modern cyclist. 70 or 80 miles could be covered in a day but the itineraries in the journals show that Hoare usually had stages of only 15 miles or so between the places he visited.

There is much information about inns in the diaries. Apart from the normal coaching inns there was a lower grade of inn, the 'single house'; I take it a converted private house. For long stays, as at Cheltenham, he would take lodgings for himself and his servant. The descriptions of the stays at the Spa towns of Cheltenham and Harrogate are among the most interesting in the journals. The use of the word 'hotel' is another subject of interest. Hoare may speak of 'the hotel, a good inn'. The 'tourists' had created a demand for a standard of comfort higher than that of the ordinary traveller's inn. Lord Uxbridge had built an hotel at Caernarfon (now the Royal Hotel) to cater for just that need (p. 70), and the itinerary for 1799 shows that hotels existed in some large towns. Usually they were purpose-built establishments with grander accomodation and there was not more than one in a town (Hereford seems to have been an exception).

Rather than moving constantly from inn to inn it would be simpler to create a permanent base in Wales from which excursions could be made on horseback. Hoare took a particular liking to Bala Lake as early as 1796 (p. 62) and spent two or three weeks there each year. In 1799 two inns are mentioned at Bala in the itinerary so he still had to rely on them for accomodation. Evidently the idea of constructing himself a summer retreat overlooking Lake Bala was prompted by what he saw of similar residences constructed in some numbers on the English lakes when he visited there in the following summer (p. 129ff.). As an admirer of the picturesque and an environmentalist he disliked conspicuous houses and was particularly struck by the low structure of Lord Gordon overlooking Derwent (p. 135). Accordingly he chose a site on the east side of Lake Bala, 'Fach Ddeilliog' ('Leafy Nook') where the hillside could be dug out (below an older building) to create a level platform on which his one-storey bungalow-style building (fig. 1) was erected. At the back the ground surface is level with the roof but at the front the lake is faced by a verandah of cast-iron columns sheltering the sash-windows behind, a large bow window projecting from the middle. It had a corridor at the rear linking the five rooms each with its own fireplace and chimney with a cast-iron pot. The addition of two-storeyed transverse wings at either end at a later date has altered the external appearance of Fach Ddeilliog but the internal arrangements are very clear in what is now the dining room and lounge of a motel. Hoare did not set a fashion for the building is curiously isolated on the east side of the lake. Richard Fenton has left us a vivid description of the 'elegant villa', probably written in 1802:

> 'On the south side of the lake, embosomed with wood on an elbow of the hill, prettily recessed at the head of a lawn gradually inclining to the margin of the lake, and having in front the fine range of the Arrenig Mountains, stands the villa of Sir Richard Hoare, who we heard was there: so we took the liberty of calling. We found him with a gentle-man, a friend of his of similar pursuits. They were just going to take their usual evening diversion of perch fishing in a commodious boat belonging to the baronet. We were pressed to join them, and had we not had sport the luxury of the scene would have amply gratified us. There was not a breeze to ripple the azure mirror of the lake, in which

1. 'Fach Ddeilliog'-bungalow-style house with verandah facing Lake Bala erected by Hoare as an unobtrusive Summer retreat.

the inverted landscape was beautifully shewn, and its boundaries charmingly gilded by the setting sun'.[22]

Nature and the Picturesque

The description just quoted of Fach Ddeilliog shows us at once what it was that attracted Hoare to Wales: the scenery of mountains, trees and water. One's first impression of the Journals is indeed of interminable descriptions of views and an indiscriminate use of hyperbole and superlatives to describe them. No hill or mountain was too high to climb to see the view. One feels indeed that he was intoxicated with the landscape. No doubt an intense feeling for nature was a characteristic trait of the period and deliberately cultivated. There was clearly much common ground between Hoare and the Wordsworths, but with the former there was a contrived and artificial stance to which we must now turn out attention.

While no two people held exactly the same opinions there was a conventional view that clearly formed the basis of Hoare's attitude to the scenery around him. The gradations of aesthetic experience that had started with Edmund Burke's *Inquiry into the Sublime and Beautiful*[23] had been extended by the insertion of the Picturesque. The Sublime was rarely encountered by Hoare and indeed in view of the terror that according to Burke it produced this was perhaps just as well. Gordale Scar (p. 128) is the most interesting case. Sometimes when Hoare seeks overhanging rocks that are about to fall (p. 190), to induce the sublime as it were, the absurdity of the notion is only too apparent.

The Picturesque is a different matter. Theoretically it meant training the eye from the landscape as represented by certain French or Italian painters so as to see similar features in nature. Hoare was a collector and authority on paintings and just occasionally actually notices direct resemblances, as at Denbigh where he made the apt comparison with Poussin (p. 173). It must be remembered that he was an artist, his main object being to sketch, so that like the photographer today he was concerned with best view of the subject; that is literally a picturesque or drawable view (p.256).

However response to the picturesque was something that went very much deeper with Sir Richard. Scenes were almost measured by their degree of picturesqueness. A cathedral without tombs, like Peterborough, lost greatly in picturesqueness and so value. Chepstow Castle was more picturesque than Raglan Castle. He was entranced by Conwy Castle from first sight, but Caernarfon he virtually ignored before 1810 because of its lack of picturesque quality. It was almost an ultimate measure of aesthetic value.

We have seen that the first journal was written in the year following the appearance of Gilpin's *Essays on the Picturesque* (p. 16). Hoare did not return to Wales for three years until 1796 and it was possibly the outburst of interest in the Picturesque during the intervening period that prompted him to renew the tours. In 1794 Uvedale Price published his *Essays on the*

Picturesque and Payne Knight *The Landscape*, a poem on the same subject
dedicated to Price. Both men had estates on the Welsh borders and Price had
built a castellated house on the front at Aberystwyth (on which Hoare com-
mented in 1796, p. 63). Wales and the Marches evidently played a big part in
the thinking about the picturesque. Gilpin had been a schoolmaster and had
to look to natural landscape, but his two supporters were landowners and
used the picturesque to attack the work of the 'improvers' of landscape,
particularly Capability Brown. It need hardly be added that the improvers
replied.[24] Hoare as the owner of Stourhead lake and grounds had an interest
in landscape gardening, and has a lot say when he visited other people's on
the tours, usually of a very critical nature. The journals leave no doubt that he
took a keen interest in the subject and was steeped in the literature of the
picturesque.

Probably the most coherent account of the 'picturesque' is that given by
Uvedale Price in his first volume. Variety and intricacy are the essential
elements of the picturesque:[25] 'intricacy in the disposition and variety in the
forms, the tints, and the lights and shadows of objects, are the characteristics
of picturesque scenery: so monotony and baldness are the great defects of
improved places'. One can see why mountains and trees were so dear to
lovers of the picturesque. It required a kind of exaggeration of certain
characteristics: the lion's mane makes it picturesque, as do the antlers of the
stag. 'A temple or palace of Grecian architecture in its perfect, entire state,
and with its surface and colour smooth and even, either in painting or
reality, is beautiful; in ruin it is picturesque. . . . Gothic architecture is
generally considered as more picturesque, though less beautiful than Grecian;
and upon the same principle that a ruin is more so than a new edifice'.[26]
Gothic architecture and ruins were *ipso facto* picturesque.

The point is a crucial one for understanding the journals. Hoare's prime
interest in a ruin was the aesthetic pleasure that it gave him; that is why he
drew it. He did not try to survey it or make a ground plan, except a rough
sketch. This brings us to what we may regard as the text for this book.

The response to picturesqueness is curiosity: 'Those who have felt the
excitement produced by the intricacies of wild romantic mountainous scenes
can tell how curiosity while it prompts us to scale every rocky promontory,
to explore every new recess, by its active agency keep the fibres to their full
tone: and thus picturesqueness when mixed with either of the other characters
corrects the languor of beauty, or the tension of sublimity. . . . It is the
coquetry of nature. . . . Again by its variety, its intricacy, its partial conceal-
ment, its excites the active curiosity which gives play to the mind, loosening
those bonds, with which astonishment chains up its faculties'.[27]

It might have been the picturesque, aesthetic quality of the ruin or barrow
which attracted Hoare in the first place but for the active mind curiosity
became the overpowering sensation. To satisfy this curiosity quite unpicturesque methods might be necessary, such as the exploration by
excavation of barrows that followed Hoare's meeting with Cunnington
(p. 161). We can see this in the journals: the aesthetic response to the

2. Blaenavon Ironworks with the furnaces in operation.

picturesque turning to curiosity about the picturesque object, a change from sketching to exploration, from the artist to the antiquary. Hoare always had a predilection for the ancient but its picturesque quality did not satisfy the curiosity that had been aroused; the artist was drawn more and more into becoming the antiquary and archaeologist.

The Early Industrial Revolution

No traveller in the areas reached by Hoare could at that time have ignored the activities of the early Industrial Revolution. Although Sir Richard did not like the noise and bustle in the inns he stayed at in commercial towns, as we might expect, his rather puritanical temperament approved of industry. One of the most striking passages in the diaries is where he compares the similar topographical position of Halifax and Bath in deep hollows, but contrasts the honest labour that was the foundation of the former and the dissipation of the latter (p. 154–5).

On the whole natural scenery is static except for the movement of water and clouds. Waterfalls had a particular fascination for Hoare as they did for the Wordsworths. Industrial activity could produce not only movement but also noise, smoke and flame. All the tourists were fascinated by blast furnaces, and Hoare described those at Blaenavon making the contrast with the peace and quiet of his usual ruins (p. 98) and drew them for Coxe.[28] The 'railed roads' for removing the iron pigs with the 'carts' racing down the gradients controlled by a brake man also fascinated him (p. 97).

The scale of industrial structures also impressed our traveller, notably the great cloth halls at Halifax and Leeds (p. 123). He found the cast-iron bridge at Ironbridge rather too spindly to be picturesque (p. 167). His journeys to Bala coincided with erection by Telford of the two great aqueducts near Chirk on the Ellesmere canal. He was greatly impressed by Telford's masterpiece at Pontcysyllte enhanced by the wooded background of the Dee valley; how he reacted to its completion with iron trough is not known. His visits also coincided with the great reclamations taking place at what is now Porthmadog by W.A. Maddocks culminating in the closure of the estuary by the present causeway (p. 190).

Two extractive industries seem to have made the greatest impression, since their picturesque quality outdid nature. In 1800 he descended in a bucket into a Cheshire salt mine (p. 159) and the glinting of the myriads of salt crystals made a deep impression. They tended to overshadow the experience of the sublime that he had had on the same tour at Gordale Scar, and this was even more so the year following when he tells us that the Parys copper mine in north Anglesey caused the experience at 'Maum Tarn' to be rendered almost insignificant (p. 188). Art had indeed triumphed over nature. This experience casts an extremely interesting light on the real nature of the 'sublime' and the 'picturesque'.

3. Chirk aqueduct under construction.

Antiquities

Sir Richard had already shown a predilection for antiquities, Etruscan or
early Christian, when he had been in Italy,[29] but in the Welsh tours it
gradually became the predominant interest, as we can see by comparing the
1793 journal with that of 1810. The association with Cunnington from 1801
was no doubt one major contributory factor, although this perhaps gave his
interests a special twist towards the prehistoric to which he had not been
drawn by his own artistic inclinations. It will be convenient to take the
antiquities chronologically.

Neolithic chambered tombs were encountered by Hoare in West Wales in
his first journey, and 'druidical relicts', *cromlechau* (the normal Welsh
word) or kistvaens (*cistfeini* in Welsh) were often encountered, as also some
circles. I do not think he had anything special to say on them except to
recognise that they in some measure were structures erected in stone corresponding to those in the form of earthworks in Wiltshire (p. 267). This was
even more so with the later remains, particularly the hut circles (*cytiau
Gwyddelod*) of north Wales whose affinity both in date and function with
Romano-British huts in Wiltshire he recognised. He visited a number of
hill-forts and was impressed with their stone construction, but was as often
more struck by the views! I think he was more at ease with finds such as
pottery, axes, gold objects than he was with the field monuments.

In the Roman period he was on much more familiar ground, having just
returned from several years in Italy. Pursuing the course of Roman roads
and indentifying the site and names of Roman forts were fascinating occu-
pations in which he indulged both in Wales and Wiltshire. Inscriptions
needless to say were an important matter. The results of these labours are set
out in the section on Roman Wales in his translation of Giraldus and constitute the first step in the subject, later so ably pursued in this century.

Early Christian remains need not detain us. He certainly mentions crosses
and inscribed stones. The period assumed much greater importance when he
went to Ireland in 1806 and was confronted by the great crosses and round
towers of that country.

Although Hoare did not use our terms for Gothic architecture, standard-
ised a little later than this period, there is no difficulty in following the
descriptions. Broad for 'Decorated' or 'Perpendicular', referring to the
windows, is not inapt. He speaks of groined where we say ribbed, and
fretted where we say 'interlace' or 'panelled'. The main difference is 'Saxon'
for 'Norman'. Wyndham always says Norman and we know from the essay
of Thomas Gray that the real dates were well understood;[30] there is a slight
affectation about *Saxon* suggesting something more barbarous and ancient.
He clearly understood that existing buildings showed evidence of reconstruction at several periods.

The English journey of 1800 had two main objectives: cathedrals and the
lakes. Starting on the east side (Peterborough and Lincoln) he swung west to
the lakes and visited variously York, Ripon, Durham, Lichfield cathedrals,

Kirkstall and Fountains Abbies. He had commissioned Turner to paint Salisbury Cathedral[31] and he no doubt knew most of the others in the south of the country. The Gothic buildings in Wales were not on the same scale. St Davids Cathedral he went to more than once with the main description in 1802 and Llandaff, St Asaph and Bangor cathdrals were also visited. He normally went to the church in each place he visited. He also of course visited ruined abbies, particularly Llanthony, Tintern, Margam and Valle Crucis. Wales is better supplied with castles than abbies; he visited all the well-known ones. Of the four famous castles of Edward I in North Wales Conwy was his favourite, about which he waxed lyrical; while Caernafon he did not come to terms with for sometime as we have seen.

His approach was aesthetic; the architecture and situation were his main interest. He had lodged in modern monasteries in France and Italy,[32] so it surprising that he had very little knowledge or interest in function. This can be illustrated by his confusion over the chapter house at Wenlock (p. 168). A special pre-occupation in later years was tombs, effigies and memorials in parish churches but these have been deliberately omitted in this book.

Sir Richard was something of an environmentalist. He speaks quite often of his regrets about woods having been cut down, and his remarks about the aesthetic damage to the castle at Conwy likely to arise from bridging the river at this point have a decidedly modern ring! (p. 181). In fact Telford erected his suspension bridge at this point twenty-five years later. He regrets the falls in the masonry at Margam and Llanthony Abbies and that they were not prevented, and wants remedial treatment at Beaumaris Castle (p. 267). He had strong views on restoration works carried out at St Davids and other cathedrals as Mr Woodbridge has described.[33] The censorious tone of his remarks has a decidedly familiar ring to modern ears!

The 'Historical Tour' and the Translation of Giraldus

The reasons for publishing an account of a tour were varied: the description of the antiquities of the area was uppermost in the mind of Leland, but Defoe or Borrow had very different intentions. The appearance of the 'tourists', forced from the Continent in the late 18th century by the 'demon Revolution', created a demand for a journal that was in effect a guidebook. In the Lake District this was recognised, while the commercial success of the Pennant's tours in both Scotland and Wales is an indication of the demand. Wyndham's *Tour* was written avowedly with the intention of attracting visitors to Wales which he regarded as undervisited,[34] and he specifically decided not to overload the text with historical information. These tours are closely related in their style of excursions to nineteenth century, or indeed, modern guidebooks.

In England the county history, a learned work based on years of research, had been established since the seventeenth century, being associated particularly with Dugdale in Warwickshire. The absence of such a history for

Lincolnshire was particularly noted by Hoare (p. 121), and he spent his later life remedying the same deficiency for his own county in the *History of Modern Wiltshire*. What he tried to do in Wales, and to some extent in Ireland, was to marry up the tour and the county history to produce 'an historical tour' which had some of the qualities of both but did not require the immense scholarly labour of the county history.

The 1793 journey was very much in search of the picturesque going to the Towey and Teifi valleys. In 1796-8 he moved to mid- and then north Wales, but one still has the feeling of a man who lacks a purpose for his journey. The turning point came in 1798 when on returning to Stourhead he found William Coxe waiting for him, and within the same month they set off for Monmouthshire. They were there again in 1799, Hoare doing the drawings for Coxe's *Historical Tour of Monmouthshire* that appeared in 1800.

William Coxe (1747–1828), a Cambridge man and Fellow of King's College had travelled widely in Switzerland and Eastern Europe. He published prolifically, sometimes work of importance. He was presented to the living of Stourton by Hoare and became Archdeacon of Wiltshire in 1804. It is important to remember the subservient position of Coxe in relation to Hoare; the dedication to Hoare in the book tells us that it was 'written at your suggestion and embellished by your pencil'. Probably it was published largely at Hoare's cost. Apart from Sir Richad's drawings it contains a number of original surveys of towns, and Coxe incorporated some interesting statistical information. Based on a few months in the county it could hardly be very profound although it is still certainly of value.

The particular interest is the effect the experience had on Hoare. The English journey of 1800 was the longest yet undertaken, while the three journals for 1800, 1801 and 1802 fill three of the six volumes of journals. The style of writing changed from the telegraphic summaries of the late 1790's to a full text, perhaps now with an eye to possible future publication. The English journey has a curious split in the middle with fresh pagination, recalling that in the *Itinerary* of Giraldus! The decision to publish an edition of Giraldus is first mentioned in 1802 (p. 201). Sir Richard's first publication of any kind was in 1800, a description of the house and grounds at Stourhead: this was followed in 1804 by his fresh edition of Powel's Giraldus[35] amplified as described above.

The reader who has been used to a modern popular edition of Hoare's translation of Giraldus, such as that in Everyman's, may have a shock if he sees the two large volumes that were published by Hoare in 1806.[36] They were not intended to be simply a translation of Powel's work since Hoare had by this time looked at the original manuscripts. There was an introductory section on the Roman conquest of Britain with a map, the most original feature in the book. Like Powel he added 'Annotations' to each chapter in the works of Giraldus, but they were much longer and illustrated by engravings from drawings by himelf or Carter. The work concludes with a section on Gothic architecture and there is a folding map in colour at the end showing the route of Archbishop Baldwin around Wales. It was an ingenious adaptation of an historic journey to the 'historical tour' of the later eighteenth century. It no doubt had serious deficiencies, particularly in the history, but given the original nature of the two works of Giraldus, which deserved a full description, the two volumes do them justice.

Almost immediately upon completing the translation of the *Itinerary* he undertook a tour in Ireland in 1806. This volume (IV) is the only part of the journals in Cardiff library that he published himself,[37] the work appearing in Dublin and London in 1807. In some ways it is the most interesting of the published tours since although he did not call it an 'historical tour' its completed form gives an insight into what he saw as the intention of such a tour. He travelled with his son, crossing from Holyhead to Dublin and spending 23rd June to 1st September in Ireland before returning by the same route. From Dublin he made one trip south to Killarney and another north to the Giant's Causeway. The picturesque clearly still played a big part, and he was probably not a little influenced by the fact that Giraldus had also been there and written about it. The book is proceeded by a long historical account indicating the extent of his reading and concludes with 'General Remarks' on Irish archaeology and indeed Ireland generally and what it has to offer the reader. There is strong guidebook element in the book although we may suspect it was far too learned for the ordinary visitor.

We must now turn to Richard Fenton (1746-1821), or Counsellor Fenton as Hoare called him when he first him in 1793 (p. 45). Born at St Davids Fenton was educated at Haverfordwest, and then went on to London and the Middle Temple. Returning to Wales he practised on the Welsh circuits, living first at Machynlleth and then, during the time of Hoare's journals, at a house he built for himself at Fishguard. He had had a circle of theatrical and literary friends in London and was himself a modest poet and linguist. He had the resources to give up practice in middle age and then had somewhat grandiose proposals for histories of the Welsh counties. This was the common ground with Hoare in which their friendship grew and ripened.

Although they were friends from 1793 Hoare and Fenton did not travel together until 1804. Fenton's accounts of this and subsequent tours with Hoare were extracted from his notebooks and published by John Fisher in 1917. Hoare did not bind the journals from the time when he started travelling with Fenton, except for 1810 in the quarto volume (VI) and 1804 and 1808 in folio volume (III) for which there is no contemporary records. The accounts given by Fenton give the impression of two middle-aged undergraduates riding about Wales! Fenton had also been at Stourhead and on excavations with Cunnington, so they now did occasional digging in Wales. His journal is of quite a different character to that of Hoare with more emphasis on extra-curricular activity, so to speak, such as who was at dinner in the evening and so on. It is much less impersonal and not pre-occupied with the picturesque.

Fenton's *A Historical Tour through Pembrokeshire* was published in 1811. Although its author was a native of the county and it is based certainly on a much deeper knowledge of the area than Coxe had in Monmouthshire, yet it is, I think, less successful. Coxe had an historian's skill and a writer's experience so he is less discursive and rambling than Fenton. Coxe had a better idea of what the reader wanted to know and how to tell him it succinctly. Both books were illustrated by Hoare but Coxe's had its valuable town plans. Fenton's was also dedicated to Hoare to whom the author was 'indebted for its birth to your suggestions, for its maturity to your fostering encouragement, and for its chief embellishments for your fine taste . . . and recollecting the numerous journeys in which we have traced together the vestiges of antiquity . . . the thousand offices of sympathy and benevolence with which you have dissipated the gloom hanging heavily on my mind . . . the friend of my fortune and my life.' Although the wording is effusive it probably gives some indication of the relationship between the two men, as comparison of their two journals for 1810 shows.

Hoare's 1810 journal suggests that some kind of 'Historical Tour' of Caernarvonshire and Anglesey with comprehensive coverage was planned. We have the list of 'iters' *(itinera)* which by analogy with the tour in Pembrokeshire were to be the chapter headings (p. 245). The point that emerges is that it was Hoare who was designing the book and taking the lead, and indeed from Fenton's journal one would hardly know what was intended. Nothing more clearly illustrates how chimerical were Fenton's proposals for a history of the Welsh counties; without the push and drive of Hoare we may doubt whether he would have completed even the Pembrokeshire history.

Although not a tour in the sense that we have used the word the *History of the County of Brecon* by Theophilus Jones, pubished in 1805-09 may owe something to Hoare or more likely Hoare to it. Jones and Hoare met in 1803 (p. 236) when Jones advised Sir Richard on Giraldus, and the other project was no doubt discussed.

Wales and Colt Hoare

If there is a particular Englishman that we associate with Wales it is George Borrow who tramped its hills fifty years after Hoare, and recorded his experiences in 'Wild Wales'. The impression we receive from Hoare is certainly not of wildness except in some of the landscape, but rather of an extraordinary peace ruffled by little more than Methodist meetings and fairs which so disconcerted Sir Richard. Borrow was playing to some extent to the gallery since the commercial success of the book had much more significance for him than the publication (virtually private printing) of his book had for Sir Richard. Yet it may well be that Hoare's book has had the deeper influence. When we think of Wales we tend to think of Giraldus and we see the *Itinerary* and *Description* through the spectacles of Sir Richard's translation. The former is of topographical interest mainly but the latter

certainly had a place in the growth of Welsh national consciousness in the
last century.

Borrow through his command of the language had greater contact with
the people; for Hoare the material environment, the landscape and antiquities,
were almost his exclusive interests and when he puts figures in his drawings
we are made unexpectedly aware of the local inhabitants. The thought of the
shy and rather sombre baronet amongst the local population must indeed
raise a smile. In a country which 'for so many successive years has afforded
me health, amusement and information'[38] he had little contact with the local
population and on his own confession found in 1806 the expansive and
impulsive termperament of the Irish much more congenial than the tighter
Welsh one.[39] Yet one of the closest friendships of his life was formed with
that quintessential Welshman Richard Fenton.

There is something almost naive in the journals that is sometimes irritating
but this simplicity has surely an endearing aspect. Sir Richard did not have
the linguistic ability of Fenton, the piercing intelligence of Wyndham, the
historical skills of Coxe, the organising ability of Cunnington, the scholarship of Knight . . . yet he had a measure of will and application denied the
others which combined with the financial means at his disposal could trans-
mute ambitious schemes in the head into the black and white of the printed
word. Sir Richard was not merely an interpreter of the Welsh landscape but
made a solid contribution to the study of its past by stimulating the publication
of two 'historical tours' and of course by his study of Roman Wales and his
annotated Giraldus. I hope that the extracts from the records of his travels in
this book will help us to appreciate his not inconsiderable achievement.

I

Journal of a Tour in South Wales. Anno 1793.

1 May.   I left Stourhead at ½ past 12, and arrived at the New Passage at nine, passing through Bruton, Cannard's Grave, Old Down and Bristol. The inn at New Passage is good.

Thursday 2nd May.   After a rough and tedious passage of two hours and a half I landed on the opposite side of the channel. I never would recommend anyone to go over in the large Passage boat (as I did) but to take a small one, as the former is generally much loaded with cattle and horses, which are not the pleasantest companions in a rough sea. In point of distance the Old Passage is preferable, but the new one is far better for embarking carriages. The inn at the Old Passage, formerly very bad, is much improved.[1]

Passing by a seat of Mr Lewis on the right I proceeded to Chepstow which breaks very abruptly on the view when you least expect it. The Beaufort Arms is the best inn. After dinner I continued through Ragland [*Raglan*] to Abergavenny, leaving the beautiful grounds of Persfield to the right of the road, and a large enclosure of wood called Chepstow Park to the left. Part of the road is rough and stoney. There is a tolerable inn at Ragland. I paid but a cursory visit to the romantic castle at Chepstow, and to the more extensive, though less picturesque, one at Ragland, meaning to re-visit them some future day. I found a good inn at the Angel, Abergavenny, but bad attendance.

Friday 3rd May.   I proceeded to Crickhowel six miles from Abergavenny where I continued till Monday the 13th., after which I paid a visit to Mr Greene at Llansanfrede [*Llansanffraed*] where I remained till 21st when our party broke up, and my friends dispersed each their different ways. The object of our visit to Crickhowel was salmon fishing, but the season was too far advanced and the fish out of season and not eatable; the proper season being the end of February or beginning of March. There is a tolerable little inn at the Bear but a large party cannot be accomodated.

Hitherto my time had been idly though pleasantly spent; on returning to Abergavenny I laid aside my fishing rod and took up my pencil. The situation of Abergavenny is fine, built on a gentle eminence above the River Uske and surrounded by lofty montains which from their bold and varied forms add much to the general beauty of the scenery. Of these the Skirid Fawr, the Sugar Loaf and Blorench are the most remarkable. I mounted the summit of the Sugar Loaf which commands a most extensive view. I was told that General Roy[2] on measuring the heights of these mountains had

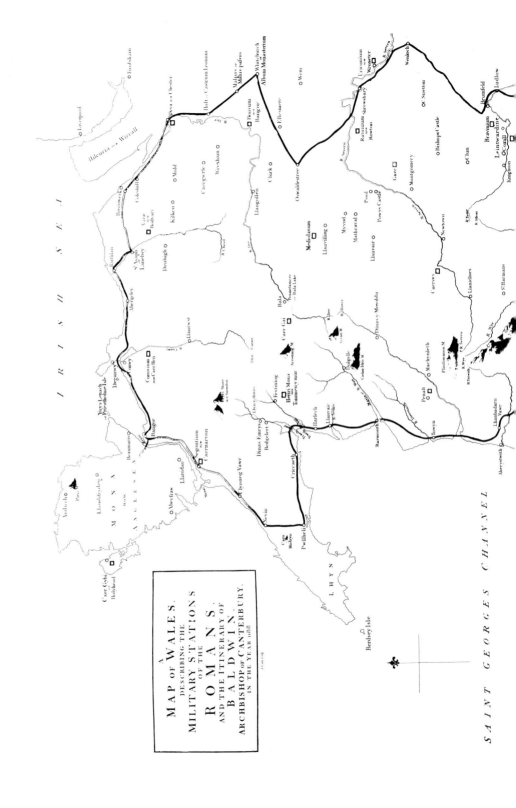

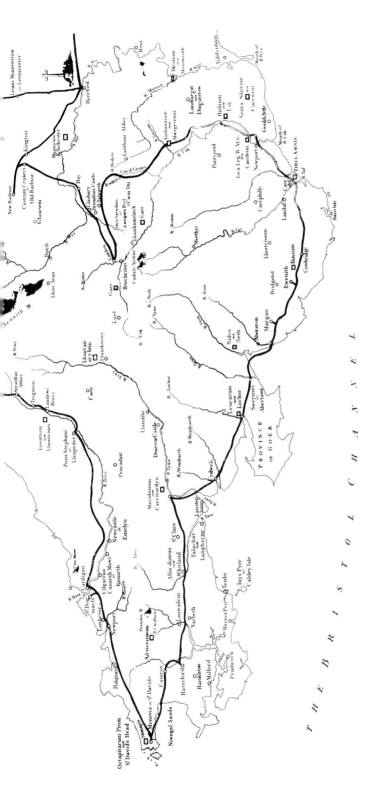

4. Map of Wales engraved by J. Cary, showing the clockwise route of Archbishop Baldwin in 1188 and Roman stations, used by Hoare in his edition of Giraldus of 1806.

found the highest pont of the Skirid exceeds that of the Sugar Loaf. The Blorench is less rude in its form but more covered with wood. The remains of the castle at Abergavenny are trifling, and deserve more attention from their pleasing situation and the prospect they command than from the merit of the building which is in a very dilapidated condition.

There are several gentlemen's seats in the neighbourhood of this town amongst which Mr Hanbury Williams' at Coldrock and Mr Jones' at Clytha, both on the road to Ragland, are the most remarkable. The latter has lately built a modern castle on a hill adjoining the road, fitted up in the most elegant style with respect to furniture, and commanding a most pleasing view of the distant mountans with the River Uske meandering through the rich and beautiful vale bencath.

Abergavenny is much frequented in Summer by invalids who go there to drink goat's milk and breathe its pure air. During my stay there I visited the ruins of Llanthony Abbey, distant about 12 miles. Leaving the great road to Hereford near M.V opposite to the old seat of the Oxford family (Llanvihangle where there are some of the largest Scotch firs I ever saw) I turned off to the left. From thence the road becomes very indifferent, and so narrow in some places as not to leave room for a foot passenger to pass a chaise, the hedges nearly meeting, and the road often overhanging a steep precipice,[3] notwith-standing it is turnpike and such a one never surely was seen before. Had I previously known the state of it I certainly should have taken a horse as my conveyance, instead of a chaise.

Friday 24th May.   Returned to Crickhowel. The entrance into Wales and Brecknockshire is between this place and Abergavenny through a spacious and well-cultivated valley, surrounded by lofty mountains and watered by the Uske. . . .

During my second visit to this place I made several excursions. The River Uske as far as New Bridge and higher presents many picturesque scenes of wood, rock and of water. Between four and five miles to the SE is a very pretty cascade called in the language of the country Pwll y Cwn or the Dogs' Pool. . . . The scenery around it is wild but its scale is more adapted to a garden than a country wild and mountainous as that in which it is placed. . . .

Sunday 26th   This day I spent amongst the ruins of Llanthony Abbey. The road I went (on horseback) is calculated at eight miles but the badness of it heightened the distance considerably; indeed this noble ruin is accessible only with difficulty. The description of Giraldus Cambrensis who visited Wales in 1188 is so accurate and truly expressive of the situation of his abbey that I am tempted to transcribe it as it has been copied by Camden:

'In the low vale of Ewyas, which is about a bowshot over and enclosed on all sides by high mountains stands the church of St John the Baptist covered with lead and considering the solitariness of the place not unhandsomely built with an arched roof of stone . . . a place fit for the exercise of religion, and the most conveniently situated for canonical discipline of any monastery

5. Llanthony Abbey, Gwent, its west front.

in the island of Great Britain, built first (to the honor of that solitary life) by two hermits in this desert, remote from all the noise of the world upon the River Hodeni. . . . The monks sitting in their cloysters, when they chance to look out for fresh air have a pleasing prospect on all hands of exceeding high mountains, with plentiful herds of wild deer feeding aloft at the furthest limits of their horizon. The body of the sun surmounts not these hills, so as to be visible to them till it is past one o'clock, even when the air is most clear. . . . "All the treasure of your Majesty and kingdom would not suffice to build such a cloyster". At which both the king and courtiers being astonished he at last explained that paradox by telling them he meant the mountains wherewith it was on all hands enclosed.'

The above account of Giraldus is in general very correct. No place was ever better adapted by Nature for celibacy and monastic retirement. The modern little churchyard testifies by its monumental inscriptions the salubrity of the climate and its tendency to longevity. Our author seems to have erred only on one point respecting the late appearance of the sun . . . at nine o'clock in the morning I was obliged, when drawing, to have recourse to the umbrella to shelter me from its scorching rays.[4]

This abbey is still magnificent even in its ruins, though clearly decaying from the neglect of its owner. It presents a mixture of Norman and Gothic architecture, lower arches of the latter, the upper of the former order. . . . With great regret I heard that the beautiful arch of the eastern front had fallen last year of which a very exact view by Grimm . . . has been given by Mr Wyndham in his *Tour through Wales*. Few ruins present themselves in a more striking manner to the eye chiefly owing to their isolated situation where all the surrounding objects appear characteristic of the building, and suited to its original destination.

There is nothing but a miserable little ale-house there where the traveller who is not overnice may eat his cold meat within view of the ruins, or if he wishes to be better accomodated he may use his endevors to prevail on the farmer to receive him into his house, which is annexed to the abbey.

Thusday 30th May. I quitted Crickhowel with regret for few places contain so many natural beauties, and so pleasing a mixture of wild and cultivated nature. The industry of the inhabitants is very conspicuous in cultivating the mountains as high as the soil will admit of, and if the summits of them were cloathed with wood (as they once apparently were) the scenery would be complete. The extensive ironworks in the neighboring hills require such a consumption of charcoal that the woods are sadly massacred and even the virgin oaks do not escape the stroke of the axe. A little way from Crickhowel on the left of the turnpike road is a supposed druidical relict, consisting of a circular stone supported by others of smaller size beneath it[5] and between Crickhowel and Newbridge there are two other upright stones. . . .

About two miles on the right of the great road is the village of Tretower also a castle in tolerable preservation and of a singular construction, being a

strong circular tower enclosed within another of irregular form.⁶ It consisted
of two or more stories, and two large fireplaces remain which would not
disgrace the Abbot of Glastonbury's kitchen. Artificial means of defence
seem to have been employed in the construction of the tower, as the natural
situation of it was weak being in a level plain commanded by hills. . . .

Here I must mention a particularity in the Welch language which strongly
marks its originality for every name of a place or town has its meaning and
generally expressive of its situation. About the XIIth milestone, on the left
of the road, is the seat of Mr Gwynne, on the banks of the Uske. At the
XIVth on the same side of the road is one of the circular columns mentioned
by Camden, with an inscription on it written downwards-*VICTORINI*-in
bad character.⁷ . . . The road is good from Crickhowel to Brecknock and
generally in sight of the Uske.

The town of Brecknock is pleasantly situated on a gentle eminence above
the River Uske. There are still the remains of the castle and priory founded
by Bernard Newmarch, a Norman, and of the college founded by Henry
viii. The priory stands on the most elevated part of the town, and the well-
shaded walks around it on the banks of the River Hodeni [*Honddu*], which
were formerly laid out and kept at the expence of a private family, have been
justly and universally admired. The priory church under the appellation of
St John's is used as parish church and there is another called St Mary's. In
the former the service is performed in Welch and frequented chiefly by the
lower class of people but the general place of burial is here. . . . This church
was formerly much larger, the adjoining cloysters having been taken down
but a few years ago. Visitors [*are*] shown the mutilated tomb of its original
founder, Bernard Newmark. The castle is also situated on an elevated spot
but its remains are not very considerable.

During my stay at Brecknock I visited the Roman station called *Y Gaer*
about two miles and a half distant from the town, where I saw some of the
bricks lately dug up and inscribed LEG.II. AUG. ie *Legio Secunda Augusta*.⁸
The earth of which they are made is heavy and not of a good color. I was
there informed that these bricks were continually dug up and that coins had
also been found of gold and silver with the name of the Emperor Nero on
them but I cannot vouch for the authenticity of this information . . . in the
road leading to the *Gaer* is the stone mentioned by Camden, between six
and seven feet high, with two figures rudely worked on it. . . . The situation
of this camp is very pleasant, the Beacon Hills rising over a beautiful grove
of oaks feathering down to the River Uske. . . .

Saturday June 1.   Left Brecknock, dined and slept at Llandovery, 19 miles.
The only high mountains are to the south of Brecknock, called the Vann
[*Pen y Fan*] or Beacons. They are bold and broken in their forms. The
country in general well cultivated and has some fine groves of oaks to boast
of. . . .

Sunday 2nd June.   Left Llandovery and proceeded to Llandilo, 12 miles;

6. Carreg Cennen Castle, Dyfed, seen from below by the River Cennen.

road good; inn the Bear, good. The country about this place bears a better appearance. The village is built on an eminence over the River Towy where there is a bridge and (like most of those in Wales) of narrow dimensions. The beautiful park belonging to the Rice family at Newton adjoins the village. Few places can boast of such natural beauties of situation: wood, lawn and water are here in the greatest perfection. The former consisting chiefly of fine oaks has been preserved with a parent's eye from the destructive axe. The ground is very uneven never rising to a mountainous elevation nor sinking into dead flat. The River Towy meanders through the vale beneath and adds much to the beauty of the surrounding scanery. The architecture of the house is not unpicturesque, being built in the form of a castle with battlements and four turrets with small cupolas at each angle. But the object which adds the greatest beauty and interest to this place is the old castle, proudly seated on a lofty knoll, covered with thick wood, formerly the royal residence of the princes of South Wales, and from which their successors, the Rices, have taken the title Dynevor. . . .

The wood has nearly oertopped the castle, [so] that the summits only of it are visible, and I could have wished that a little more of this classical and interesting object had been exposed to view. This beautiful hanging wood is seen to the best advantage from the meadows below near the river, from which it appears to be that the poet Dyer in his poem called Grongar Hill drew the following natural and beautiful description:

> Gaudy is the opening dawn.
> Lies a long and level lawn
> On which a dark hill steep and high
> Holds and charms the wandering eye
> Deep are his feet in Towy's flood,
> His sides are cloathed with waving wood
> And ancient towers crown his brow
> That cast an awful look below . . .

On the opposite side of Llandilo there is another object which merits highly the attention of the traveller, the castle of Caer Kennen [*Carreg Cennen*]. A little rivulet which runs near it gives it the name of the Fort [*Rock*] on the Kennen.[9] It is distant about four miles from Llandilo, the road rough and stoney and accessible only on horseback. This castle is remarkable for its bold and singular situation; built on a high, projecting, isolated rock, strongly fortified by nature and even inaccessible on three sides, accessible only on the side facing the north. Great part of the walls still remain and a perforation to a considerable depth (I should imagine fifty or sixty yards) is made in the natural rock, for what purpose is not known, perhaps to procure water for the garrison. . . . Perhaps its singular natural strength prevented it being attacked and thus the silence of the historians may be accounted for. . . .

Wednesday 5th June. Left Llandilo; dined and slept at Carmarthen, road good but hilly; inn, Ivy Bush, 15 miles. On leaving Llandilo and ascending the first hill beyond the Park there is a most advantageous view of the grounds at Newton where the beautiful woods appear at the greatest perfection. Near mile V on the left of the road is Grongar Hill, in Welch the round *gaer*. . . . A little further on on the same side of road is Drusllwyn [*Dryslwyn*] Castle,[10] situated on a bold isolated hill projecting over the River Towy. A small portion only of the old walls remain. The badness of the weather prevented my visiting this ruin. . . .

Near Carmarthen is Abergwylly [*Abergwili*], the seat of the Bishop of St Davids. The river here takes a singular zig-zag course. The vale leading to Carmarthen as well as the greatest part of the road thence to Llandilo, but more particularly the latter part of it, is very pleasing and well-cultivated. I lamented only that the road had not been made nearer the river (as from Trecastle to Llandovery) by which means several sharp hills might have been avoided.

Carmarthen, for a Welch town, is the best I have seen in my tour; the buildings more regular and the streets wider. The town hall is a regular Doric building. The town is situated on the banks of the River Towy over which there is a bridge, narrow like the generality of those in Wales; the river is navigable as far as the town. Here I first saw the fishermen make use of coracles and with wonderful dexterity. They are small wicker boats (or rather large flat baskets) covered with leather, just large enough to contain one man, who guides it by paddling with one short oar. There are some trifling remains of the old castle near the bridge.

Thursday 6 June.   Left Carmarthen and pursued my journey to Newcastle Emlyn, 20 miles. . . . Newcastle is a small village on the banks of the River Tivy [*Teifi*] over which it has a bridge, dividing the counties of Carmarthen-shire and Cardiganshire. Adjoining the town are the ruins of an old castle seated on a knoll and from its architecture not of a very ancient date. I found it mentioned by Powell in 1215. This place is said to derive the name of Emlyn from the river's taking the form of the letter M in its course near the town.

From this place I fished down the river to Gelly-Dowyll, the seat of my friend Captain Lewis. This place signifies in Welch 'the dark grove', and is still applicable to its present shady situation. . . . About half a mile from hence is Kenarth where the salmon leap mentioned by Giraldus is situated, of which he gives a particular description . . . the boldness of the rocks in the river, and two fine hanging woods, which meeting in a point enclose the river, form a very picturesque scene. . . . Giraldus also mentioned that this was the only river in Wales which produced beavers. . . .

Sunday 9th June.   We rode, partly by the side of the river, to Llechryd where there is a bridge over the Tivy, and some iron and tin works, and from thence to Coidmore, the seat of Mr Lloyd from whose grounds are seen the most beautiful views of Kilgerran Castle,[11] situated on a high rocky

7. Cilgerran Castle, Dyfed, looking up from the right bank of the River Teifi.

knoll on the opposite side of the river. No description can give an adequate idea of the beautiful scenery on the banks of this river, nor could the most ingenious artist or the man of the greatest taste have placed a ruin in a more happy spot. The river though influenced by the tide still preserves its beautiful sea-green color. . . . It winds its various turnings through a narrow channel, surrounded by hills, feathered with wood to the water's edge though a beautiful wood has just been cut and will not recover its pristine foliage for many years. In the hands of a man of taste and fortune Coidmore might be rendered one of the most beautiful spots in Europe. The castle belongs to Mr Lovedene and is a considerable building. Two large round towers remain with a staircase entire.

I was so delighted with this enchanting spot that I visited it three times and viewed it in every possible direction. It can ony be seen to advantage by water. At high water the boat may go as far as the ironworks at Lllechrid; and of the many beautiful points of view which the castle presents perhaps it appears nowhere to greater advantage than on coming down from Llechrid bridge towards Cardigan.

The town of Cardigan was anciently known by the name of Aberteifi being situated near the confluence of the River Tivy with the sea. There are many other towns in Wales whose names begin with *Aber* which implies any place where a smaller river discharges itself into a greater, or into the sea. . . . The walls of this castle are washed by the tide. The ruins are trifling and do not form a picturesque object. There is a platform at top commanding a good view of the river which is distant about three miles to the mouth where it discharges itself into the sea. It still (as in the days of Giraldus) maintains its character for good salmon.

At a short distance from the town are the ruins of the ancient abbey of St. Dogmael, surrounded by some fine old ash trees.[12] Its architecture was Gothic. These ruins are not very picturesque and form the best subject for the pencil when seen from a hill behind them with the river and Cardigan at a distance. . . .

The town of Cardigan may be classed amongst the neatest in Wales, and the Black Lion is a good inn. A modern Gothic house has been built on the ground adjoining the old priory, the eastern front of which with part of the church annexed still remain. NB. The inhabitants of Saint Dogmael (a fierce and hardy race) seldom connect themselves with their neighbours but intermarry entirely amongst themselves. They subsist chiefly by fishing.

Wednesday 12th June. I left Cardigan and proceeded through Newport to Fisgard [*Fishguard*] where I slept. . . . I quitted my carriage and turned off to the left to a farm house at Pentre Evan from which at a distance of near a mile towards the south, on a rough and stoney common, is a Druidical relict, known by the name of *Y Cromlech*, and by the common people perhaps better by the appellation of King Arthur's Quoit.[13] It consists of one large stone about eighteen feet long, supported by three others about eight feet high. There are others placed under it but of no use, as the great stone does not rest upon them. The upper stone [*sketch*] . . . broad towards the south and tapering towards the north, and inclining downwards about a foot towards the latter point. The forms of the stones underneath vary: those which support the great stone are pointed, others rounded which appear never to have supported any part of the stone. The breadth of the large stone is about eight feet. In the field adjoining some large stones lying on the ground seem to indicate the existence of another similar monument of antiquity.

From hence I went on a little further in my chaise, and then quitting it and sending it forward to Newport I turned off to the right to the little village of Nevern situated close to river bearing the same name. I visited this place on account of the antique monuments which are mentioned by Camden as existing there in his time. I found the cross still there in the churchyard. . . . A gentleman in the neighborhood told me that he dug down seven feet under this cross into the ground without reaching the foundaions of this stone. I could gain no intelligence respecting the inscriptions mentioned by Camden as existing in the churchyard.

Newport is a small village, and very populous, situated near the sea. Its name in Welch is *Trefdraeth*, the town in the sands. According to Camden it was built by Martin de Tours whose posterity made it a corporation, granting it several privileges: they constituted therein a Portrieve and Bailiff and also built themselves a castle above the town. . . . Great part of it situated on an eminence above the town still remaining and forms a picturesque object, its south front consisting of two tall towers. . . .

In a field between the town and the harbour I saw another druidical relict, resembling in some degree the one at Pentre Evan but infinitely smaller in its proportions.[14] The upper stone resembles an umbrella, or mushroom. Though there are several stones underneath, some fallen to the ground and others standing, it rests only upon two. But as it is evident that some have given way it is impossible to say how many it was formerly supported [*by*]. I here heard that there was another small monument of this kind beyond Pentre Evan and another large one (mentioned by Camden under the name of *Llech y Drybedh*) about two miles distant from Nevern in a direction towards Cardigan. This also has the general vulgar appellation of quoit. There near the monument at Newport as I could procure no provisions whatever (not even fish) I proceeded on my road to Fisgard, where after some difficulty and much patience I got some eggs, fish and potatoes.

. . . I should observe that as the traveller in this and other parts of Wales where there is deficiency of wood will frequently see upright stones (and sometimes of large dimensions) placed in the middle of fields he must not attribute them to the remote era of the Druids; as they are frequently placed so by the modern farmers to supply the place of rubbing posts for their cattle.[15]

The roads from Cardigan to Fisgard are very rough and stoney, the country generally laid out in large enclosures surrounded with high banks planted with furze. The features however of the country were not bad if they

8. St Davids Cathedral, Dyfed, the then ruined east end.

were varied with wood. The mountains to the left are lofty and rocky, and the most remarkable of them are the Cwm Kerrwn [*Cwmcorwyn*] and Priscelly [*Preseli*].

I found a decent bed at Fisgard and a letter from my friend Captain Lewis procured me the acquaintance of Counsellor Fenton[16] from whom I gained much information respecting my tour, no one being more versed in the ancient history and records of his native country. . . .

Thursday 13th June. I left Fisgard and proceeded to St Davids. The roads are better but the country still more open and dreary, inclosed with high banks and stone walls. How melancholy and at the same time how true a description does Giraldus give of this place.[17]. . . Nothing can be more dreary than the country about St Davids; not even a hedge can be reared on account of the high winds which prevail here. Much however might be done by human labour and industry towards recovering the bad character it has born for so many centuries. The residentiary canon, Mr Holkham, has planted some trees near his residence which thrive well (their situation is however well sheltered) and the crops of corn, where the land is properly cultivated, are good. The barley of these parts is of a particularly fine quality and in great request.

Saint Davids however, on account of its ancient name and high character in the Welsh Annals deserves the attention of every curious traveller; but few I find ever visit it. This church was originally founded by St David whose bones rest under its roof, and till the year 1101 was the Metropolitan Church of Wales; about which time it became subject to the see of Canterbury. The shrine of this saint was frequented by numerous crowds of pilgrims and even kings came penitent and barefooted to pay their devotion to it. The value of the relicts and offerings daily received was so great that they were weighed and divided amongst the monks every week.[18] In short it was the British Loretto.

The church as well as all the adjoining buildings are either in an absolute state of ruin, or decay. The cathedral is still made use of as a place of religious worship and service is performed in it both in the English and Welch languages, though owing to the bad ground in which it is built its existence is in a very precarious state. There is a very great settlement in one of the arches supporting the steeple. The architecture is a mixture of Norman and Gothic; the arches are finely proportioned and many of the ornaments are very elegant. The pavement is sadly disfigured by the custom generally adopted through many parts of Wales of digging graves within the church by which its level is raised and rendered very uneven. . . .

Bishop Gower was the last great improver and restorer of the church and is said to have erected the Bishop's Palace,[19] magnificent still even in its ruins. Bishop Vaughan lies buried in a most beautiful chapel built by him and bearing his name. Above £2,000 have been lately expended in repairing the west end of this cathedral and I wish I could add with good taste and judgement. A compilation of Gothic, Norman etc ornaments introduced into the modern front now supply the place of the fine Norman facade which was so universally admired and regretted by those who see the wide difference between the antique and modern workmanship and design.

The adjoining ruin of the College built by Bishop Houghton presents an elegant specimen of fine Gothic architecture, and the Bishop's Palace adjoining is a still grander object. A range of open Gothic arches runs along the parapet, the use of which (from a part left entire) seem to have been to strengthen the battlements above them, as this place answered the double purpose of a fortification as well as episcopal residence. In the interior quadrangle of his building is a hall of large proportions, over the entrance door to which are said to be the statues of King John and his Queen. On the other side of the quadrangle are the bishop's apartments: hall, kitchen etc in which were some chimnies of a curious construction, now fallen down.

This noble building owes its ruin to Bishop Barlowe who lived in the time of Queen Elizabeth and procured leave to strip the lead from off the roof of this palace, and with which he is said to have portioned his five daughters to as many bishops. He is also said to have alienated another episcopal palace at Lantphey, which became the possession of the celebrated favorite of the Queen, the Earl of Essex, and to which he retired after his disgrace. But the epoch of the fall of St Davids was at the Reformation when the offerings to the holy shrine, the relicts, indulgences etc etc came into disrepute. A tower is here shown, said to have been the birthplace of Saint Patrick; though other countries contend for that honor Erasmus quotes him as a Welshman by birth.

Thus much for St Davids and its church which to a lover of antiquities is highly gratifying, and affords to the painter a variety of picturesque architectural subjects. Its situation is so flat and surrounded by so many stone walls, modern buildings etc etc that it requres no short time to discover the most favorable points of view. Its history has been written by Brown Willis who never saw the place till his book was published. . . . Few churches, considering the very early [*date*] of its foundation and its great celebrity, would furnish more interesting records and historical anecdotes, but the materials are lost, and this once celebrated sanctuary remains unfrequented and unknown. . . .

The village consists of a few straggling, wretched houses, and one long wide irregular street commanding a distant view of the sea. In this street is situated the inn (Black Lion) if it deserves that appellation, for it is by far the worst I ever met with. I was very unwell and much discontented with my situation, yet resolved to put up with my accommodations, homely and bad as they appeared. I was soon however relieved from my anxiety by the kind invitation of Canon Holkham who insisted on my lodging in his house. Thus was I once more indebted to the family of Holcombe, for some years ago, together with many of my family, I was overtaken by a dreadful storm at night on Milford Haven and received shelter in the house of an uncle to the Canon.

During my stay here I rode to the most western point of the island, called

9. Haverfordwest, Dyfed, the castle and bridge from across the river.

St Davids Head, the *ultima thule* of Wales, composed of a bold promontory
of rocks and huge stones thrown about in wild confusion. At this further-
most extremity on the western point, where the land contracts itself into a
very narrow point, and is on three sides surrounded by a deep precipice of
perpendicular rocks, is a Druidical monument differing from any I have yet
seen. It consists of six distinct circles of no very large dimensions with stones
set around them, most of which are now displaced.[20]. . . No place could ever
be more suited to retirement, contemplation or Druidical mysteries, surrounded by inaccessible rocks and open to a wide expanse of ocean. Nothing
seems wanting but the thick impenetrable groves of oaks which have
generally been thought concomitant to places of Druidical worship and
which, from the exposed nature of this situation, would never, I think, have
existed here even in former days. There is a singular *lusus naturae* in the
rocks which project towards the sea on the most westerly point of land;
which forms the perfect profile of a venerable old head such as I could have
fancied a Druid's character.[21] [*sketch*]

The air of St Davids is esteemed very healthy but on account of the want
of trees and other shelter very high winds prevail. This neck of land is also
very subject to fogs coming in a direction from Ireland which come and
disappear very quickly, whilst other places three miles only distant are free
from them.

A singular method is adopted here for feeding sheep and cattle arising
from necessity and the want of fences and proper inclosures; they are yoked
in pairs and fastened to the ground by a long peg and a cord. And a tall
upright stone supplies the place of a tree for a rubbing post in almost every
field.

There is a tolerable good beach for bathing near St Davids, and the coast
abounds with the finest fish but the want of a market (there being none
nearer than Haverfordwest by which families can be supplied) prevents the
fishermen from going out. Lobsters are the only fish at anytime plentiful.

Having spent five days very pleasantly with the worthy Canon Holkham
and his family, and having this morning assisted at the marriage of one of his
daughters on *Tuesday 18th June* I proceeded on my road to Haverfordwest.
The first object which attracted my attention was the picturesque little
harbour of Solvath [*Solfach*] situated in a deep narrow cove surrounded by
high rocks. I afterwards crossed the sands at Newgal, respecting which
Giraldus says that at the time when Henry the Second was in Ireland the
sandy shores of this coast were laid bare by the violence of the storms, and
the face of land together with trunks of trees etc. which had been acovered
by the sea for many a year re-appeared. A similar circumstance is said to
have happened here about 1590. A little further to the left of the road is
Roch Castle and village. The former, not large, of an irregular form, is built
on one of those land rocks with which the country (and about St Davids
particularly) abounds; and cannot be deemed picturesque. The country
improves on approaching towards Haverfordwest and trees begin once more
to make therir appearance. The road is tolerable; two steep hills, the one by

Newgal and the other by Solfath.

Haverfordwest is a large town built on a very uneven situation on the declivity of a steep hill, at the bottom of which runs the River Cleddau which the tide renders navigable up to the town. A large square castle (made use of as a goal) in a commanding situation overhangs the town, and in several points of view, but more particularly from the London and Cardigan roads, and from the meadows north of it, form a very picturesque object. . . . On the banks of the river adjoining the town are the ruins of an old priory.[22]

This part of Wales was formerly called Rhos and was colonised by Flemings; *vide* Powell and Giraldus: 'AD 1105, the next year a very dismal and calamitous accident happening in the Low Countries proved very incommodious and prejudicial to the Welch. For a great part of Flanders being drowned by the overflowing of the sea the inhabitants were compelled to seek for some other country to dwell in, their own now being covered with water, and therefore a great many being come over to England they requested of King Henry to assign them some part of his kingdom which was empty and void of inhabitants where they might settle and plant themselves. The King taking advantage of this charitable opportunity and being in a manner assured that these Flemings would be a considerable thorn in the side of the Welch, bestowed on them very liberally what was not justly in his power to give: and appropriated to them the country of Rhos in Dyfed or West Wales where they continue to this day.' (Powell)) The inhabitants differ to this day from their neighbors as they speak only English. . . .

Saturday 22nd Left Haverfordwest and went in my chaise to Picton Castle where I quitted it and sent it forward to meet me at Slebech. Picton Castle, the residence of Lord Milford, is an old castle modernised and rather too much to render it an object of antiquarian research. The walk from thence to Slebech is very pleasant. I prefer this place to the former as it commands a fine view of the river. . . .

Sunday 23rd June. I spent the morning at Lawhaden [*Llawhaden*], a few miles distant from Narbeth. I am surprised that these ruins have not been more noticed by authors and travellers as in point of situation and structure they are superior to many in Wales better known and more frequently visited.[23] This castle belongs to the see of St David's. [*It*] is strongly situated on a high hill, a great part of which is covered with thick wood. It is a mixture of round and pointed architecture; the gateway remaining entire is round. It appears to have suffered less than many of the Welch castles. . . .

Monday 24th June. I left Narbeth and proceeded on my road to Pembroke. Very considerable improvements have been made within these last few years in the lands round Narbeth, which were all waste and in common but now produce excellent crops of corn. The method used in their cultivation is first burn-raking, and then liming which is procured at a very

10. Pembroke Castle and town from across the river.

cheap rate owing to the plenty of culm and limestone in the neighborhood. Good crops are also by these means produced. The road is in many parts very rough.

Five miles from Pembroke is the village and castle of Carew which highly deserves the traveller's attention. . . . The castle is a magnificent building; the front facing the north and the river is the most perfect and commanding. Its architecture also is singular: at each extremity are two large round towers and further on at equal distances are two round towers of smaller dimensions, which have this particularity, *viz.* that the windows are continued entirely round the curve of the bow. The space of wall intervening between the towers is filled with large and lofty windows. This front has a very grand appearance when viewed from the opposite side of the river. To Cromwell we owe the demolition of the southern front from which side it was battered; its picturesque appearance is however increased by this circumstance as it has opened a view into the interior parts of the building which otherwise would not have been seen. The front facing the east where the entrance appears to have been is also picturesque, being irregular in its form and finely overspread with ivy. The last front facing the west has a different character, is more simple and perhaps more majestic in its parts, consisting only of two fine, round towers and battlements between them.

On the roadside adjoining the castle is a cross ornamented with fretwork and characters which I could not distinguish sufficiently to copy, similar to that before mentioned in the churchyard at Neverne.[24]

This part of Wales was known by the name of *Dimetia* and afterwards called *Dyved* by the Welch. The town of Pembroke is situated on long neck of land extending for a considerable way in length and sloping down to the river which flows here from Milford Haven. The original foundation of the castle is attributed to Arnulph de Montgomery, brother to Robert Earl of Shrewsbury who gave the command of it to his constable and Lieutenant, Gerald de Windsor, who defended it gallantly, and considerably added to its fortifications. This Gerald was an ancestor or relation of my travelling companion Giraldus Cambrensis, in whose *Itinerary* some interesting anecdotes are related concerning him.

The castle of Pembroke is one of the most interesting in Wales, both in point of size and situation. Built on a high rock and nearly surrounded on three sides by the river, it is seen to best advantage from the opposite shore, or on approaching it by water from Milford Haven, where the ruins form three distinct masses and each is a respectable relict of antiquity. The principal features of these ruins are the chapel facing the river, the two round towers and southern gateway and the large round tower rearing its head above all the rest; the whole finely varied with ivy and [*not*] too much which is the case with several of the castles of Wales. It appears to have been battered from the south. The round tower has its stone-vaulted roof remaining; [*it*] was divided into three stories besides ground floor and had two chimnies. Its walls are of immense thickness. Underneath the chapel is a large natural cavern called the *Wogan* which opens towards the river, and by a staircase has a communication with the buildings above it. It appears nearly circular and whether excavated or not in former times for the sake of the stone (which is freestone as I was informed) is uncertain. It bears however a very natural appearance and very much resembles grottos I have seen in Italy which were called *nymphaea* and used by the Romans as places of amusement and retirement from the heat. . . .

During my stay at Pembroke I made an excursion to the sea coast about seven miles distant: first to the Eligug Stack[25] which are two insulated rocks rising out of the sea in a pyramidical form at a very short distance from the land, and deriving the above name from the astonishing quantity of eligugs [*guillemots*] resorting thither. . . . The number of birds is so great that these two rocks are so completely covered with them that in parts no rock whatever is to be seen. All the chasms are also filled with them from the top to the bottom but they abound the most on the bare summit where they have no shelter whatever. They stand upright and hold the egg under their foot, and seem to avoid the land as if conscious of the weakness of their legs; they fly from cliff to cliff not crossing any part of the adjacent land. And many are continually on the wing besides thousands on the sea, as they never go to the land their food must of course be procured from the water.

The cliffs here are the most romantic in their forms and color of any I ever beheld and I lamented much that owing to the steepness of them there was no possibility of descending to a level with the sea, where these, as well as the Eligug rocks could have been viewed to much greater advantage. My guide pointed out to me a piece of rock of a very singular nature; in appearance it resembled exactly a piece of goose's dung. On examination it appeared to be a petrafaction of sea weeds. From thence I went to St Gowen's point distant about two miles. The cliffs still maintain their beautiful form and hue. In a narrow gorge between them stands a little chapel dedicated to St Gowen who still maintains his credit in the country; for his well and chapel are frequently visited by the infirm in hopes of finding a remedy for their complaints. There is a well of red, muddy water adjoining the chapel of which those who have faith in the saint drink. . . .

In my way to and from the coast I passed by an old-fashioned mansion house of the Owen family called Orielton, and Stackpole belonging to Mr Campbell. Round these two places are a few woods bearing the desolating marks and effects of the sea breeze. The country is otherwise composed of large enclosures with a mixture of corn and grass, and very little wood. . . .

Friday 28th June.   I left Pembroke and proceeded on my journey to Tenby, 10 miles; road good; inn, White Lion, good, in a charming situation overlooking the sea. Two miles from Pembroke and at a very short distance from the great road is Llantphey [*Lamphey*] Court belonging to Sir Hugh Owen. It resembles in miniature the episcopal palace of Saint Davids; the same low, flat situation encompassed by numerous walls and similar in its architecture. It was built by Bishop Gower. . . .

Leaving this place I again deviated from the great road on the right to see the ruins of Manorbeer Castle situated at a short distance from the sea shore. After the fine castles of Carew and Pembroke Manorbeer must appear to a disadvantage. Its form is massive, its architecture heavy, its shape approaching to the square or rather oblong; without any windows on the outside except those of a modern date, so that it appears to have been considered more as a fortress or *place d'armes* than as a princely residence, like the other two castles. On an adjoining hill is the parish church containing the effigy of a cross-legged knight with a lion at his feet, which the common people converting into a bear from thence find a derivation for the name of this place. Giraldus Cambrensis has drawn a very faithful description of this place and castle.

The town of Tenbigh [*Tenby*] is delightfully situated in a neck of land surrounded on three sides by the sea. At the extremity of the point are the remains of the castle, in themselves trifling but crowning and adding an orament to the verdant knoll on which they stand. On the western side of the town is a long range of old walls and round towers. . . . In a part of these walls the landlord of the White Lion (Saer) when building the new Assembly rooms found a 32lb. canon ball enclosed between the stones, one of those probably used by Cromwell in battering the town and castle.

The church highly merits the traveller's attention. It presents a mixture of Gothic and Norman architecture and evidently has undergone many reparations from the dissimilarity of the arches, windows etc, etc. It was clearly a collegiate church, not a monastery, for the older stalls remain with the modern pews carved underneath with grotesque devices. The roof of the chancel is curious on account of its carved work and proves also that is was a collegiate church, for the ribs which support it spring from the heads of canonical priests who have their hair round and not shorn like monks, and hold escutcheons in their hands designed for their arms. The living supporters of the Church are gone but their wooden representatives remain in a high state of preservation. . . .

To the south of Tenby is Caldey Island belonging to Lord Warwick near which were caught the large oysters used for pickling. During the fishing season the coast is much frequented by the Devonshire fishermen. No place can be better adapted to sea-bathing. The shore is so regularly shelving and well sheltered that you may bath at at any hour of the day, on which account the little town is now much frequented during the summer months. Lodgings are made more convenient and the town is daily undergoing improvements and additions to its buildings. The water is said to be so pure and strongly impregnated with salt that it weighs heavier than that at Weymouth.

The country around Tenby is uninteresting, being rather destitute of wood, but the immediate environs are very beautiful; and most particularly the rocks and cliffs on the sea coast, whose forms and tints are very picturesque and harmonious from being covered with a short brushwood and a variety of other low plants and an abundance of ivy, which takes off their barren appearance. The walks under them are varied and convenient though the substance of the sand is not sufficiently hard. At Spring tides they may be traversed as far as Laugharne, a distance of sixteen miles.

Tenby is open to the eastern sea. The bay which is very spacious is formed by a projecting neck of land on the Glamorganshire coast, and is much enlivened by the number of fishing vessels which are continually going in and out of the harbour. Their arrival is announced by the town crier through the streets. I was informed that here (as well as on the coast near Saint Davids, Newgal etc) the trunks and roots of large trees have been found under water.

Friday 5 July. I left Tenby and proceeded on a rough, hard road for six or seven miles when it unites itself with the great road leading from Narbeth to Carmarthen. No post horses being kept at Tenbigh I was obliged to send for them from Tavern Spite, 13 miles off. . . .

I was prevented making several excursions from St Clear by the badness of the weather. To Laugharne three miles, and to Lanstephan a little further, at both of which places there are remains of ancient castles;[26] and also to Whitland five miles, the celebrated spot where Howel the Good formed his code of Welch laws. On approaching Carmarthen the country improves and becomes more woody.

Saturday 6th July Left Carmarthen and proceeded to Kidwelly (9 miles); road good and not very hilly; a tolerable inn but a pair only of post horses are kept. A fine rich view on the road looking back towards Carmarthen. The castle at Kidwelly, of Gothic architecture, is a large and respectable ruin.[27] Several round towers are standing and in many points of view it presents itself in a picturesque form. On one side a river washes the knoll on which it is built; the tide comes up to the town. This castle belongs to Mr Vaughan of Golden Grove who unlike most of the Lords of Welch castles does not suffer these interesting and national monuments of antiquity to go to decay. . . .

I dined at Kidwelly and proceeded in the evening through Llanelly to Pont ar Dylas [*Pontarddulais*], a single house near the bridge over the River Lloughor. Road good and more interesting on account of some pleasing points of view which occur in this tract, particularly on the mountain three or four miles from Kidwelly, and on descending from it towards Llanelly where the sea forms a large bay on the opposite shores. . . .

Sunday 7 July. Now entered Glamorgan and proceeded on my journey through Neath to Pile. Both roads and inns and country mend; the country is in general more wooded and more covered with the gentlemen's seats, manufactures and population. In the churchyard of Llangevelach [*Llangyfelach*] I observed a square block of stone ornamented with knots of fretwork which I imagined to have been part, perhaps the pedestal, of a Saxon cross,[28] similar to those before-mentioned at Nevern and Carew. Pass the seat of Mr Morris in a fine situation, well-wooded, and commanding a beautiful view of the surrounding country. Beneath it is a town of his creation called Morris-town, where extensive copper works are carried on. Beneath it runs the River Tawy [*Tawe*] over which there is a bridge of one large arch with two circular funnels in the piers to let the water pass in time of floods.

Here the Swansey road joins that from Neath. The ruins of Neath Abbey which are considerable are on the right hand of the road about a mile from Neath, where there [*are*] the small remains of a castle. The whole neighborhood of this town abounds with forges and copperworks etc. A little on the other side of the town is Knoll, the seat of Sir Robert Mackworth and a little further on the road is Bretton Ferry, the property of Lord Vernon, surrounded by beautiful hills covered with wood, which do not here as in Pembrokeshire feel the pinching influences of the sea breezes. On the right a large marsh, then Aberavon at the confluence of the Avon with the sea. Extensive forges and a new village have arisen here within these few years. The road continues flat to Margam under the magnificent hanging woods of Mr Talbot, and from thence to Pile where the same gentleman has lately built a most elegant and convenient inn.

Monday 8 July.   In the morning I returned to Margam which I found much altered since the time I last saw it: the mansion house nearly pulled down, a magnificent greenhouse of the Doric order erected for the reception of the fine orange trees, which had considerably decreased in beauty and luxuriance. I viewed also with grief the ruinous state of the chapter house, once the most elegant and most perfect specimen of Gothic architecture existing in Wales. During the two last winters two of the arches have given way and a third and fourth are approaching to the same fate. Still by a timely assistance the building may be saved, as the centre column has not yet given way. By removing the heavy mass of earth which weighs down the roof, and the shrubs and plants whose roots have penetrated it and admitted the wet, and substituting a thin covering of copper and lead this beautiful, and I may say unique, building may yet survive for many succeeding centuries.

The front of the parish church maintains its original and very ancient facade of Norman architecture, and some of the inside arches are of the same order. It contains many fine monuments in marble and alabaster of the Mansel family. In the street of the village are the base and top of an old Saxon cross ornamented with fretwork like those at Nevern, Carew etc and the base resembles that I saw yesterday at Llangevelach.[29]

In the evening I proceeded on my journey through Cowbridge . . . is situated in a bottom and consists of one long street. The inn is indifferent. Ascending from hence a fine view of the Bristol Channel presents itself. NB. From this hill in a former tour I once thought I could discover my tower at Stourhead and from this tower we think we can see the large ash trees on this elevated spot. The country becomes more populous and the landscape is much enlivened by the whitened and numerous cottages dispersed over the face of the country. I entered Cardiff near the fine old castle and found a good inn at the Cardiff Arms.

Tuesday 9th July.   Proceeded on my journey through Newport to the New Passage, leaving Tredegar, the seat of the late Mr Morgan (now of Sir Charles Gould), to the right, an old-fashioned brick house, grounds finely wooded. At Newport are the remains of an old castle adjoining a wooden bridge over the River Uske. See on the right a large house belonging to Mr Salisbury, on the left the ancient city of Caerleon. Passed through Caerwent, once a Roman station and where a fine mosaic tessellated pavement is still extant. See on the right near the Passage the ruins of Caldicot Castle.

There are many castles and situations which I have not mentioned in the latter part of my tour which was performed in a hurry and of course imperfectly since I quitted Tenby. Glamorganshire deserves particular attention from having been the seat of the Normans at a very early aera of whose forts and castles there are numerous remains, particularly in the neighborhood of Cowbridge. This county and Monmouthshire are reserved for some future tour.

[*Hoare apparently did not visit Wales in 1794, nor in 1795*]

II

1796: MID-WALES

Sunday, 19th June, 1796.   Left Stourhead, dined with Mr Champries at Orchardley House, near Frome.

Monday 20th.   Rode to Mr Horner's at Nells Park; to Nunney where there are the ruins of a fine old castle and to Marston.

Tuesday 21st.   Left Orchardley, breakfasted at Bath, dined at Rodborough. Beautiful country, much peopled, great cloth manufacture. Walked to the churchyard where further excavations are making to ascertain the limits of a Roman villa of which great vestiges have been been found, and will be published, under the inspection of Mr Lysons.
   Arrived in the evening at Cheltenham. Delightful drive from Rodborough. Lodged at the Plough, a good inn.

Wednesday 22nd.   Took a lodging at Mr Pope's, pleasantly situated not far from the well or town, yet quite in the country as to prospect and retirement. Terms: two guineas a week, viz half a guinea each for two rooms for myself, the same for one for my servant and the kitchen; the usual price of the lodgings here during the Summer season. The place begins to fill with company.
   . . . The hills afford a constant variety of the most rich, extensive, beautiful views I ever beheld; not to be equalled in any part of England I have visited but in Devonshire on the hills beyond Exeter near Teignmouth. . .
Rides:
   To Tewkesbury eight miles. The abbey, lately new fitted up. Several curious monuments. The largest parish church in England except St Albans. Venerable Saxon architecture. . . . .
   To Gloucester nine miles. The cathedral. The new goal, well worth visiting; its good arrangement, cleanliness and management; cost £26,000, raised by the county. Llanthony Abbey in ruins half a mile out of town and adjoining the new canal from Berkeley. Little of the building remains except a magnificent barn and part of the entrance gateway with three escutcheons with arms over it. One of them the arms of Bohun Earl of Hereford. . . .
Half a mile beyond Llanthony Abbey is Newark, a large house situated on an eminence, commanding a fine view of the city and environs, said to have belonged formerly to the Prior of the Abbey. . . .
   Winchomb, a long scattered village. Numbers of children in the streets. Remains of the abbey enclosure, well built. Grotesque heads about the church. No very curious monuments. An ancient house adjoining the

churchyard now converted into a poorhouse. Inn: White Hart; tolerable.

Sudeley Castle, belongng to Lord Rivers. Fine ruin but not very pictur-esque; few points of view in which it appears to advantage. Chapel the most perfect part of the building. Some part of it appears as a castellated mansion, the other as a place of defence or fort. An uncommon fine crop of cone wheat[1] in the left hand field leading from the town to the castle, some of it higher than my head, six feet at least. Remains of a noble barn.

Hales Abbey, two miles beyond Sudeley; bad road. Situated on a fine rich plain, surrounded by hills. The remains of the abbey trifling, yet worth visiting.[2] It was formerly a rich and mitred abbey. . . .

To Charlton Kings, seat and park of Mr Hunt. Old London Road, up the hill to the seven springs, supposed to be source of the River Thames; return by the Balloon public house and the Bath road. . . .

I made an excursion to Park Corner, a tolerable inn. From thence to Sapperton a mile and half: famous tunnel of the canal through the hill. From thence through Oakley Woods to Cirencester 5 miles. Noble plantations, the work of one man, Lord Bathurst. Ten vistas meet at one broad point. The wide left-hand walk leads to Cirencester . . . a large town. Fine porch to the cathedral [*parish church*]; not many curious monuments, those of Brydges and Master the most so. Hungerford chapel more richly orna-mented in its ceiling than the rest of the church. One pointed window. From Cirencester to Fairford 8 miles; beautiful church, time of Henry vii . . . river made a fine sheet of water, full of trout. Good hothouses.

To Painswick, eleven miles by Birdlip, one of the pleasantest rides in England, through a wild forest of beech wood and juniper bushes. A noble view from an old camp, double-ditched, a mile from Painswick. . . .

The carriage roads near Cheltenham are in general bad, except those leading through the vales to Gloucester and Tewkesbury. The country is very accessible on horseback and without a horse the finest views (perhaps in England) cannot be seen to advantage. The country well peopled and cultivated, the soil sandy and absorbent. The cone wheat, or bearded, is in general sown, a proof of the goodness of the land; it sells at a higher price and yields more per acre. The vales are a very deep clay with a mixture of sand. Great tracts of beans, few oats and little barley. Those grains mostly cultivated in the Cotswold Hills, looking over these rich vales. The hill farmers reckoned better than in the vales; land in the vales (arable) letts for thirty shillings and upwards (a tenant of Lord Sherborne's rents above 4,000 acres in this county). . . .

From the hills (owing to the quantity of the trees in the hedgerows) the country bears a very woody appearance; few houses are distinguished. But on riding through the lanes in the plain the population and wealth of the yeomanry and peasants show themselves, and, if I may judge from the appearance and frequent succession to each other, the farms are of moderate extent. The soil seems particularly adapted to the growth of trees; elms and oaks grow to a very great size. The fields and hedgerows are in general very well wooded. There are few large copses. Property much divided.

Way of Life:

Spa opens at seven in the morning. Company meets from that time to nine.

Plays: Tuesday, Thursday, Saturday [Best actors and actresses: Rupell, Old Shute, and Mrs Bonneville and Mr Fox].

Balls: Monday and Friday. [Balls end at eleven at night].

Rooms for cards every night.

Rooms for tea on Sundays.

Bowling Green for ditto on ditto.

A coffee room with newspapers for ladies only at the Bowling Green; public breakfast there on Thursdays.

Coffee room with newspapers at the Plough Inn for gentlemen: subscription 5 s. Sun, Star, Times and Morning Post.

[For drinking the waters usual price 5 s. per week; a fee to Mrs Forter who pumps it; 5 s. for the music; 2′ 6″ for the walks; and a guinea to the master of ceremonies].

No public ordinary as at Harrogate. The town well-paved; the lodgings in general very neat and clean; provisions plentiful and not extravagant in their price.

Tuesday 20th July   Left Cheltenham after breakfast; rode to Tewkesbury, 8 miles. . . . To Upton 7 miles, a picturesque old bridge over the Severn. To Little Malvern, 6 miles On a near approach these magnificent hills lose somewhat of their apparent height, probably owing to a long and gradual ascent towards them. The Well House, a large single brick house situated immediately under the hill. Company board and live together as at Harrogate and Matlock; the terms reasonable; the table very well served. At a little distance is the Spring, and a cold bath, of the purest water without any taste of mineral.

I do not hesitate in giving the preference to the views on the Herefordshire side of the mountain. The view is more varied by a diversity of little hills all covered with wood. Numerous farmhouses and orchards are interspersed and the scenery is finely terminated by the Welch mountains: the Sugar Loaf near Abergavenny, the Black Mountains in Brecknockshire etc. The opposite side presents an immense plain with the cities of Worcester and Gloucester at the opposite extremities, and the foreground has the disadvantage of a large tract of uncultivated commons.

At Little Malvern there was formerly a convent of Benedictines founded about the year 1171. It was rebuilt (the church) about the year 1482 by John Alcock, Bishop of Worcester. It is now in a ruinous state but has a picturesque appearance. Adjoining it is an old house belonging to Miss Williams. . . . Between the house and the mountain is a beautiful little glen, well worth visiting. The trees, particularly the oaks are remarkably fine and natural. . . . In the midst of these solitary groves we met a Carthusian émigré, brother of Miss Williams, deep in meditation with his book in his hand. No place was ever more adapted to such a man and such a pursuit.

Wednesday 21st.   Left Little Malvern and breakfasted at Great Malvern. I prefer the situation of this place; the scenery is richer, the place more peopled and chearful. The church is a fine majestic object situated just under the mountain and overlooking the extensive plain . . . a fine building but hastening quickly to its dissolution. A mixture of Saxon and Gothic architecture; the lower arches are low Saxon. . . . There is a good hotel here, very well situated, and in every respect, for rides, walks etc I prefer as a residence Great to Little Malvern. . . .

Dined at Worcester. To Bromsgrove 13 miles. Inn: Golden Cross. Red soil inclined to sand. Pasture and corn, the latter very fine. Country inclosed. To Stourbridge 10 miles. . . . To Wolverhampton 10 miles. . . . Great ironworks in neighborhood. A large populous town. . . . To Stafford 6 miles. . . . Small for a county town. Handsome town hall now building; infirmary and goal out of the town lately built. From Wolverhampton hither the country inclosed, cultivated with corn, and pastures. Hedgerows well wooded. To Stone 7 miles; Crown Inn; a neat town and church. Country rather more wild and open. . . . To Newcastle 9 miles; inn: Roebuck. Large and populous town. Hat manufactory. All the above towns being built of brick have a dark and dull appearance. . . .

To Tabley House 2 miles. The country mends; more wooded, but still flat and wet. Tabley House, seat of Sir John Leicester: large and handsome brick house with stone portico, friezes of Doric order. Capital offices, stabling etc. Park flat and rather thinly wooded, ground wet. Large piece of water. Old house and chapel remaining on an island moated round. . . .

Saturday 30th.   Left Tabley in morning. To Northwich, 5 miles; to Chester 17 ditto. To Northwich a paved road. . . . Great Saltworks. . . .

Chester: one of the oldest and most singular cities in England. Walk through many of the principal streets under old-fashioned low porticoes. Cathedral singular in its appearance from the nature of the stone with which it is built. Mouldering away. Deep red color. Walk round the walls. Good inn-hotel. Stay too short to see the town. Form of the race ground like that of a Roman amphitheatre; appearance during the races very picturesque and singular.

To Wrexham 11 miles. . . . Good road. Fertile soil, well cultivated. From a hill a fine view: Beeston Castle at a distance on a bold isolated hill. Fine church at Wrexham. Wynstay, seat of Sir Watkyn Williams Wynne on left. Descend to a handsome stone bridge over the Dee.

First romantic appearance of country. River Dee running rapidly at the bottom, fine hanging woods above. Prospect terminates with the mountains about Llangollen: Castle Dinas Bran on the summit of a lofty conical mountain. This entry into Wales fine. Canal on right. Great lime works on right. Good road, that to Oswestry on left.

Llangollen, 11 miles and half. Inn: Bloody Hand. Neat. People slow and

11. Valle Crucis Abbey, Powys, the west end of the church before restoration
by Scott.

tardy in their manoeuvres. Picturesque situation. Alpine appearance. Village built on the banks of the Dee; falls rapidly above the bridge, which is handsome and well built.

Sunday 31st.   After breakfast went to Valle Crucis, two miles on the road to Ruthin. Fine ruins situated in a deep vale and too much surrounded with trees to have a good view of them. An old cross with an inscription at a little distance.[3] To Corwen 10 miles . . . a little village under a wild rocky mountain like some in Switzerland. River Dee very fine for fishing.

Saturday 6th August.   Left Corwen in the evening. To Bala 12 miles; road not bad, one long hill. Country for the first part well-cultivated, afterwards wild and mountainous. Good view of Bala Lake before you descend to the village. One long broad street; singular mixture of old and new houses; street rather picturesque. Lake about half a mile off; River Dee issues from it at the end near the village; length about 5 miles, banks not rocky but cultivated. Two inns: Bull and White Lyon, the last reckoned the best. Two pairs of post horses only kept here, and these at the Bull.

Sunday 7th.   To Dolgelly [*Dolgellau*] 18 miles; three hours and a quarter with a pair of horses. The road leads along the right bank of the lake. The parish church of Bala about a mile from the village on this road. High mountains on the right. End of the lake where several rivers enter it. Sir W. Wynne's steward's house, who on application will give permission to have the lake drawn with a net.

Dolgelly, a little village in the vale at the foot of Cader Idris. Inn: Golden Lyon; bad. About 4 miles to the highest summit of the mountain.

To Machunleth [*Machynlleth*] 18 miles; 4 hours with 4 horses; that number absolutely necessary. Long and steep ascent winding round the mountains. Stoney open country without trees; wild and romantic scenery; fine successive range of mountains in perspective; little lake in the valley beneath. Steep descent through a narrow gorge; perpendicular cragged mountains above. Turn off to the left, leaving the lake to the right. Wild country. Descend into another valley; fine handing woods, torrent at bottom. . . .

To Aberystwith 20 long miles; four hours, four horses, went quick. Ascend a steep hill hanging over the River Dovey, navigable to this place, ships and boats. Wild rough ground. Sea. Hills covered with copse. Embouchure of the river into the sea. . . .

Aberystwith: a little seaport in Cardiganshire, situated on the River Rheidiol though its name applies to the River Ystwith which runs at a little distance and unites itself with the Rheidiol just before it empties itself into the sea. Both these rivers have little water during the summer months. The situation of the town is very healthy. The castle (whose ruins are very trifling) stands on the most elevated ground and commands a noble sea view. . . . In a clear day all the mountains in this point of land which projects appear like so many islands. . . . The beach is good for bathing; four machines kept. Pleasant walk in the castle. Two inns; the Talbot the best. Few good lodging houses and those not commanding a sea view, except a good family house belonging to Mrs Corbet in which I had apartments. Mr Price of Foxley, Herefordshire, author of the *Essay on the Picturesque* has built himself a house in the form of a castle projecting immediately over the rocks near the old castle.[4]

Very little trade carried on except in lime and slate. The rocks are in general of a slaty nature which gives them a form very far from picturesque. At the back of the town is a large plain called the Marsh in which is a spring of strong chalybeate. Another of the same sort, but not so strong, adjoining the Machunlleth road. Little variety of rides and those not very interesting. The country in general cultivated with corn and thinly wooded. Post comes in Monday, Thursday and Saturday. Balls weekly at the two inns. Apothecary: Mr Williams and Partner. Four or five posthorses kept. Not much fish. Sewen in both rivers. Singular method of catching them when the water is clear by spearing.

The two principal objects of the traveller's attention are Hafod and the Devil's Bridge. Hafod, the seat of Mr Johns, has, with regard to the beauties of its local situation been so exaggerated by Mr Cumberland that everyone who has an eye to see, and a judgement to discriminate the beauties of nature must, like myself, be much disappointed in viewing it. After crossing some of the most dreary and barren mountains imaginable you enter a valley, apparently well-wooded at a distance. . . . The scenery or beauties of this place consist in walks out through the woods on each side of the river which with other streams form in different places some pretty cascades. The house is of a singular, and not an elegant, species of Gothic architecture. . . . One room fitted up with very fine Gobelin tapestry. The library circular in its form with a gallery supported by marble columns of the ancient Doric order without bases; the proportions much too heavy. Conservatory of above a hundred feet in length joins the library. There is a good picture of Vandyke. . . . The house is certainly not very advantageously placed, facing a barren mountain; nor do I think (owing to the small extent of this woody valley) could it have been placed so as to have had the barreness of the adjoining country totally concealed. The largest trees are sycamore, which I have always thoughts the hardiest of all trees.

Hafod is about fifteen miles from Aberystwith and five from Devils Bridge. The bridge has probably gained its name from its singular situation being thrown over a chasm of an immense height. The old bridge being apparently in a state of decay a new one was thrown over the old one which still remains, and adds to the picturesque appearance of the whole. The River Monnoch [*Mynach*] roars at a considerable depth below, and forms a very long cascade which, at the time I saw it, was too destitute of water to give it the effect I could have wished. It is well surrounded by wood but the form and nature of the rocks is not very good. There is another waterfall adjoining which, though it cannot vie with the above for magnitude and is not so often visited by travellers, yet has infinite more beauties of variety. . . .

the masses of stone scattered about the bed of the river is as fine as ever I saw, and particularly adapted for the studies of an artist.

The whole scenery about the Devil's Bridge is very fine and infinitely, in my opinion, superior to Hafod. There is a decent little inn on the spot with two very good bedrooms. By following the bed of the Rheidiol and fording it at different places there is a much pleasanter ride to Aberystwith than by the usual carriage road. Hafod and the Devil's Bridge are too much for one day.

Thursday 1 September.   Left Aberystwith at six in the morning; breakfast at Cwm Ystwith, 15 miles. Road good but hilly. Lands cultivated. Buckwheat used as a manure by ploughing it in. Lands pared and burned. . . . . Enter a narrow valley, the picture of barrenness and desolation; totally void of wood. River Ystwith at bottom. Lead mines on left. Road continues to Rhaeder 15 miles. . . . Cwm Elan, so called from being situated on the River Elan, is an estate of 12,000 acres, lately purchased by my friend, Mr Grove of Fern in Wiltshire; where he has built a new house and by introducing the English mode of agriculture has already made a very considerable improvement in his land, particularly by draining, folding, turnips, cabbages etc. . . .

Saturday 3rd September.   Left our quarters at six but obliged to return to them in few minutes; on descending a steep bank into the river the pole of my carriage broke. At eight it was repaired. Arrived at Rhaeder at 9½. Inn: Red Lyon; bad. Imposing landlord (with regard to my posthorses). Situated on the Wye, an insignificant stream.

Country better than from Aberystwith but not very interesting. Cultivated to Penybont. A single house where we baited the horses for half an hour. Bad quarters. From thence through New Radmor to Kington in Herefordshire, 5 hours and a half in all from Rhaeder. Country wilder after Penybont for some distance. . . . Adieu to rocks and mountains! A good road with few hills leads us to Hereford. Rich country well wooded and well cultivated. Foxley, the seat of Uvedale Price, eight miles from Hereford on left.[5] Fine woods. Two good hotels at Hereford: City Arms and New Inn. I lodged at the latter — good. The former appears the largest. Stay too short to see any of the town.

Sunday 4th September.   Left Hereford; to Ross, 14 miles; 2 horses, road good. Country woody and well-cultivated. Hop grounds and orchards. Fine views of distant country. Wilton Castle on the left near Ross before the bridge. A modern house built in the middle of the old ruins — dreadful! Cross the Wye, several pleasure boats. . . . To Gloucester 16 miles, 2¼ hours. . . . To Petty France 13 miles, 1 hour 25 minutes. . . . Noble wood of beech trees on left on mounting the hill. A most dull country succeeds: cornfields enclosed by stone walls, the most hideous af all fences. Badminton, the seat of the Duke of Beaufort on the left close to Petty France.

To Bath 15 miles, 1 hour 35 minutes. Road good. Same dull country.

Came remarkably quick the whole day; 4 horses to chaise. York house. To Warminster, Deptford Inn; and Stourhead.

III

1797: NORTH AND SOUTH-EAST WALES

Tour in the Summer of 1797

Left Stourhead on *Thursday morning 15th June.* Breakfasted at Orchardley. From thence to Bath; dined at Petty France; slept at Gloucester. . . .

Country round Bath pretty, hills finely varied. Approaching to Gloucestershire country becomes dreary and few trees; stone walls supply the place of hedges. . . . Prospect changes instantaneously; sudden descent into one of the most beautiful vallies I ever beheld, singular in its nature and gay in its appearance. Consists of narrow dale or glen, well wooded, a rivulet running through the bottom. The sides of the hills interspersed with numberless houses, neat in their architecture and whitened walls. This little valley appears the seat of ease, comfort and opulence. Inhabited by clothiers. Reminds me much of Locle and La Chaux de Fond in Switzerland. Inn at Rodborough in the midst of the valley. . . .

Friday 16th. Left Gloucester; breakfasted at Ross; dined at Leominster; slept at Church Stretton. . . . From Ross to Hereford: first part of the road dull; about 4 miles from Hereford a fine view; descend rather a steep hill; the city appears well and country about it. Approach to the town favorable: the square tower of the cathedral appears exactly in the center between two other spiry steeples as its supporters.

From Hereford to Leominster road rather better. At VIIM. an old mansion house on the left under Dinmore Hill concerning which there is the following note in Paterson's *Itinerary*: 'Burghope, an ancient mansion, formerly the seat of Sir John Dineley Goodyere Bart. who was murdered by his brother, Captain Samuel Goddyere. From the above event it bears the character of being haunted by spirits and of course uninhabited and falling to decay'. The woods around it are beautiful and its situation fine. Long ascent and descent on Dinmore Hill which is finely wooded.

Descend at VIII 8[M], Hampton Court, the seat of Lord Malden, formerly of the Coningesby family . . . bad all the remainder of the way to Leominster. A nasty borough town and dirty inn. . . . At IVM. from Ludlow you see the lofty tower of the church. Entrance to the town pretty; some picturesque mills and waterfalls near the bridge close to the town. Steep ascent . . . Ludlow is a neat small town, not so large as Leominster.

To Church Stretton 16 miles. On leaving the town Ludlow Castle appears a fine ruin. Oakley Park, seat of Lord Clive on the left: a red brick house, bad style of architecture, backed with a fine mountain covered with wood. . .

Saturday 17th. Left Church Stretton, 18 M. (inn indifferent); breakfasted at Shrewsbury (Raven inn good); dined at Oswestry; and slept at Llangollen.

The road from Church Stretton to Shrewsbury continues for some distance winding through the valley with a range of hills on each side, affording excellent pasture for sheep. . . . Entrance to Shrewsbury over a very handsome stone bridge — modern. The city built on a hill, steep ascent to it. Built of brick. Market day: great concourse of people. To Oswestry 18 miles. Cross the Severn over another handsome modern stone bridge. Ruins of an old one on the right. At M.IV cross the river again over another stone bridge. . . . House of Industry on left nearer Oswestry . . . a neat town, houses of brick, roofs of slate. Large parish church, no ancient monuments but one with two figures kneeling. . . . Rye cultivated and ploughs used with two wheels; no one to direct them, seem to go regular and steady.

To Llangollen 12 miles. The first part of the road uninteresting. . . . Leave Chirk Castle on the left. . . . Sudden change in the appearance of the country: romantic valley; River Dee running in a rapid stream at the bottom; a lofty mountain of a conical form, on which are the ruins of an old castle, rises exactly in the center of the vale, and is backed by others more distant.

Sunday 18th. At Llangollen. Ascended the mountain on which are the ruins of Castle Dinas Bran. The remains are trifling: built of a thin slaty stone; fortified strongly to the north by nature, to the south by a deep foss cut in the rock. No very extensive view except towards Wrexham — that not very striking.

Monday 19th. At Llangollen fishing. Stormy weather. 4 small fish. My friend Leicester came.[1]

Tuesday 20th. Went to Corwen, 10 miles: fishing. . . .

Sunday 25th. Corwen to Bala 12 miles. . . . Bala Lake appears at a distance between the mountains. Road in some parts good but owing to late heavy rains now rough and dirty, the face of the country dull and uninteresting. Inn at Bala, White Lyon, John Williams, landlord: one good dining room and one good double-bedded room. . . . A sect of Methodists called Jumpers, very loud in their vociferation at a meeting house opposite the inn.

Bala Pool, or Pimble Mere, the largest lake in Wales, between 4 and 5 miles in length, near 12 in circumference, and in some places a mile wide. Fish: perch, trout, eels and *gwyniad*, a white delicate fish. The two former afford excellent sport to anglers, the latter are never caught but in nets. After heavy storms some have been found dead on the shore. Some years ago both the lake and the River Dee were full of pike; their destruction is attributed to a large flood since which none have been seen. The ride round this lake is very pleasant. At the upper end, owing to the rivers which there enter the lake, it is necessary to go as far as the village [*of*] Lanwelyn [*Llanuwchllyn*] in order to make the tour of the pool. The lofty mountans of Arrenig on the

right, and of Arran on the left add much to the beauty of the scenery, and at
the extremity of the lake (near Bala) the majestic mountain, Cader Idris, fills
up the chasm between the Arrenig and Arran. A fine sailing boat is kept
there by Sir Watkyn Wynne (the Lord of the Lake) and on application is at
the service of travellers.

There is something picturesque in the appearance of the village of Bala:
one long, wide street with some sycamore trees projecting into it; several
cottages rendered picturesque from their dilapidated state and the grass and
other plants sprouting from their thatched roofs. The chief trade of this
place as well as of the adjoining villages is woollen; stockings and gloves are
made in great perfection and very cheap.

Thursday 29th.   Left Bala to Tan-y-bwlch: 23 miles, 5 horses, chaise and
pair. . . . A few scattered, miserable habitations with little inclosures of oats
etc. Some fields have been cultivated with much care and labour, the stones
collected and put into heaps. Soil peaty, dug and used as fuel. A fine range of
mountains on the left, the most conspicuous are Arrenig. . . . A black stream
running through the meadows which, if drained, would yield excellent
pasturage. Continual hills, chiefly ascents. All cultivation ceases. Fine
mountain scene: in the foreground a wide extent of land covered with heath
and rushy grass, backed by lofty mountains of a beautiful dark purple hue
and of the most rude and picturesque forms. Herds of black oxen and wild
sheep, not a tree or a shrub to be seen. The vivid green of the moor finely
contrasted with the dark blue tints of the distant mountains. A herd of 2,000
sheep with their rustic drivers added to the wildness of the scenery. . . .

On a sudden a fine prospect of the sea coast extending towards Pwllheli;
amphitheatre of lofty mountains to the right. Village of Festiniog; an inn
there for a small party. Long and steep descent to Tan y bwlch. . . . Neat
little inn; no chaise or post-horses; two good double-bedded rooms. Adjoining to the inn is Tan-y-bwlch Hall . . . a most picturesque object from every
part of the vale. The tide comes up to the bridge over which you pass to the
inn. From the banks of the river is a fine view of the vale looking towards
Festiniog. Few and small trout but good salmon fishing in the river after a
flood. . . .

Friday 30th.   Left Tan-y-bwlch early in the morning, hiring a horse and
paniers to carry my luggage, the road being too bad for a four-wheel
carriage. Steep ascent . . . we again entered amongst the mountain, still more
deeply than yesterday. They become more lofty and rugged in their form.
View of an extensive sea coast, Harlech Castle on the left seated on a bold
rock projecting into the sea. On approaching Pont Aberglasllyn a few trees
in a thriving state. . . . Descend to Pont Aberglasllyn, a bridge of one arch
over a deep chasm in the rocks through which the river runs rapidly. Just
above it a salmon leap; too early in the season for the fish to come up in any
quantities. Mountains approach very near each other, just leaving room for
the torrent and the road on its side; rugged and void of wood but romantic

12. Caernarfon Castle in 1810 from across the River Seiont.

in their form and situation. Copper works close to the bridge.

Beddgelert: bridge, church and mountains form a pleasing landscape. . . . From Beddgelert to Carnarvon 12 miles, road good. Leads under the base of Snowdon; rather disappointed having seen other mountains apparently almost as high and more picturesque in their form. . . . Adieu to romantic scenery! Dull country, fields enclosed with stone walls etc. Church of Lanbublic [*Llanbeblig*] on right, a large building, the parish church of Carnarvon. Descend to Carnarvon. Cross the river. Road good. In the midst of hay harvest. The roads in general much improved and still improving in many of the most unfrequented parts of Wales; done by subscription and county rates. Well planned. Women bare-footed and employed in knitting.

Carnarvon: a neat town, chiefly built within the precincts of the old walls. The castle: large, massive pile of building, rather too much so to make it picturesque. A good view of it at a little distance up the river. Its chief trade in slates, of two colors, blue and of a rich purple. Over the entrance to the castle is a figure of its founder, King Edward.[2] Good view from the summit of the Eagle Tower, so called from the sculpture of a bird on its summit; part of it still remaining but mutilated. . . .

A magnificent hotel has been lately built at the extremity of the town by Lord Uxbridge. Commands a fine view of the River Menai[3] and the oposite coast of Anglesey. Very flat. Number of vessels continually passing up and down with the tide enliven the view. The landlord comes from Cheshire and has taken the inn on tryal. The little concourse of travellers will, I fear, impede his success as innkeeper. He rents a large farm and has introduced the culture of turnips which answer well. Cheap bill.

[Bill at the Hotel Carnarvon
2 large place of salmon
2 fowls
Neck of mutton
Veal cutlets
Peas-beans-potatoes
2 lobsters
Gooseberry tart
For the above we were charged eight shillings]

Sunday 2nd July.   Left Carnarvon. Saw the first wheat and barley in ear. Road uninteresting. . . . Towards Bangor we descended to a ferry and crossed the river to Plas Newydd, seat of Lord Uxbridge who is now building a large house there in the Gothic style of architecture.[4] I might rather say *mixed*, as several square modern sash windows are injudiciously mixed with the Gothic. Hall and dining room Gothic and handsome rooms. A wing of offices takes off from the symmetry of the facade. Hot and cold sea baths before the house. Stables: a picturesque Gothic building in a singular style. The stone quarried on the very spot where the house is built, of a blue slatey color. A well-preserved cromlech behind the house; some fine trees overhanging it add much to its venerable character and appearance.

The banks of the river are here well-wooded but soon, on following the course of the river, become rocky and barren. Several little rocks and islands dispersed in the channel of the river give good reason to suppose that formerly Anglesey was united to the opposite coast. They now, on account of the violent eddies, render the navigation very dangerous except to experienced pilots. A plan was once in agitation to throw a bridge across the rivr but opposed (though thought practicable) by the inhabitants of Carnarvon, who thought the navigation of their trading vessels would thereby be impeded. Herds of black cattle are forced to swim across from one shore to the other, and their course directed by boats stationed on each side.

Monday 3 July In the morning went to Lord Penrhyn's slate quarries, 8 miles. Pass through Bangor. . . . Some parts of the quarries picturesque. Country wild and barren, void of trees. Several neat little white cottages scattered on the side of the hills; one ornamented belongs to Lord P. who has made several new plantations in these parts. . . . Ascended the sides of a steep mountain . . . I have seen no scene as yet during my journey so wild and romantic, or situation so high that at times we were quite envelopped in clouds. One point of view very striking: on one side a long range of the most rugged mountains, rearing their lofty summits above the clouds, not a tree or bush to be seen; on the other side a view of the verdant valley through which we had passed, terminated by the coast of Beaumaris and the Menai. Nothing in the wilds of Merionethshire appeared so sublime as the above scene. A good road goes by the banks of the lake to Capel Cerrig [*Curig*], and from thence there is a horse road to Llanrwst.

Thursday 4 July. Spent the morning and dined at Lord Penrhyn's. House in a very exposed position, lately faced with Southampton tiles. Built in the form of a castle.[5] Offices very complete: chapel, stables etc. Slate used in a variety of forms, as paling etc. etc. The outside of the stables are faced with slate which is screwed down to strong wooden plugs sunk into the wall. The hot and cold baths near the sea very complete. Adjoining them is a large weir of wickerwork on the sea coast, where the sea, on the going down of the tide, leaves great numbers and variety of fish. Lord P. has made many young plantations which seem in their present state to thrive well, but the S.W. wind here has great power over them. The little port of Penrhyn from which Lord P. exports his slates is between his house and Bangor. At the bottom of his garden runs the River Ogwen where great number of salmon are caught at the end of the Summer. Water so clear that they may be seen from the walks above the river.

Wednesday 5 July [At Bangor as well as in many parts of North Wales a harper attends at the inn and plays to company during their meals; the best we heard was at this place]. Left Bangor Ferry Inn; good but rather dear. To Bangor 2 M. No curious monuments in the cathedral; no effigies except of

13. Looking down the River Ogwen towards Pont Talybont with (the earlier) Penrhyn Castle beyond.

two bishops who have lost their heads. Plain church and very unlike a cathedral. Neat little church at Llandegai which contains the effigies and monument of Archbishop Williams. . . .[6]

Pursue the road to Conwy. A fine range of lofty mountains in front, one of which, called Carned[d] Llewellyn, is reckoned the second in height to Snowdon. . . . At MILE IX begin to ascend Penmaenmawr, long ascent over a steep and rugged mountain; few signs of vegetation; many large masses of rock detached from their original rock and fallen on the declivities of the mountain. Good road with a parapet wall on the edge of a steep precipice. Ascend another steep mountain and then descend to Conway. Nothing picturesque in the approach; enter through one of the old city gates. From Bangor to Conway 15 miles; country badly cultivated; some corn; road good.

Conway. The castle built by Edward 1 nobly situated on a bold rock projecting to the river which washes its walls. The architecture varies in this respect from Carnarvon Castle (which was built at nearly the same time) that all the towers are circular instead of square.[7] On these towers are built others of smaller dimensions which give a very light appearance to the building. One of the large circular towers is in a state of ruin owing to the rock having been taken away on which its foundation rested; the upper part of it hangs together suspended in wonderful manner. The form of the rooms remains very perfect: the most remarkable of these is the great hall with its chimney pieces and arches on which the ceiling was supported still remaining. . . .

This magnificent castle appears to great advantage wherever it is viewed; but the best points of view are from the fine woods of oak leading up the hill towards Mr Pryce's house, where the entrance to the river, the opposite coast and castle form a most pleasing and well composed picture, and from the opposite side of the town where the castle presents itself backed by the fine woods above-mentioned. They belong to Lord Bulkeley and are the principal ornament of the place.

The parish church bears some marks of antiquity in its appearance, and with the fine trees in the churchyard has a picturesque effect. . . . Many ancient houses in the town: the Plas Mawr in the street a little above the Harp Inn, built by the family of Wynn, the old inhabitants of Gwedir. One curious large room within with stucco, arms etc.

The town carries on but little trade. Some vessels load with stone for paving to Liverpool. Formerly some little trade was carried on with pearls. They were found in the muscles [*mussels*] which were caught in great numbers by the women and children, and when boiled each shell produced a pearl. They were sold to the apothecaries who made of them testaceous powder. This trade is now at an end.

On the opposite side, at the entrance of the river, was another ancient castle of Diganway, of which some trifling remains are still visible. . . .

Sunday 9 July. Left Conway, to Llanrwst 12 miles. Good view of Conway Castle. Afterwards the River Conway appears to advantage in a broad sheet

14. Conway Castle from the south-east across the River Gyffin. Note the tower with collapsed base.

of water, tide being full. Follow the course of the river on the left [*west*]. Lands on each side well cultivated. Caer Hun; some antiquities (supposed Roman) have been found here [*see pp. 179, 250*]. On approaching to Llanrwst valley becomes narrower. Large masses of rock fallen from the mountains, large blocks of slate. At different points some good views of the river. Fine wood of Gwedir near the town. Pass over a handsome bridge of three arches. Road good.

Churchyard on the banks of the river picturesque. Gwedir chapel, designed by Indigo Jones (as well as the bridge)[8] contains some very curious brasses and monuments of the Wynne family, but rather in a neglected state. . . . Stone coffin of the Great Llewellyn, Prince of Wales, brought from Conwy Abbey. . . .

Monday 10 July. From Llanrwst to Yspytty Evan [*Ysbyty Ifan*] 12 miles. Cross the river. Pass through the fine woods of Gwedir; plantations continued along the sides of the mountains by the present possessor, Lord Gwedir. Many fine weeping birch trees. River Conwy on left. Little village of Bettws [*Betws y Coed*], romantic bridge over the River Llugwy. Scenery very grand. River forms a fine fall over large masses of rock. . . . Fine pools in river out of one which a man has just caught a salmon of 23lb. In the latter part of the summer these fish come up in great numbers. . . . take the left hand road. Country now becomes dull and in some places bad even for a horse. Handsome bridge of one arch over the River Conwy and apparently a good road leading on the other side of it to Llanrwst . . . Yspytty Evan, a little village situated in the midst of a wild mountainous country, on the banks of the River Conwy, here much diminished in size and running over a rocky bed.

Tuesday 11 July. At break of day mounted my horse to go to Llyn Conwy; steep ascent; cross a wild and boggy moor; walk a mile. Llyn Conwy, about 3 miles in circumference. Situated in the midst of a boggy and peaty moor, its sides rocky and indented. Several wild sea gulls making a great noise. River Conwy issues in a small stream from this lake. Wind too high for fish to rise. The trout in this lake are reckoned amongst the best in Wales. Descend about two miles to the nearest house where the horses could be put up.

In the evening I left a most miserable inn, which nothing but its vicinity to the lake could make supportable and rode to Bala, twelve long uninteresting miles through a wild moorish country. . . .

Friday 14 July. In evening left Bala. Tumulus on the right at the extremity of the town.[9] . . . It is intended to make a carriage road from Corwen to Bala through this valley by which means all hills will be avoided. Some part of it is already done. Arrived at Corwen at the conclusion of the fair.

Sunday 16 July. From Corwen to Llangollen 10 miles. Fine valley. Pictur-

15. Valle Crucis Abbey, houses in the cloister with the church behind.

esque open wood of oak and birch on the right. . . . Few places in Wales can boast of so many natural beauties as Llangollen; amongst the many picturesque vales watered by the Dee I prefer this.

The remains of the celebrated abbey in Vale Crucis are about two miles distant and, though not so well preserved as their beautiful architecture should have merited, still merit the attention of every traveller who will view them as an artist or antiquarian. To the former they will afford much employment for his pencil. The ruins are surrounded by fine old ash trees whose delicate taper corresponds well with the elegant light Gothic architecture of the building, but I could wish one or two of them removed to admit a more perfect view of the fine western front. This abbey, formerly the residence of a numerous fraternity of [*Cistercian monks*] is now converted into a farmhouse.[10] The modern buildings intermixed with the old architecture have not a bad effect. A little rapid brook runs near it. It is backed by a lofty mountain covered with fine wood and the situation is such as the monks generally selected for their habitations; who in this respect at least knew how to mix the *utile* with the *dulce*: a good soil, fine water, and a sheltered and secluded spot.

Tuesday 18th. From Langollen to Wrexham 13 M., road good. The beauty of this valley still continues undiminished till I arrived at the turnpike. . . . The church of Rhuabon contains some good monuments of the Middleton family. Extensive coal works in the neighborhood. Wynstay, the seat of Sir Watkin Wynne, on the right. Road to Wrexham flat and dull. From Wrexham to Chester 12 miles, road flat and good. Church at Wrexham the handsomest I have seen in Wales: rich ornamented Gothic architecture. A very good print of it just published in aquatint (price 9d). . . .

Chester. Hotel, good inn. . . . Cathedral: fine Gothic carve work in the choir of wood; arches on the two sides of the choir differently finished; chapter house an elegant building; the ancient shrine of St Werburg now made the Bishop's seat. . . . It appears that the roof of the nave and aisles was never finished, stones left from which arches must spring. Fine old abbey gateway. Walk round the walls of the city very singular, as well as that under the rows. Fine goal now building. . . .

Saturday 29 July. Left Tabley. From Tabley to Northwich 5 miles. Visited the salt works of which there are many in this neighborhood. They are distinguished in [*by*] brine pits and rock pits; the former are round pits into which the salt spring is introduced and from thence conveyed into large square receptacles of beaten iron, then heated by large fires beneath. On the boiling of the saltwater the saline particles sink to the bottom and form the salt. These are emptied twice a day, and produce from four to six tons of salt. The pits of rock salt are, I believe, peculiar to this part of England but I did not visit them [*p. 159*]. They are sunk several yards under ground. When the spring in the brine pits is not sufficiently strong rock salt is sometimes added. A navigable canal is made close to these works and a cotton work

16. Ross-on-Wye as seen across the bowling green of the King's Head Inn in 1797.

17. Goodrich Castle, Herefordshire; view in pencil in the courtyard looking towards keep.

adjoins. . . .

To Whitchurch . . . Hills well coverd with oak on the right. Enter the great road leading from Whitchurch to Chester at the 13th milestone from Chester; road better. On arriving at Whitchurch I found the landlord had imposed on me by recommending this road for which I was obliged to take four horses. . . .

To Wem 10 M. Road sandy. Fields of buckwheat, hemp and rye; pasture lands foul as I observed them to be in Cheshire . . . a small town and indifferent-looking inn.

Shrewsbury . . . Castle modernised with Gothic windows; good view from the summer house.[11] Pretty walk round the quarry. Fine avenues of lime trees on the banks of the Severn. Walk round the city walls as at Chester but not so clean. 2 very fine bridges; the old Welch bridge nearly pulled down. The large stone bridge built in 1774. New goal. . . . Ludlow . . . environs very pretty. . . . Castle a large pile of a building situated on a rock; river at bottom; pleasant walks round the castle, several waterfalls on river. . . .[12]

Monday 31 July. To Leominster 10 miles. . . . Church burnt down, rebuilt partly; the old part Saxon, the new a rich Gothic. It has a good effect when seen at a little distance out of the churchyard, the front well broken by trees. . . . Town hall: curious piece of old woodwork. . . .[13]

Hereford: City Arms Hotel, New Inn. Cathedral: contains beautiful specimens of old Saxon architecture; has undergone a thorough repair under the direction of Mr Wyatt. Part of it which fell down has been restored in the Gothic style which I think is rather too light for the fine massive Saxon near it.[14] Arches between the principals which support the tower very ugly. In the library a curious chapel dedicated to the Virgin Mary left in its old state, painted. Many effigies and brasses, many of the latter in a state of decay. No good account of the monuments and church; Parker, a bookseller, means to undertake one. . . .

Monday 31st.[15] Ross. Went to Goodrich Castle[16] by land, 5 M. Large building on an eminence surrounded by trees, rather too much so for drawing. The inside presents some picturesque studies. The keep apparently of Norman architecture and much more ancient than the other parts of the building. Cross [by] ferry; road nearer to Ross. The castle appears to advantage on the opposite side. . . .

Wednesday August 2. From Ross to Monmouth by water 25 M., by land 10 m.[17] Wilton Castle on right. Wilton Bridge over the Wye. Village of Pencreek on an eminence to the right. Fine bank of wood to water's edge. Newhouse, belonging formerly to the Swift family. Goodrich Castle: good point of view under the wood where the castle and well-wooded hill fill up the center of the landscape; the ferry house and boat beneath add to the picturesque effect. Goodrich church and priory on the right. Here the river

18. Looking across the River Wye towards Goodrich Castle by the ferry, with boats.

takes so winding and circuitous a course that from the above ferry to another further down the river the distance is seven miles, whereas by land the distance is only one mile.

Division of the two counties a hedge running in a straight direction up the hill; on the Hereford side fern and wild ground, on the Monmouth side copse wood and timber. A little further on the left the counties of Hereford and Gloucester are divided by a little brook. Quarry on the right from which Bristol bridge was built. Mr Vaughan contracted for quarrying the stone and conveying it down to the river, and I was told that he lost considerably by the contract. Bishop's Wood furnace on left; iron ore here melted into pigs. Courtfield house on right: Mr Vaughan's. Village of Librook. Vessels laden with coal from Forest of Dean. Valley more narrow. Welch Bicknor. A conical hill in front called Rosemary Topping.

Coldwell Rocks, a grand scene of wood and limestone rock. Symond's Rock, here again the river takes a very winding course: 4 M. by water, 1 M. by land. Large masses of rock fallen down on the left from the mountain. Here again the spire of Goodrich Church appears on the right and soon after the ferry above-mentioned. Banks of the river uninteresting. Halfway house on the Monmouthshire road which here comes near the river. Church of Whitchurch on the right. New wear [*weir*]. A striking scene: fine cliffs and wood, waterfall and iron forges. A grand animated scene!

The boat passes a lock. River closed in by a fine amphitheatre of wood and rock. New house built by Mr Atley on right. Monmouth road close to it, 2½ M. to Monmouth. Fine woods on right and left. Hadnock (Dr Griffith) on left. Come in sight on Monmouth town bridge. Low situation backed by wood. Dixton Chapel on right. 5 hours.

Inn at Monmouth: Beaufort Arms, good. Two bridges: one over the Wye, the other over the Monnow. Church modern. Handsome town hall. Heath, printer, has published several tracts respecting the topography of this neighborhood and intends to add more. Saxon architecture in a church adjoining the bridge over the Monnow. Few remains of the castle and those not very picturesque.

Thursday August 3. From Monmouth to Chepstow 25 miles by water, 16 by land. Good view of the town. Troy House (Duke of Beaufort) on right. Pretty bend of river, banks well-wooded. A flat stone in the middle of the river called Cowman which according to vulgar report divides the counties of Gloucester and Monmouth. Village of Redbrook. Banks finely cloathed with wood intermixed with pastures. Duke of Beaufort's property on the right, Lord Gage's on the left. Whitebrook on the right. A paper mill a little way up the valley.

River presents a fine sheet of water; broader, fine wood in front. Village of St Briavel's on a hill on the left; a house of General Rooke's in the bottom beneath. Left: Brickswear. Village of Llandogo: number of little houses scattered on the declivities of the hill. Spring tides come up here and vessels of 100 ton burthen. Village of Brockway on left, that of Tintern on right.

Banks begin to be muddy and sedgey.

Tintern Abbey[18] no longer decked with the fine woods which surrounded it some years ago and almost concealed it, having been lately cut. Nothing can be more striking than the first entrance through the western gate. The four arches which supported the tower are uncommonly grand, as are those of all the windows, one of them beautifully overhung with ivy, as well as the aisle of the abbey. In some parts I think the ivy conceals too much of the building, as none of the architecture or stonework can be distinguished. The many shabby cottages which surround the abbey diminish much from the grand appearance which it would assume, if they, as well as other obstacles, were removed, and the building could be viewed at its proper distance. But now it can only be viewed at too near or too distant a point of sight.

It looks well from the opposite side of the river; the building is here less covered with ivy, but its form is rather too straight and uniform and the beauty of the architecture not sufficiently discernible. But nothing can possibly exceed the beauty and elegance of the interior part of the building. The old ferryman (with his bottle-nose), 70 years old, remembers when the ivy was constantly cut and carried away by people to burn and feed to cattle in winter. He says that the clearing of the rubbish from the building cost the late Duke of Beaufort £150. I wish he had still completed the improvement by removing the cottages and orchards round the building.

From hence to Chepstow 9 M. Wood and rock on left, sedgey bank on right. Fine semi-circular range of woods where the grounds of Piercefield terminate. Rocks beautifully peeping through the thick foliage; perpendicular rocks on the left. Small chapel on left. River widens. Look back on a noble range of white rocks, finely contrasted with hollow woods on left. Chepstow castle comes in sight. I could wish the bank before it on the left were covered with wood, as it appears in part only over a narrow neck of land not in a very advantageous point of view; whereas it would break on the sight most nobly and surprize every beholder if it could possibly be hidden till the boat turns the angle.

Approach to town very picturesque: the wooden bridge, vessels, fine castle, etc etc. Church partly modern and partly antique; the doorway, fine rich Saxon or Norman with receding columns. Castle not very picturesque within its walls; dungeon; chapel; room where Henry Marten, one of the judges who tried K. Charles I was confined for 25 years; walls of great thickness; good view from the summit of H.M.'s Tower.[19]

Beaufort Arms — good inn. 5 hours from Monmouth. Price of boats: 1.11.6 to Monmouth, 10 s. for watermen's victuals; the same from thence to Chepstow. The men were well satisfied with 10/6 which I gave them extra. Eight boats kept at Ross.

Friday 4 August.   From Chepstow to Newport 16 M. . . . Caerwent: an old Roman station on a slight eminence surrounded by a stone square wall of great thickness.[20] Great part of it remains and surrounds in part the churchyard and orchard where the Roman pavement was discovered about

19. Tintern Abbey from across the River Wye.

20.   Chepstow Castle and Bridge across the River Wye. Note stone piers on Monmouthshire half of the bridge.

the year 1777. I had seen it soon after its discovery, when every care was taken to preserve it by the owner who erected a covered building round it. I was sorry to find it in so very ruinous a state at present. The roof of the building has been removed, the owner thinking that it would be less liable to injury, as the worms by working under the pavement had raised great part of it. But now the grass and weeds have the same bad effect, and, by being exposed constantly to the weather, the materials of which it is composed have lost the brightness of their colors, and the pattern is not so easily traced. The greatest part of it is loose and threatening a speedy annihilation.

Another pavement of a larger pattern has been discovered in the same orchard since the former, and another in some part of the village on which I was told there were a hare and hounds. The materials of the first red brick, a grey limestone and another of a light yellow cast.

The poor inhabitants of the place offered me for sale several old coins dug up in the village, but though evidently Roman I could find none whose inscription was legible, except one only, viz a Bristol farthing (Armes of Bristol; C.B.1662 on reverse).

At M.8. Penhow Castle on an eminence to the left of the road above the turnpike. Little remains of the ancient part being intermixed with a modern building. . . .[21] Descend to Newport. Old wooden bridge, boards loose; new one of stone now building; shell of old castle adjoining it, its walls washed by the river. The road in general good. Some steepish hills. Country well cultivated. Cattle in abundance. . . . Inn: Cardiff Arms, good.

Saturday 5th August.   From Cardiff to Llandaff 2 M.; turn off to the right one M. on the Cowbridge road. Village prettily situated. West front of the old cathedral bears a picturesque appearance. It is in a state of ruin. Three doors of Saxon architecture remain. Within this front another church is built, or part of the old cathedral modernised, in a style corresponding very badly to its ancient architecture. The while building is modern but the most glaring defect, and what I never recollect to have seen in any other church, is the altar, which is placed under a regular Grecian portico. In short a heathen temple is introduced within a Christian one. It contains several fine monuments executed in a very good style of sculpture. . . . I was sorry to see that many of these fine monuments were in a very neglected and ruinous state. . . . The houses in the village are all whitened and bear a neat appearance. . . .

Sunday 6 August.   To Caerphilly 8 M. Road good for a carriage; halfway ascend steep hill. Village of Caerphilly, its castle and a rich and well-cultivated country beyond it. Fine view. Mountains tilled up to their summits.

Castle:[22] a large pile of building, not very picturesque in form or situation; being low, surrounded by a marsh; walls very extensive; fine hall, clustered columns remain from which the roof sprang, gallery all round, one long avenue of which remains; large inner court; at the front was a drawbridge; the other entrance towards S.E. near present village; the leaning

21. Newport, Gwent: looking down the River Usk with bridge under construction and castle. Note how the unfinished stone arches of the bridge are spanned by timber.

22. Llandaff Cathedral: the west front in ruin before the construction of the
south-west tower.

[*tower*] projects above eleven feet; trees wanting to render the views of it more picturesque; built of rough dark colored stone, not cut in regular forms; more a castle of strength than of beauty.

A tolerable inn now at C. Houses neat and white. Road bad from the ascent. Return to Cardiff. On the summit of the hill an ash tree, from which there is one of the finest views I ever saw looking towards the Channel. . . . The tide was high by which the Severn lost in great measure its muddy hue. The views in general of this country are much improved and enlivened by the cottages and other houses which are universally whitened and have a very gay look.

Monday 7 August. From Cardiff to Pont y Pridd 13 M. Road good for carriages. Road not particularly interesting, but in some parts pretty, the river Taaf [*Taff*] running near it. The remains of a small castle called Coch Castle[22] on the side of a hill to the right, backed with wood.

Pont y Pridd: a bridge universally admired and visited from the boldness of its arch, its singular form and picturesque situation. [Dimensions of the arch: 35 feet high, 140 ft. span of arch, 9 ft. circle the large hole, 8½ the second, 4½ the third).[23] I was sorry to see it rather neglected; great part of the parapet wall being suffered to fall down and remains unrepaired. But this neglect rather adds to its picturesque appearance on paper by breaking the uniformity of the lines. The best point of view is from the bed of the river where it is backed by a lofty mountan of a steep and rugged form and well wooded.

A tolerable inn has been lately built about half a mile from the bridge. A canal follows the course of the river and from the number of its locks and the difficult country through which it passes well deserves the notice of the curious traveller.[24] Its distance from Merthyr Tydvil to Cardiff is 25 miles in which distance there are 52 locks, the fall of the water about 544 feet. 3 M. from Pont y Pridd there are 16 locks to be seen one above the other. . . . There are very curious works and machinery at Merthyr. . . .

Cardiff: a small neat town; two good inns: Cardiff Arms and Angel. The situation of the first is the pleasantest. The castle was modernised by the late Lord Mountstewart but his untimely death prevented its completion. Within its walls a very pleasant walk has been made and is open to the public. The keep on a mount appears the most ancient part of the building. The dungeon is shewn in which Robert son of William the Conqueror was confined. . . . Several portraits of the Windsor family by Sir Godfrey Kneller. . . . Church: a neat Gothic building, the turret of the steeple richly ornamented with Gothic fretwork. The windows here as at Llandaff are worked in stone openwork which has a good effect. Neat inside. . . . A little way from the town is the shell of the monastery of Grey Friars where the Herbert family probably lived as they bear the title Herbert of the Friars. . . .

Tuesday 8 August. From Cardiff to Cowbridge 12 M. Two extensive views towards the Channel. . . .

Wednesday 9 August.   To St. Donats VI miles. Good horse road. Village of
Llantwit [*Major*]: some curious inscribed stones in the churchyard, which
have not been decyphered ornamented with fretwork. Nothing striking in
the approach to St Donats. Castle large and picturesque in many points of
view, from the valley and field opposite. Some fine trees, many of which
have already fallen victims to the destructive blasts of the sea breezes and
others are sharing the same fate. . . .

Friday 11 August.   The morning employed in the neighborhood of Cowbridge. Penllyn Castle on an eminence to the right of the great turnpike
road, a modern house supplying the place of the ancient building, of which
part only of an old wall and turret, apparently of a more modern date,
remain. . . . From hence I crossed the turnpike road and went to Llanblethian
[The castle and lordship of Llanblethian were given to Sir Robert St Quintin,
one of the twelve knights who accompanied Robert Fitzhamon]. Church
prettily situated on an eminence, small remains of a castle. On the other side
of the little river which runs through the vale are the ruins of another castle
called St Quintins. These are generally confounded with Llanblethian. . . .
The country here is prettily varied with fine woods belonging to a Mr Talbot
of Margam. Corn, pastures etc, soil good and strong. Enter the road leading
to Llantwit; turn off to Bewpere [*Beaupré*] where there is an old mansion
belonging to the Bassett family formerly.[25] The porch in the inner court is a
curious piece of ornamented architecture and worth notice. . . . Cowbridge,
a long town. Inn: the Bear; rooms and beds good, attendance bad. No
manufactures. An academy founded by Jesus College sends six monitors
every year to the University.

Saturday 12 August.   To St Donats again to copy the inscriptions. . . .
Between the castle and the sea a large oblong inclosure with remains of
extensive buildings round it. Supposed to have been barracks for garrison. . . .[26]
Stopt at Llantwit to see the church. . . . There are three inscribed stones in
the churchyard: one standing upright in the yard; another (which has been
lately found) with a long inscription, upright also against the wall of the
church near the porch; another lying flat seems to have been the upper part
of a cross[27]. . . . In the evening went to Cardiff.

Sunday 13 August.   To Newport 12 M., to Uske through Caerleon 12
M. . . . to Ross 10 M. . . . All this country is well cultivated with corn; arid
soil and finely wooded. . . .

Monday 14 August.   Spent the morning at Goodrich Castle. . . . Ross
church: a handsome stone building with a lofty spire; good view from it;
fine trees in the old churchyard planted by the Man of Ross, his monument
within. . . .[28]

Wednesday 16 August.   From Ross to Ledbury 13 M.; road in some parts bad; pretty approach to Ledbury; fine corn country and well wooded. . . .

(*September 7* — Slept at Gloucester; *8* — arrived at Stourhead).

IV

Tour in North Wales — June 1798

Sunday 24 June. Left Stourhead in company with my friend Sir John Leicester.[1] Slept at Bath.

Monday 25 June. Left Bath after dinner. Slept at Rodborough, Gloucestershire.

Tuesday 26 June. Dined and slept at Hereford.

Wednesday 27 June. Dined at Shrewsbury. Slept at Oswestry.

Thursday 28 June. Dined and slept at Llangollen. Hitherto I had not varied from the route I took last Summer. From Oswestry we deviated a mile from the road to see Chirk Castle, lately the seat of Col. Middleton, now belonging to his three sisters, left joint co-heiresses.[2]

The castle is a low, heavy building consisting of several round towers, a quadrangle within and a lofty arch where the portcullis was placed. Within are four very excellent apartments: dining room, saloon, drawing room and a long gallery of a hundred feet in length fitted with family and other portraits. These apartments and the staircase are much better arranged than I thought possible from the exterior appearance of the building. The approach to it on that side where the offices stand through a fine grove of oaks is striking and well-adapted. The removal of the stables on the left and a terrace wall substituted in their place would be an improvement.

The castle stands on a gentle eminence, commanding a very extensive and distant view, the ground around it well varied and planted. A piece of water, badly planned and managed, made on a hill, contrary to nature. It has been too general a custom first to think water absolutely necessary for the ornament of the park or garden, and then to form it on places where nature never designed it or would have placed it. Thus two errors are committed: Nature outraged, and a defect created instead of a beauty. A very handsome gateway of cast iron conducts you into the park.[3] The Doric lodges on the side are not massive enough in their proportions to correspond with the gates.

In the valley below Chirk, and on the road from Oswestry, an aqueduct is now constructing to convey the water of the canal across the valley.[4] From the level of the canal which is now nearly brought to this spot the arches of the aqueduct must be of a very considerable height, and I doubt if two rows of them must not be erected, similar to those of the *Pont du Gard* in Languedoc. From the length of this building, the straight lines and light piers which intersect the valley it has a pleasing effect even in its present imperfect state. When finished it will have the most grand and picturesque appearance, the background being finely wooded and the foreground also; from the winding of the road downhill and the sudden and unexpected appearance of the aqueduct forms a fine subject for a picture. [*Fig. 3*] On the road to Llangollen there is another aqueduct over the valley where the River Dee flows, on a similar plan and equally advanced, but not so long. These form part of the Ellesmere Canal leading from that place to Chester.

Friday 29th June. Went to Corwen.

Sunday 1 July. . . . Two miles from Corwen . . . mill of a most picturesque and rustic form; above it a fine stream issues from a deep chasm amongst the rocks, which are well overhung with wood, and forms a fine cascade. The masses of rock are large and well-shapen. I have seen few such perfect rural scenes confined within so narrow a spot. . . .

Tuesday 3 July. Went to Bala. Found the road on the left banks of the Dee much advanced since last year. Found much better lodgings at the Bull Inn (I. Randles) than at the Lion. Remained at Bala till *Sunday 8th July.*

8 July 1798. Rode from Bala to Mallwyd, 28 miles. . . . Moors of marshy ground, fed by sheep and black cattle; begin shortly to descend into another valley which bursts unexpectedly on the sight and presents a noble range of mountains richly varied. This new road is also cut on the side of the mountain but not so judiciously as the other, the turnings being short and steep. I have been informed that its direction is to be altered. Near the bottom another valley opens to the right. Picturesque subject for a drawing: a rustic cottage and romantic birch trees near the road. . . . Dinas y mawddu [*Dinas Mawddwy*]: a little village in a very romantic situation immediately under a fine mountain which in some points of view on approaching towards it appears like an immense barrow or tumulus thrown up by art. Cross the clear streams of the River Dovy. . . . Arrive Mallwyd, a single house and tolerable inn. From thence there is a road to Welch Pool and Montgomery. . . .

Monday 9 July. Fished the River Dovy. At a short distance from the inn is a salmon leap and weir where great quantities of fish are caught at this season after hard rains. . . .

*Tuesday 10th July.*1 Fished a lake near Mallwyd. . . .

Wednesday 11 July. Returned to Bala.

Friday 13 July. From Bala to Festiniog 18 miles. I followed the same road

as last year . . . few rides of 18 miles more dreary. Stopt about three miles
short of Festiniog to fish a lake about quarter of a mile from the road, Llyn
Morwynion [for an account of the tradition respecting this lake and origin of
the name *vide* Pennant, Wales, vol. 2, p. 130], the Maidens' Lake; the fish
are not very large but the best in flavor I have tasted in Wales. . . .

Saturday 14th.   Fished two lakes, Lynns Mannod [*Llyn y Manod*]. The
first is about three miles from Festiniog in line with Lyn Morwynion and is
situated between two mountains which bear the name of Mannod. The
people of the country tell strange stories about the immense size of the fish
in this lake lake but I could not get any positive proof of this assertion. In
this lake we caught eight trout. . . .

Sunday 15th July.   Ride from Festiniog to Harlech 10 miles. Descend a
long hill. Turnpike road and bridge on the right leading to Tan-y-bwlch inn
and hall. . . . Maes y Neuadd, old seat of the Wynne family. Fine woods of
oak and some good timber, probably spared owing to the owner's being
settled in the Indies. Leave the mountain road to Harlech and follow a horse
track leading there on the right through the fields, the worst and most
rugged imaginable. The castle placed on a bold rock towering above an
extensive plain beneath appears in many favorable points of view. Barren
and stoney approach to Harlech.
   Harlech Castle,[5] as well as Conway and Carnarvon Castles, were built by
Edward the First. It cannot boast of the same extent as Carnarvon, nor the
elegance of Conway, but in point of bold situation it may vye with either.
Its architecture is similar to the others, having small towers issuing from the
larger. It is built on a steep and lofty rock at no great distance from the sea
coast, inaccessible on one side by nature, and rendered so on the other near
the town by a deep foss cut in the rock. A large flat marsh extends for a great
distance towards Carnarvonshire; the soil is good and if the sea were banked
out much valuable land [*would be*] made productive.
   A curious ceremony had just been performed before my arrival at
Harlech: an old man of upwards of eighty years had been baptised in a pool
near the castle. The sect of Anabaptists has increased very much in these
parts of Wales within these few years, and this ceremony of adult baptism,
which four or five years [*ago*] was scarcely heard of, is now become very
general. . . .
   Leaving Harlech I pursued a different road home over the mountains with
a view of visiting several pools on them. At a little distance from Harlech
observed a long upright stone near the roadside, and on asking my companion
(the landlord of Festiniog who had been educated in this neighborhood) the
meaning of it, he told me that a curious history was annexed to this stone:
that the parish of Harlech gave five shillings to everyone who would stand
with their head upon this stone, and that he, when a boy, had done it and
received the reward. . . .
   From the ridge of these mountains is a most singular and beautiful view of

the coast of Carnarvonshire, and I believe for variety of rock, water and mountains scarcely to be equalled. . . . The mountains are of the most varied and majestic forms amongst which Snowdon reigns as Sovereign. The long neck of land in Carnarvonshire extending from Pwllheli towards Bardsey Island. . . . Descended from the mountains by a steep path and came into the old road by the little lake before-mentioned at Llyn Tegwyn [*Tecwyn*]. After passing the dreary waste between this lake and the beginning of the descent towards Tan-y-bwlch one of the most singular and beautiful views imaginable bursts upon the sight, and which by not looking back would have escaped my attention before. . . .

The country round Festiniog is of the wildest nature; rock, mountain and rivers abound in all their different forms and the beautiful little vale beneath adds a pleasing variety to the surrounding landscape. The inn at Festiniog commands from its high situation a fine view of the valley. The civility of the landlord could scarcely repay me for a bad night's rest; the convenience, however, of the situation for the lakes I wished to visit overbalanced the inconvenience of bad accomodations. . . .

Tuesday 17th. Returned to Bala. Fished for a short time in the Maidens' Lake, and about five or six miles from Bala deviated to the right to see a lake situated under the lofty M. Arrennig. It is a fine piece of water of the most transparent color abounding with trout of a large size and fine flavor but not to be caught without the greatest difficulty.

Saturday 21 July. Visited a lake situated under the lofty M. Arran. . . . Caught 14 trout 5½ lb., black. The mountain opposite to this, separated by a brook, abounds in fine marble, several specimens of which are seen dispersed about the country in the beds of rivers, walls etc.

Monday 23 July. Left Bala; slept at Corwen. It has rained *every* day more or less since I came into Wales.

Tuesday 24th. Dined and slept at Chester.

Wednesday 25th. Dined at Tabley and remained there till *Wednesday evening.*

1st August. The second day of Knutsford Races. Pursued my journey through Holme Chapel to Newcastle [*under Lyme*] where I slept. . . .

Friday 3 August. From Worcester to Tewkesbury, Gloucester and Rodborough, where I dined, to Petty France and Bath and Stourhead.

During my whole residence in Wales it rained more or less every day; the foliage of the trees uncommonly fine.

Tour in South Wales or rather Monmouthshire — August 1798.

Rev. Mr Coxe, my son and self.

Monday 20th August.   Left Stourhead after dinner. Slept at Bath.

Tuesday 21st August.   Left Bath, pursued the road to Bristol . . . from thence to the Old Passage. Crossed the Severn in quarter of an hour in the small boat. A good inn at Beachley. From thence to Chepstow three miles. The Seve[r]n forms a fine bay on the right; to the left the River Wye with its embouchure into the Severn. Steep descent to Chepstow. Beaufort Arms Inn.

Wednesday 22nd.   Left Chepstow, pursued my journey to Ragland [*Raglan*]. Many steep ascents and descents, road rough and sandy. Fine view of the Severn behind, and fertile and extensive view on the left. Beaufort Arms good little inn.

Ragland Castle

The ancient seat of the Marquis of Worcester still exists, and though in a very dilapidated state, presents a large and interesting mass of ruins.[6] The approach to it is very striking; the three hexagon towers, grand and well built, are so entirely covered with ivy that not a single stone of it can be discerned. The cornice of the towers more worked than generally in Wales. View of the inner court is picturesque. Great Hall: a fine room with the arms of the family on the wall at one end. Kitchen on the right. Enter another court. Little more than the foundations of the chapel appear, and at the upper end, in line with the walls of the chapel are two figures fixed against the wall, apparently male and female. Much hid by ivy they seem to have belonged to a room on an upper story. The traces of many other apartments are visible.

   The citadel suffered much at the time of its siege, nearly half of it having fallen to the ground. On the terrace adjoining the castle is an elm of uncommon size. From this side is a good view of the country and mountains and Abergavenny; the other views in general from the castle are uninteresting. It is situated on a gentle eminence, not very strong by nature. The architecture bears the marks of different aera; the three towers at the entrance appear of the most ancient date and are very grand.

   Ragland church contains nothing worth notice but two mutilated alabaster figures lying on the ground. . . .

Thursday 23rd.   Left Ragland, pursued the road to Abergavenny. Pass Clytha, the seat of Mr Jones, a modern castle built by him, to the left, and a Gothic entrance to his grounds on the right lately erected from a design by Mr Nash the architect. It appears to me too light and airy for a similar purpose, and more appropriate as an approach to an abbey through a thick wood than to a plain simple house near the turnpike road. Dined and slept at Greene's Llan St. fraid [*Llansan'ffraed*].

Friday 24th. A large party sallied forth from Llan St. Fraed on an excursion to the mountains. Passed through Abergavenny. Follow the road to Crickhowell for about four miles and enter Brecknockshire, the crossing marked by a boundary stone near the roadside. Ford the River Uske to which place a railed road leads from the mountains. This road is made at the heavy expense of a thousand pounds a mile and its utility consists in transporting very heavy burdens with few horses. It is formed by long bars of iron cramped together, and strengthened by others fixed crossways. A deep cart with iron wheels is made to fit exactly the iron track. The friction is by this means so small that they run with the greatest facility. It is curious to see a number of these carts laden with ironstone etc running with great velocity down the sides of the mountains without any horses. One or two men stand behind the cart and by means of a lever stop the motion of the wheels instantaneously. These carts carry the weight of three ton. We followed this road for near four miles.

Ironworks in the bottom on the left. Turned down to the left by a steep path to see the cascade . . . the form of the rocks is in general good, the fall of the water well-broken and the trees particularly well-adapted (in form) to the surrounding scenery. Our party consisting of above twenty dined under the canopy of the skies. Our cloth was spread on a large flat rock. A rapid rill running at its foot cooled our wines and afforded us a delicious beverage. The scene was Alpine and gay, such as I could have fancied oft occurred in Switzerland, but in its past happy days.

We returned in the evening to Abergavenny.

Saturday 25th. After breakfast went in a chaise to Pont y Poole, 10 miles, a long village scattered on the declivity of a hill. Formerly a brisk trade was carried on in Japan goods, called Pontypoole Ware but now it is reduced to a very low ebb, only eight hands being employed on it. There are several iron forges in the neighborhood, mines of coal and iron in the mountains. We saw the greatest part of the town in driving to the inn, from whence we took the landlord as our guide to the church over a mile distant. . . .

Leaving Pontypool we proceeded to Usk seven miles, where we dined. This town is pleasantly situated on the banks of the river of the same name, over which is a handsome stone bridge of five arches. There are the remains of castle on a hill commanding the town, but neither elegant or picturesque in their appearance. The church is large and of a very picturesque form. . . . The remains of the priory adjoin the church. The church is a mixture of Gothic and Saxon architecture and was of greater extent than it is at present. . . . The porch is an insulated building and has a pretty effect when grouped with the fir trees around it. . . . Uske is mentioned in the *Itinerary* as a Roman station.[7] After dining at Uske we returned to Abergavenny, 8 miles. The country through which we this day passed was pleasant, finely varied with wood and corn. . . .

Sunday 26th.   After breakfast went to Llanthony Abbey. Turned off to the left by the side of an old decayed oak. Road narrow and bad. I had visited these ruins three times before [*p. 34*] and viewed them again with fresh pleasure. They owe their beauty to a variety of causes and effects. In the first place no natural situation can be more appropriate to the holy institution formerly established there: surrounded by fine mountains, a rich cultivated vale watered by a limpid stream — the *Religio loci*.

The architecture is grand and simple. The breadth and massive appearance of the tower has a good effect rising in the midst of the vale and well relieved by the mountains in the background. [The fine mellow, yellow tints with which the greystone is tinged add much to the general effect of the building. Many parts of it, disjointed by trees and other plants growing in the fissures between the stones threaten a speedy dissolution.] I might add they received in my eyes an additional good effect by not being covered with ivy as the ruins in Wales generally are. I approve of ivy when it hides deformities, not when it conceals beauties.

We dined at the door of a little public house in full view of the ruins on a cold collation we had brought with us, a necessary precaution for every traveller as nothing can be procured in this remote and solitary spot. . . .

Monday 27th.   After breakfast visited the ironworks of Mr Hopkins at Blaenavon, about five or six miles distant from Abergavenny. Cross the bridge over the Uske. Good road for a mile. Ascend to the right. Rugged and steep. Several fine points of view. . . . The summit of the hill commands a most beautiful and extensive view. The road then pursues a track over a dreary, barren and stoney country, rich however under the surface.

Tempted by the great richness of nature on this spot Mr Hopkins about ten years ago established [*a*] very considerable ironworks here.[8] The same rock produces the iron and coal in one spot. I saw two strata of coal rising in a mound considerably above the surface. The whole is a busy scene: the noise of the forges, the fire and thick volumes of smoke occasionally bursting forth from the furnaces, the numerous mules, assess and horses employed in carrying the lime, coal etc., the many cottages and habitations disposed all around; together with the very picturesque forms of the buildings, being very irregular, massive and ?decisive in their forms, produced a new and pleasing effect and a perfect contrast to the deserted castles and solitary abbies we had lately been visiting.

We returned by the same road having a distant view of the Severn etc on the right. The descent steep, long and very rough. Dined at Llan San Fraed.

Tuesday 28th   After breakfast went to Uske and employed the morning in taking views there.

Wednesday 29th.   After an early breakfast went on an excursion to White Castle. . . . Ascend towards White Castle,[9] a large building on an eminence commanding a fine view of the adjacent country. The castle consists of six massive round towers connected by square and circular walls, varying according to the nature of the ground, with strong outworks. It bears the marks of great strength and was evidently designed only as a fortress, not a habitation, there being no windows and only the marks of two small entrances. It is built of rough stone without any attention to ornament.

We descended by a narrow and dirty and stoney path into another turnpike road which in five miles led us back to Abergavenny . . . after dinner visited the two churches of St Mary and St John. The former is a handsome Gothic building and bears the appearance of a cathedral in miniature. The choir with its old carved woodwork still remains with the seats appropriated to Bishop and Dean. . . . There was another handsome church in Abergavenny dedicated to St John, now converted into a free school.

Thursday 30th.   Employed the morning in taking views at Abergavenny. Met a party from Llansanfraid at Llanvihangel, and dined on the banks of the Hodni.

Friday 31st.   We revisited the ironworks at Blaenavon. [A singular sight presented itself to us on mounting the hill; on a sudden I heard a great hissing and looking down observed close to my horse's feet an immense snake who had seized a toad. On seeing us he loosened his hold but so intent on his prey that he pursued the toad for considerable distance laying hold of him several times. Till at length the toad jumping under our horses' feet alarmed its pursuer and escaped. The eagerness and velocity of the snake were astonishing and on coming near the horse's leg he reared his crest and I thought would have attacked the horse.]

From thence followed the rail road to Pontypool, six miles. The road leading through a narrow valley well cloathed with wood on each side, varied by many white cottages, and little patches of cultivated pastures and cornfields amongst the woods. A most pleasing scene reminding me of the vallies in Switzerland in the Jura Mountains. A stream runs in the bottom. The rail road joins a canal at a short distance from Pontypool. The whole of this ride is one of the most delightful I ever took. Returned to Abergavenny.

Saturday 1st September.   Left Abergavenny at seven in the morning. . . . Grosmont Castle[10] church and village. There are considerable remains of the former, though not very picturesque; a curious stone chimney remaining entire. Church large and of a picturesque form. . . . Leaving Grosmont we followed narrow and stoney lanes, ascending and descending, which led up to Skenfreth Castle, 4½ M. . . . This castle[11] as well as that of Grosmont are situated in the River Monnow which divides the counties of Monmouth and Hereford. The situation of Skenfrith is more picturesque than Grosmont though the ruins of the latter are more conspicuous and varied. Those of Skenfreth consist of semi-circular towers attached to square walls with a round tower standing isolated in the center of the area within. The castle, bridge and river united with a background of well-wooded hills form a good landscape. The church is of a picturesque form. The mixture of elegant stonework forms a good contrast with the woodwork which forms the upper part of the tower. It is a handsome building within but in a most shameful state of neglect and almost ruin. . . .

Sunday 2nd September. At Monmouth.

Monday 3rd September. Employed the morning taking views at Monmouth; the environs, particularly the meadows beneath the town, afford many picturesque points. The old bridge over the Monnow has been a favourite subject with all artists and deservedly so. . . .

Tuesday 4th. At Chepstow. Environs and situation most picturesque; the castle proudly seated on a perpendicular rock. The bridge is of great length and from the variety of its architecture affords a fine object for the pencil.[12] The piers on the Monmouth side are of stone, those on the Gloucester side of wood. . . . One of the great beauties of this scenery is owing to the harmonious and mellow tints with which the stone is colored and the variety of herbage which overhangs them and grows amongst their fissures. A variety of shipping animates the scene, and nothing but a clearer stream is wanting to render the landscape perfect.
   The church contains in its porch a fine specimen of Saxon architecture. . . The interior of the church is in much more ancient style than any we have yet seen during our tour; it was evidently all Saxon though some of the windows have been converted into Gothic. Still the Norman prevails throughout. To a certain height of the building all is Saxon and easily perceptible in the facade of the church on which is opposed a horrid imitation of Græcian or medley architecture. The simplicity of the building would be very striking if several of the finest arches were not intersected by pews — galleries etc. The lofty roof with its plain unadorned ceiling has a good effect. . . .

Wednesday 5th September. Visited Caldicot, 5 miles from Chepstow, where there are the remains of a large and ancient castle. At a distance it forms a fine mass, the stone being variegated with ivy. Its size appears to greater advantage from being situated in a flat meadow. In general it is very well built, the entrance grand, one tower entirely covered with ivy. . . . the parish church adjoining is a handsome building. . . . From Caldicot we followed the same road back again. . . .

Thursday 6th September. I spent the morning at Tinterne;[13] went there by land. . . . Reviewed with pleasure these elegant and wonderful remains of

Gothic architecture and monkish grandeur. No ruin I have seen in England has so striking effect on the mind and senses as that of Tinterne when the door first opens and presents the whole extent of this most beautiful Gothic aisle, overhung with ivy in the most picturesque manner, and terminated by the magnificent eastern window through which is seen a distant hill covered with copse wood, on which fortunately there are no buildings or breaks to disturb the repose and tranquillity of the scene. So much for the interior which is unique and I believe not to be equalled in this kingdom.

There are many objections to the exterior. The situation is naturally fine on the banks of a rapid river which here is of good color, backed by a hill covered with hanging wood and coppice. But it is so surrounded with ragged cottages and orchards that half of its height is completely hidden by them. But the principal deformity arises from the four pointed roofs [*gables*] which rise from the building in a very unpicturesque form, and make the want of a tower much to be regretted. The western front as well as the eastern (but particularly the former being more ornamented) would be a most beautiful object could it be seen in its proper point of view, which now it cannot owing to the obstruction of the cottages and orchards.

Friday 7 September. Left Chepstow early in the morning. Caerwent: visited the Roman pavement and walls, the former visibly in a worse state than last year. Turned off to the right on the Uske road. Llanvair; a little village; ruins of a castle on a small eminence; a round tower is the most perfect part of them; are so overgrown with weeds and choked up by rubbish that it is impossible to examine them accurately. . . . Ascend and enter an extensive woody country. . . . At the edge of this woody district are situated the remains of Strighil Castle, belonging formerly to Strongbow, Earl of Pembroke, from which he took one of his titles. Being in a low marshy situation and possessing no natural or local strength I should imagine it to have been an habitation rather than a fort. The remains are trifling but in some points rather picturesque, and interesting from having belonged to so celebrated a personage. From hence we left the Uske road to the right and descended through a narrow lane to Barthelly the seat of — Thomas Esq, beautifully situated on a gently rising ground commanding a most delicious view of the valley of the Usk beneath it and the distant mountains. Backed by a rich hanging wood in front of the house the Usk forms a singular bend, nearly a complete circle. . . .

In the evening walked about Caerleon, a large town on the Uske over which there is a wooden bridge, like in construction to that at Chepstow, supported by ten wooden piers. The ruins are very trifling. Those that remain are of high antiquity. Of these the amphitheatre is the most remarkable[14]; its shape, which was nearly circular, remains entire in a field near the town, and now vulgarly called Arthur's Round Table. Near it part of the Roman walls are visible but in a more imperfect state than those at Caerwent. The site mentioned by Mr Wyndham many years ago is still preserved in the house of the same shoemaker[15]; it was probably (from the ledges on each side) used to convey water. The ground only on which the castle stood is now visible. There is a round tower near the inn and the remains of another close to the bridge on entering the town, both of which were probably erected to guard the pass of the river. We found a comfortable little inn and much civility at the Hanbury Arms close to the bridge. We walked on the banks [*of*] the Usk opposite to St Julians, formerly the seat of the famous Lord Herbert of Chirbury; much [*of*] the ancient habitation has been pulled down.

Saturday 8 September.   Early in the morning left Caerleon . . . we entered an extensive flat marsh; passed by a handsome new-built house of Mr Philips on the left, and arrived at Goldclift. Here stood formerly a celebrated priory of which we hoped to find some remains; a modern farmhouse now occupies its scite. A small portion of old walls hanging immediately over the clift and forming part of the barn is the only relict of this priory. It is built on an eminence rising gradually on the land side and ending in a clift towards the Channel. Its height appears from 50 to 60 feet. Pieces of stone found on the shore and which contain some sparkling yellow micae have given rise to the vulgar report of their containing gold, and from thence the name of the place is derived The rocks are limestone of a light yellow color which at sea with the reflection of the sun on them may have given a golden appearance.

However disappointed in the principal object of our journey we were repaid by a sight of the sea walls, constructed for the space of nine or ten miles to keep out the sea from the adjoining level or marsh. They are really a stupendous work and probably begun by the monks of Goldclift. From Goldclift we returned back to Llanwern and then turned off to the right a little up the hill. Llanmartin, a handsome church. . . . Here we had again occasion to lament the wretched state of the churches in this diocese, many of which are in a most ruinous condition.

At a short distance from hence are the ruins of Pencoed mansion and castle which struck us more forcibly as they have been little mentioned, and the castles which had been lately the object of our researches had contained little of the picturesque; here however we were very agreeably surprised in finding a most beautiful pile of building. The gateway is perfect, one tower like those of Ragland and Caldicot completely covered with ivy. A round tower adjoining has a good effect. The outward walls being broken down admit a view of the old mansion behind which is well built of grey stones and well varied with ivy. The windows are particularly picturesque, also the porch. They present [*from*] several good points a view for the pencil. We were the more pleased here as we expected but little . . . to Penhow, which I had before visited, and the New Passage.

On arriving at the New Passage I found it high water. Passage ¾ hour. A little wind. Excellent inn on the other side.

Sunday 9th September.   After breakfast went to Clifton. Hard rain.

Monday 10th.   Stourhead.

Here ended one [of] the pleasantest excursions I ever remember to have taken during which we had not been interrupted in our plans for a single hour, having had a continual succession of fine weather. The object of our tour was a thorough investigation of the antiquities and history of the county. The time allotted was rather too short but we visited every object worthy of attention of which we could gain information.

V

1799: THE MARCHES AND NORTH WALES

Tour in South and North Wales, 1799.

I left Stourhead on *Monday 15th day of April.* Dined at Deptford Inn with the Club.[1] Slept at Bath the same night.

Tuesday 16th. Proceeded through Petty France, Rodborough and Gloucester to Cheltenham (Plough Inn). Remained there till Friday 10th of May. Snow on the hills on the 18th of April and remained for some days. Lodged at No. 12 High Street. Paid six guineas for the house, Mrs Forty at the well a guinea, including 3/6 subscription to the walks. . . .

Friday 10th May. At Gloucester (King's Head).

Saturday 11th May. In the morning walked to view the ruins of Llanthoney Abbey.[2] This abbey was removed from Monmouthshire to the neighborhood of Gloucester; its ruins are now to be seen at a short distance S.W. of the city, adjoining the new canal. They consist of a very large enclosed area, a magnificent barn, strengthened with fine buttresses and two handsome doorways of the broad Gothic architecture. Part of the old gateway remains consisting of part of a large arch and a smaller one on its side to the right. The latter is perfect and over it are three escutcheons of arms.
  Mr and Mrs Fortescue joined me at dinner.

Sunday 12th May. Rode to Ross and staid there that night (Kings Arms).

Monday 13th May. Rode to Monmouth. In my way took views of Wilton Castle and bridge over the River Wye. . . . Slept at Monmouth (Beaufort Arms/Watkins).

Thursday 14 May. One of my horses being ill I took a chaise to Chepstow. Stopt at the village of Trelleck five miles from Monmouth. At a short distance to the left of the turnpike road beyond the village in a meadow are three curious stones (probably monumental). The church is a handsome stone building. Near the entrance to it and on one of the pedestals of the gateway of a free school is a pedestal over which is a dial [*drawing*] . . . on one of these pedestals is the date 1687. . . .[3]

Wednesday 15th May. Remained at Chepstow, the day too cold to draw.

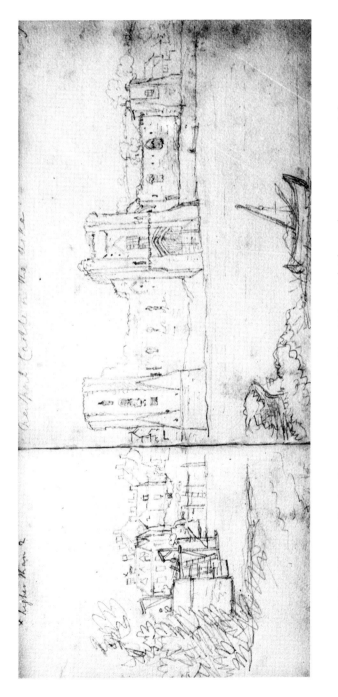

23. Newport Castle, Gwent, seen across the River Usk with bridge under construction on left.

Thursday 16th May. Rode to village of Portskewit, not far distant from New Passage. At a little distance from it on the sea coast are the remains of a fine encampment, and close to it the ruins of a picturesque little chapel called Sudbrook. . . .

Friday 17th May. Left Chepstow. Beaufort Arms, (George). Rode to S. Pierre, the seat and park of the Lewis family. . . . Dined and slept at a little inn, the Rock and Fountain. . . .

Saturday 18th May. We found a good parlor and a good double-bedded room[4] at the Rock and Fountain. . . . At M.Vl from Newport I turned off to the right through the fields to examine a building which at a distance seemed to be an old ruin but in near inspection proved to be only an old house. It is called the Folly[5]. . . . I was fully repaid for my trouble in ascending to it by the very beautiful view which the summit of the hill presented, commanding on one side the extensive vale of the Uske and on the other the country bordering on the Severn. . . . Descending again to the turnpike road you see Pencoed Castle on the hill. . . .

I neither found the bridge or inn at Newport completed; a temporary passage for horses over loose planks is left open. In the evening we walked up to the church of St Woollos on the road leading to Cardiff, a curious old church with Saxon columns and some dilapidated old effigies on monuments. A very curious old Saxon arch unlike the generality of those I had before seen. The view on each side of this church, which is built on an eminence, is very fine and extensive; the town of Newport appears to great advantage. Inn at Newport King's Arms (Chambers.)

Sunday 19th May. In the morning visited an old seat of the Morgan family at Machen about six miles distant from Newport. Left the road leading to Cardiff at Bassaleigh [*Bassaleg*] and turned off to the right. . . . On our way home stopt at Bassalech where there was formerly a religious house; a school adjoining the church but detached from it probably was a part of the old building. From hence we returned to Newport through Tredegar Park. The house is large, built of brick, heavy, massive architecture; the rooms large and fitted up in an equally heavy style.[6] Several family pictures but none very good. Situation flat. The park abounds with very fine trees: oak, Spanish chestnut etc.

Monday 20th. At Newport; employed the morning in drawing the church of St Woollo's, and a curious Saxon or Norman porch within it. . . .

Tuesday 21st May. After breakfast left Newport in company with Mr Evans, the vicar of St Woollo's. Malpas: a very curious old church a short distance on the right of the road to Caerleon. This church though small is one of the most curious Saxon buildings I have seen in Monmouth. Many very elegant ornaments are carved on the doors and windows, some exactly like the Etruscan. And there is a singularity in the sculpture of them which I never observed before; that the two columns in the door and windows are dissimilar and have different ornaments sculptured on them.

A violent rain came on and prevented our accomplishing the remainder of the tour destined for this morning which was to visit Llantarnam, the scite of an old Cistercian monastery etc. We made the best of our way to Caerleon where we found the same comfortable little inn and kind attention at the Hanbury Arms (John Charles) which we did last year. In the evening drank tea with Mr Nicholls who possesses a curious intaglio on a grey stone representing Hercules strangling the Nemean lyon, found at Caerleon with its original gold setting.

Wednesday 22nd May.   After having taken a view of the bridge and town I left Caerleon in company with Mr Nicholls . . . to Tredaneck [*Tredunnock*] church . . . has within a curious inscription. . . .[7] Two miles from Uske turned off to the left in Llangibby, the seat of Mr Williams. On an abrupt hill rising immediately behind the house and well cloathed with fine trees are the remains of a castle, inclosing with its walls a very large flat area at the summit of the hill. There are considerable ruins of the walls, towers etc., but not sufficiently high and too much interrupted by wood to render them picturesque as a view. . . .

Thursday 23 May.   Employed the morning taking views at Uske. Dined and slept at my friend Mr Greene's at Lansanfraed.

Friday 24 May.   Breakfasted at Abergavenny (Angel Inn/Saunders). Proceeded on the Hereford road to Llanvihangle. . . . The object of this journey was Oldcastle, formerly the residence of Sir John Oldcastle, but we found nothing either in the house or church to awaken our curiosity. . . . Dined with Mr Waddington at Lanover on the opposite side of the Uske from Llansanfraed. From the lawn before the house the range of mountains, viz the Blorenche on one side, the Skirid on the other and the Sugar Loaf in the center, form one of the grandest outlines I ever beheld, particularly when they assumed the grey and sober evening tint. Walked home to Lansanfraed 3 miles.

Saturday 25th May.   After breakfast rode through Colebrook grounds to Abergavenny. Colebrook is the seat of Mr Hanbury Williams. The house has some tolerable good portraits. The shrubbery and pleasure grounds pretty. . . .

Sunday 26 May.   Breakfasted at Uske. . . . New Passage: crossed in 40 minutes, nearly high water, rolling sea.

Monday 27 May.   Arrived at Stourhead before ten. . . .[8]

Tuesday 28 May   After dinner left Stourhead. Slept at Bath. . . .

Wednesday 29 May.   . . . New Passage . . . dined at Chepstow.

Saturday 1 June.   Inn at Hereford: New Inn (Green). After breakfast went
to the cathedral with Mr Waller, an intelligent man, to see the cathedral.
Some very fine specimens of Saxon architecture in the rich ornamented style.
The effect and solemnity of the cathedral much injured by its being painted a
dead white. The upper rows of arches over the Saxon (added by Mr Wyatt)
are much too light in their construction. The ceiling by the same hand is
better. A beautiful little chapel in the left aile. A variety of monuments and
effigies and brasses, many of the latter taken away. The cloysters rather
heavy in their architecture. A picturesque remnant of the chapter house. The
library and monuments within it deserve notice. *NB*. When the cathedral
was repaired an immense quantity of the brasses was sold at eight pence per
pound of which Mr Waller purchased a large quantity and sent to Mr Gough
the antiquarian.
    Afterwards proceeded on my journey through Leominster to Ludlow.
Crown Inn. In my last year's tour I mentioned the picturesque situation of
the town of Ludlow. . . . I also visited the church, a large spacious building
of light airy Gothic architecture. . . .

Sunday 2nd June.   After breakfast went to Downton Castle, the seat of
Richard Payne Knight Esq six miles from Ludlow. Leave the Shrewsbury
road at M.11, turn off to the left after passing the bridge. A picturesque
church, some ruins annexed to it, an old porch etc denote antiquity. Leave
the great road to Knighton and turn off to the left to Downton Castle.
    This place has been justly celebrated by travellers for its picturesque
situation and the taste shown by its owner in having laid out the grounds
according to the true dictates of Nature.[9] The house has great variety in its
architecture. Built of a yellowish stone of a good color it has a round, square
and octagon tower, a Gothic porch, Gothic and modern sash windows etc,
all embattled. Of the interior apartments the most conspicuous is an elegant
rotunda, used as a dining room, fitted up with niches supported by columns
representing porphyry. In each nich is a bronze figure holding a light. The
cieling is ornamented with compartments. The whole room is very similar to
the Pantheon in my garden at Stourhead and I have heard that the idea was
taken from thence. It has also a large window commanding a fine view
which is opened, or shut occasionally. The other rooms are nothing remarkable. The house is placed on a natural terrace with a broad gravel walk before
it commanding a fine view.
    The River Teme running through a fine meadow in the vale beneath from
whose opposite banks a fine range of mountains rise immediately. The view
towards the east is particularly grand, the form of the mountains finely
varied and covered with most beautiful groves of oak. In the background the
Clee Hill forms a charming contrast with its broken shape and beautiful grey

tint. From the house I descended to a stone bridge over the River Teme and entering a narrow walk followed its left bank for a mile and a half till I came to a rude and picturesque wooden bridge thrown across the river. On this spot the scenery is grand, pleasing and romantic. The rocks on the opposite bank are of a considerable height and perpendicular. The scene is animated by some picturesque cottages and a mill and a waterfall occasioned by a weir, where the water is penned up for the mill. Above the bridge it flows in a clean tranquil stream. Crossing over the bridge the path leads back on more elevated ground above the river. The trees are finer and the scenery totally different from that on the opposite side.

This walk of three miles affords a constant succession of natural beauties. Here nature reigns alone; the works of art are scarcely discernible except in the forming of the walks which are done with great judgement and the most picturesque eye. The present owner claims all the merit: he built the house; he laid out the grounds. Though the river nearly runs in a straight direction it never offends the eye by a sameness of appearance. The walk leads sometimes on its banks, at another time in a more elevated direction. The river also varies in its course; at one time expanded, at another flowing more rapidly through a deep and narrow channel amongst the rocks. These though rather of a slaty nature form good masses and are picturesque in their tints. Wild mountain sheep and ocasionally a herd of deer add much to the wildness of the scenery.

Whoever views these grounds must consider that the owner here intended that nature should have no ornament but those peculiar to herself, no trappings borrowed from her rival, art. View Downton with these ideas and no one will be disappointed. If criticism can anywhere be well founded it is on the house which I do not think quite adapted to the genius of the place. Too great a variety of different architecture of different aera — it is neither an ancient castle nor a modern house but a mixture of modern and antique. The want of trees near it has rather a naked appearance at present, but this objection will be removed when those now planted are grown up. The view immediately opposite the front of the house is also rather naked and appears the more so from the uncommon richness of that on each side, but particularly that to the east.

I returned to Ludlow through Oakley Park, belonging to Lord Clive and now the residence of his mother, the Dowager Lady Clive — a modern brick house. Some fine oak trees in the park etc but seen to great disadvantage after Downton Park. In the evening I proceeded on my journey to Bishop's Castle, 17 miles . . . I entered Lord Clive's park at Walcot, a large brick house and piece of water before it. Far inferior in point of situation to Oakley Park where he and Mr Knight uniting their property might make the most beautiful succession of rides and walks imaginable. . . .

I found a comfortable inn (the Castle) where I met my friend, Mr Frowd, who has the living of Bishop's Castle. The inn, its garden and bowling green above occupy the space of the bishop's castle. Here the bishop formerly resided till about the time of Q. Elizabeth. The town is a borough commanded

24. Powis Castle; Hoare regarded it as over-modernised.

by Lord Clive. Dreary and dull. The ground around it is uncommonly rich and valuable owing probably to the quantity of manure running down on it from the town on all sides. (Inn good).

Monday 3rd June. After breakfast left B. Castle. . . . Here we entered Montgomeryshire. . . . [On the range of hills to the right are several mines of lead etc. They were probably worked by the Romans, as in this neighborhood was found a pig of lead with the characters *ADRIANI* marked upon them. I am informed it is still in the possession of Mr Probert near Shrewsbury] . . . a little further on the right in the parish of Church Stoke the ancient Offa's Dyke crosses the road . . . turned off to the right to see an old mansion house at Lizner Park. . . . It presents a curious specimen of the style of architecture used in this county at the aera of its being built. Its construction is of timbers and plaister with several gable end roofs. It bears the date 1675. . . . The County town of Montgomery is small and prettily situated between two hills on one of which is placed the church and on the other the castle. . . . Its remains are trifling, a few ruined walls[10] only standing, but which still have a good effect when united with the church on the opposite hill and the town between them. Leaving Montgomery I pursued my journey to Welch Pool, 7½ miles. . . . I again saw Offa's Dyke on the right. . . . This dyke formerly extended from Chester to the mouth of the River Wye near Chepstow and was made as a boundary between England and Wales. . . .

The town of Welch Pool consists of one long broad street, the houses of brick; a new town hall of handsome proportions is now building. It is advantageously situated for trade, being a short distance from the Severn and close to a canal. It derived its name probably from a Pool which is supposed to have been in a meadow on the left of the direct road leading from the town to Powys Castle. . . .

Wednesday 5th June. The day was so bad yesterday that we only could extend our walk as far as the church. This morning I again visited Powys Castle.[11] With every local advantage which an elevated situation commanding a distant view over a rich and fertile vale bounded by high mountains can afford, this building is not in itself a picturesque or very striking object. It arises from its little extent in length, the multitude of high narrow chimnies and modern sash windows some of which are of very large proportion. The stone also of which it is built vies with brick from redness of color. This noble situation to do it proper justice would require a castle of bold and massive architecture. Having been modernized in order to render it habitable little of the antique appearance remains.

The inside walls are of an uncommon thickness, so thick as to admit closets being made out of them. It contains some good rooms. The gallery, called the ballroom, is a long narrow apartment well calculated for the use it is now put to, picture gallery. All Lord Clive's collection has been deposited here during his absence in India. The most remarkable are a St

John, whole length by Giacomo Bassano, whole family by Rubens, a beautiful little picture by Fra Bartolomeo etc. In the Powys collection there are several portraits. . . .

The castle is built on a solid rock of a very red hue. A terrace guarded with balustrades joins the house and commands a most delicious view with the noble mountain, Breidden, directly in front. The gardens were laid out in the foreign style with terrace above terrace, vases, statues, parterres, fishponds, etc. The traces only of these remain at present. I regret that the modern taste of gardening has entirely put this old mode of laying out grounds out of countenance, for certainly it has a great dignity of character in it. It will not suit all situations but it is the only one fit for Powys Castle, from whence you could descend by no other means into the gardens but by a long flight of steps. This still remains as an approach from beneath. The walls overhung with fine ivy etc have a very good effect, but the gardens and terraces are in a very neglected state.

The grounds unite a variety of natural beauties . . . the finest feature of the place and that to which the eye almost irresistibly turns every moment and never quits but with regret is the Mountain Breidden, rising immediately above the town of Welch Pool which fills up the vale in a very picturesque manner and tends to enrich the surrounding scenery. I neve saw a mountan in England or Wales whose form was more beautifully varied and contrasted. One point rises majestically like a volcano while the opposite extremity is of a more massive shape and sinks more abruptly into the vale beneath. On this latter northern point a column is erected to the memory of our naval hero, Rodney, so small from the elevated ground on which it stands that it is but just visible. This mountain even exceeds the everchanging Skirrit in Monmouthshire.

The views near the castle are domestic and confined. . . . The chimneys are also so close to each other and so numerous that I should think that two or three or more of them might be cased round and united into a small tower, the good effect of which is seen particularly at Conway Castle where small towers arise out of the larger ones. I would also reduce the number and size of the windows and if possible render them of a form more adapted to the building. I think the approach also to the Castle might be mended and rendered more striking by turning the road off to the right on entering the park, winding it round the hill so as to come up to the castle through the old stone quarry. This my companion, Frowd, told me was Lord Powy's idea, far better than that of Mr Eames who planned the present approach. . . . I would also drain the two pieces of water in this same valley. . . . I cannot approve of the different plantations which skirt this delightful terrace on each side. They are disposed in clumps of fir, beech and oak, quite in the modern style of planting and according to the modern customs also, not thinned sufficiently early. Having suffered so much myself by these modes adopted in plantations I speak feelingly of others. Here particularly the ground required a large range of plantation *en masse*. . . . More of the birch trees should also have been planted for no tree is more suited to a wild country. . . .

All was noise and bustle this day at Welch Pool being one of their fair days of which they have six each year. After dinner proceeded on my journey to Oswestry, 16 miles. . . . I was obliged to make a little detour at the village of Lanymychan [*Llanymynech*] as the waters of the Verniew [*Vyrnwy*] were so high as to render the ford impassable. By this detour I saw a handsome stone aqueduct of five arches made to carry the canal over the river. . . . On the left above the village, Lanymychan, the whole range of mountain is limestone. The differet kilns ranged along its sides appear like so many habitations. Since the cut of the canal into this country many advantages will result: the introduction of lime into Shropshire which before was dear and scarce, the reduction of horses and consequent consumption of oats, the roads bettered etc, etc.

Thursday 6th June. After breakfast proceeded on my road to Llangollen, 12 miles. On my way stopped to take a view of the noble aqueduct forming across the valley under Chirk to convey the waters of the canal over a wide and deep valley.[12] It consists of ten arches, half of which are nearly turned and some few finished. They are grand in their form and received an additional beauty in picturesque light by the soft mellow yellow tint of the stone. On winding down the hill and just seeing this noble aqueduct (which for grandeur will vye with Roman works of the same sort) the eye is sensibly struck with this new object; its present unfinished state renders it perhaps more picturesque to the painter's eye.

. . . I turned off to the left to have a more complete view of Chirk Castle. I approached it in a different and much grander direction through a noble grove of lofty and aged oaks, and where I saw with regret the ravages lately occasioned by the axe. In the midst of this grove stands a figure of the Nernese Hercules on a spot where that of an ancient British Druid would [be] more adapted. Chirk Castle is built on an elevated situation commanding a rich and extensive view. Its architecture is very massive, almost approaching to squatness. . . . By being placed on high ground and the eye being always obliged to look up to it the defect of the lowness of the building is in great measure removed. Such a building would have suited the proud terrace of Powys and would have been grand beyond measure. . . .

From hence I descended into the beautiful Vale of Llangollen whose beauties though so well known to me struck me with fresh pleasure and delight. I lodged at my old quarters, the Bloody Hand (Parks). I remained here till *Sunday the 9th June* when I proceeded to Corwen. On *Thursday 13th* went to Bala where I staid till *Sunday 30th June.*

Sunday 30th June. From Bala to Tan-y-bwlch.

Monday 1 July. Tanybwlch inn. Fished Llyn Morwynion.

Wednesday 3 July. Rode to Harlech. . . . Noble castle built by Edward 1 about the same period as Carnarvon and Conway. It is proudly situated on a lofty steep rock and has a very majestic appearance from the extensive marsh and sea coast beneath it.[13] The principal entrance to it was from the side adjoining the town, which was defended by by a drawbridge and foss. Harlech sends one member to Parliament. The parish church is at some distance from the town. The soil very rocky and destitute of trees. The town not affording any tolerable accomodation for the night I procured a guide to conduct me over the sands to Penmorfa.

The first passage of the sands is over the Traeth Bach, through which the river (descending from the Vale of Festiniog) runs. The next (which is divided by a narrow neck of land from the former) is called Traeth Mawr through which the river coming from Pont Aberglasllyn runs. This passage over the sands and across these two rivers is very dangerous without a proper guide, as they abound in quicksands which shift continually with the Spring tides. . . . I would recommend everyone going from Tan-y-bwlch Inn to Harlech to procure a guide and take the road over the sands instead of that over the mountains; the one is perfectly level and smooth, the other hilly rough and bad. . . . At Penmorfa I found a tolerable little inn. . . .

Thursday 4 July. I deviated from the great road which leads from hence to Carnarvon and turned off to the right to fish Llyn Cwmstrallyn [*Cwmystradllyn*]. . . . A steep descent conducted me to the pretty little vale in which Bedgelert is situated. Here I found a comfortable bed and little parlour. . . .

Friday 5 July. I visited two lakes in the neighborhood. . . .

Saturday 6th July. Left Bedgelert and fished Llyn Cywellyn [*Cwellyn*] in my way to Carnarvon. . . .

Sunday 7th. At Carnarvon.

Monday 8th. Made an excursion to Llanberris lakes. We found a boat ready on the lower lake which conveyed us to the other end of it, about three miles in length. The shores are rocky but not bold in height or form. We were very unfortunate in our weather as the whole scenery was enveloped in in a thick fog [*so*] that at times we could not see across the lake. We met with a friendly and hospitable reception from Mr Wright who attended us on this expedition; and who has lately built a small house on the most beautiful spot which the environs afford, on the neck of land which separates the two lakes and exactly opposite the picturesque remains of Dolbadarn Castle.[14]

Just before our dinner the clouds suddenly dispersed and to our great pleasure and astonishment disclosed one of the most magnificent scenes I ever beheld. The upper lake is truly grand: immense moutains rise immediately from its banks and Snowdon displays its lofty summit to the greatest advantage. At the upper end of this lake is the village of Llanberris and from thence there is a passage between the mountains to Capel Cerrig [*Curig*] and Llanrwst. On the sides of these lakes are fine slate quarries and also copper mines.

Tuesday 9th July. Bangor. A pleasant drive along the banks of the Menai and a good road. The inn being full at Bangor Ferry I was obliged to go to the town, where I found good accomodations. . . .

Wednesday 10th July. Wishing to vary my route to Llanrwst I took a nearer and shorter road over the mountains. . . . I pursued my course to Capel Cerrig. A magnificent road is now forming between Llyn Ogwen and Capel Cerrig by Lord Penrhyn who in his public works is a great benefactor and ornament to this country. He is now building an inn of Gothic architecture at Capel Cerrig and making a good road which will lead from thence to the foot of Snowdon. . . . Of all the points of view in which I have seen this King of Welch mountains this is certainly the most advantageous; the whole form of the mountain has a more distinct and majestic appearance. The foreground is also improved by two small lakes. After a frugal repast at a miserable hovel called an inn I proceeded on my road to Llanrwst, which after leaving the environs of Capel Cerrig and losing sight of Snowdon affords nothing very striking as to picturesque scenery. The distance from Bangor to Llanrwst over these mountains is about 20 miles or upwards, the road in some parts very good. In all, very practicable on horseback. . . .

Friday 12th July. Proceeded on my journey through Cenioge [*Cernioge*] (a single house in blank barren country) to Corwen. . . .

Sunday 14th July. Dined and slept at Chester where we remained till

Wednesday the 17th., when we adjourned to Liverpool. Crossed the River Mersey at the Woodside Ferry, the shortest passage and which with a strong wind we passed in five minutes. Lodged at Bate's Hotel, the best inn.

This town presents the most busy scene I ever beheld, particularly on the different quays. The dry and wet docks, the immense magazines of an extraordinary height, the large tobacco warehouse etc are the admiration of every traveller. I never saw shipping to so much advantage or sailing in so picturesque a manner. This arises in the first place from the extensive trade which employs so many vessels, and in the next from the depth of water close to shore, which brings the ships as they go in and out of the harbor so near the eye. The Fort is the best place to see the ships go in and out. We could not gain admittance to the French prison which is a new and handsome building. The Church of St Paul is a fine edifice. The theatre is of a good size and stands well in a large square. The weather was so very bad during the greatest part of our stay at Liverpool that many parts of the town and many objects escaped our notice.

Sunday 21.   Through Warrington to Tabley Hall where I remained during Knutsford Races and departed on *Sunday 4th August.* Dined at Litchfield, slept at Birmingham, Style's Hotel. . . . Passed through Worcester, Gloucester and Bath and returned home on Tuesday evening *27th August.*

P.S. Continual rains for the last month. Harvest very backward. Much hay still left in the fields. Just began to reap in the neighborhood of Worcester.

VI

Journal of a Tour in 1800.

Saturday 10th May. Left London at ½ p. 11 and arrived at my brother's house at Warendon between five and six. . . .

Monday 12th Fine weather. Wind NE. From Warendon to Aspley, a neat pretty village. . . . Ampthill Park, the seat of Lord Ossory, on the left. Skirt the park pale leaving the village on the right; the park finely wooded and the ground varied with pleasing inequalities. Many new enclosures lately made. Here the sandy soil ends; a flat bad country to Bedford. A handsome inn on the banks of the River Ouse which is navigable. A very fine road from Bedford to Eaton [*Socon*]; open fields and large enclosures. Cross the river at Tamsworth over a long narrow bridge of 17 arches. . . . Budgen [*Buckden*] about halfway: residence of the Bishop of Lincoln. Large enclosures, chiefly corn. Dull uninteresting flat road to Peterborough. One fine view of the distant flat country with Peterborough Cathedral at a distance. Left the great road at Norman Cross. . . .

Tuesday 13 May. Fine, wind N.E. Went to Thorney to see the remains of the abbey. Excellent road to it, flat. The most ornamented and best preserved part of this ancient abbey is the western front, but that has in later times undergone considerable repairs and alterations. It had formerly a very large Gothic window which has been filled up and one of smaller dimensions (though still a large one) inserted. . . . All this front is of Gothic or pointed architecture, and from the date of 1630 which is seen just above the entrance door to the church I should imagine these modern alterations had taken place at that time. The eastern front is also Gothic but the northern and southern sides of the church exhibit many remains of Saxon columns etc etc. . . . But the inside of the church is entirely Saxon. . . .

The Cathedral Church of Peterborough is one of the most interesting buildings I have seen, as it contains so many specimens of architecture from the early Saxon to the late ornamented Gothic . . . the abbey was first founded about the year 654. . . . But the most severe sufferings and damage this cathedral underwent in the year 1643 when many of its most beautiful buildings were destroyed, its monuments defaced and its riches taken away by the troops under the command of Oliver Cromwell. From this unfortunate circumstance we see it deprived of those ancient monuments which not only add to the beautiful appearance of the building, but throw light on the history of the times, and the state of the fine arts, in which they were erected. . . . Though still so much worthy of admiration is left in the cathedral we have to lament the destruction of the beautiful altarpiece, the cloysters, Ladys Chapel, chapter house etc, etc. . . . On first entering the close the western front of the cathedral appears in the most striking point of view. It consists of three of the finest and largest Gothic arches I ever saw, insulated from the main part of the building. They have this singularity that the centre arch is the smallest whereas in most Gothic buildings it is the largest. . . . In the inside the Saxon architecture prevails and exhibits many beautiful specimens of that style. The Library also presents a most elegant example of the ornamented Gothic in its fretted roof, light columns etc. The whole church is kept neat and clean but it wants monuments and projected chapels to render it picturesque; a long unbroken ile has a uniform and stiff appearance. The summit commands a fine and extensive view.

Wednesday 14th. Fine. Wind N.E., cold. . . . The road to Crowland for six miles is very good; through a level country well cultivated. . . . Crowland is a poor village in a low unhealthy situation. There are still considerable remains of the once famous abbey but from the cracks and settlement in the most beautiful part of the building they threaten a speedy dissolution. The western front facing the village presents a very rich specimen of Gothic architecture; it consists of a modern porch or entrance to the church; above it a large Gothic window. . . . In the middle of the village is another singular and unique piece of antiquity: a triangular bridge with the figure of King — as big as life in a sitting posture against one of the arches of the bridge.[1]

From Crowland I crossed the river and proceeded along the raised causeway with a most dreary extent of fens to my right, to Market Deeping. A long miserable village. From thence 8 miles to Stamford; the road good, by the side of a canal. Country level cultivated with corn. . . . Stamford is a large town built upon uneven ground. Has five handsome stone churches, two of them, St Mary's and All Saints, with lofty spires. Their interior does not correspond with the handsome outside for there is nothing remarkable in their architecture. . . . The only curious specimen of Saxon architecture at Stamford is the hospital of St Leonards, a short disance out of the road leading to Deeping. The facade is an elegant specimen of Saxon architecture unmixed with Gothic. . . .

At a short distance from the town is Burleigh, the celebrated seat of the Cecil family. It is a most magnificent specimen of the style of architecture used in the time of Queen Elizabeth. From its cupolas, pinnacles and projecting parts it has also a very picturesque effect; the inner court is particularly grand. Fame has so loudly extolled the collection of pictures that I must own I was much disappointed in looking them over. Every room of a large house is filled, yet there are very few of the first class of painters. The two most esteemed are by masters of the second and third class . . . it appears to me a most mistaken notion to fill up every room with pictures, for where the numbers are so great there must be a great deal of trash. How much better would it be to select all the best and fit up one or two rooms with true originals only, and to put the copies together by themselves. I do not, either, approve of mixing landscapes with historical subjects; their style of coloring is so different that the most brilliant landscape must suffer in its effect, when it has for a neighbor a rich historical subject.

A new approach is making to Burleigh house; much wanted, there being none at present worthy of the house. The architecture of the new lodges is singular and I question if they will accord with the architecture of the house. I must not forget to mention the fine old hall with its curious wooden ceiling, the only remains of the old building now extant. The park is very finely wooded with a variety of aged trees of all sorts, a particular treat to me after the dreary, flat and fenny country which I had lately traversed for many miles. There is also a fine piece of water and a handsome bridge over it; from this spot looking up the water the form of it is too serpentine in its shape. . . . Nature points out the nearest way but then her lines are always sufficiently varied and irregular. Art too often in order to avoid straight lines falls into the very error she wishes to avoid. . . . The house looks well from the opposite side of the water. The ground round it is prettily varied, beautifully wooded, neatly kept, with good gravel walks etc. etc. The view pleased me much on descending to the bridge. . . .

From Burleigh I extended my ride to Barneck [on one side of the village I observed a great tract of ground from which stone had been quarried and perhaps (as before mentioned) Peterborough Cathedral was built with it but the churches and town of Stamford would have consumed an immense quantity], a small village at a short distance from Burleigh. The parish church is a handsome stone building. . . .

On the other side of Stamford three miles on my road to Grantham I got out [of] my chaise to see the church at Pickencote — very well worth notice. I am much puzzled to give a description of it as it has lately been rebuilt, so much in the old Saxon style and so many of the old ornaments made use of and others, as I imagine, scraped so as to appear new, that it requires a very nice eye to distinguish the modern from the antique. . . . The road to Grantham is very uninteresting. Change horses at Witham Common. Open country and large enclosures but few trees. . . .

Friday 16th May. Stormy day. After breakfast went to Belvoir Castle, 8 miles, the seat of the dukes of Rutland. The road is indifferent. From its high situation it shows itself at some distance. On descending through some of the Duke's young plantations I had again occasion to remark the error into which almost all planters fall in not cutting away the fir trees from other forest plants. Fir plantations do well by themselves, and have often a very grand effect when a large tract of ground is covered with them, but no one in their senses would suffer firs to remain in preference to oak plants. . . . The road is bad, the approach very inconvenient (if you have not a servant with you) owing to the number of gates. Nothing ducal either in the approach to the castle, or in the building itself which is low and flat; no projections, towers or pinnacles to render it picturesque. . . .

I had been taught to expect much from the Burleigh Collection of pictures and was disappointed; here without such grounds of expectation I was highly gratified. I thought myself transported to some of the palaces in Italy where a variety of pictures are collected in a long extent of rooms, un-arranged with all their antique rust and mold upon them. I shall minute down those which struck me most forcibly in the order I saw them . . . [*list follows*] . . . I cannot close this account of Belvoir Castle without exposing the very great satisfaction I felt in seeing so many works of our English Raphael, Sir Joshua Reynolds, none of which (as I could perceive) have faded in their coloring. . . .

Grantham is a large town built of brick; has a church with fine steeple. [The Angel Inn[2] appears to be the oldest house in the town; groined roofs in some of the chambers etc etc] . . . to Newark — miles. Road level and good. Common field lands divided into narrow strips.[3] Open country, little wood. Newark, built with brick, is a large town; handsome town hall; fine church with a lofty stone steeple ornamented up to the top with Gothic windows at different intervals. . . . There are considerable remains of a castle on the banks of the river. The different arches and windows in it mark its having been repaired at many different periods. Some remains of Saxon arches appear. It has a grand effect when seen behind a handsome bridge of stone of seven arches.

From Newark to Lincoln 16 miles. Level, sandy and heavy road. At first the country is more woody than any part of the country that I have yet seen. At Mile IX see Lincoln Minster on a hill at a distance; cross a large heath. Steep ascent to the inn — White Hart near the Minster. On entering the town on the right is an ancient building with the remains of a Saxon porch, an ornamented frieze, and the adjoining church has some narrow Saxon windows and over one of them a figure in relief. Opposite to this building is a rich Gothic bow window in a house on the other side of the street. Further on to the right is an old church with Saxon arches in different parts of it, and a singular Gothic building facing the street and made use of as a conduit. On the coping of the wall adjoining it are two stone effigies. On going up towards the Minster by a steep ascent I observed another old house with Saxon windows and doors. Indeed the whole town of Lincoln abounds with specimens of old Gothic and Saxon architecture dispersed about in different walls and houses.[4]

To describe the many beauties of the Minster is indeed a difficult, if not an impossible task. On approaching it from Newark by the south side it appears in a very picturesque point of view; the declivities of the hill beneath it being well wooded, the ruins of the episcopal palace forming a good contrast with the regular and rich Gothic architecture of the Minster. I entered the Minster by the western door. The nave and aisles are formed by lofty Gothic arches supported by eight light columns. . . . You now come to the transept . . . the most striking object in this part of the church is the fine south circular window and beautiful stone tracery work and filled up with old painted glass. . . . Between the arches of the second story figures are introduced playing upon musical instruments. I next proceeded through the cloysters to the chapter house which is a circular building supported by an elegant column in the center branching off into the groins of the roof. . . . In the center of the cloyster court is a curious tesselated Roman pavment discovered in the year 1793. . . . The western front is rich and beautiful beyond description; the Saxon architecture is intermixed with the Gothic but the latter preponderates. . . . The great tower, which formerly supported a lofty steeple, is entirely Gothic; has a rich parapet, two lancet windows on each side and four leaden modern pinnacles. . . . The general style of the architecture is the rich light Gothic; there is but little Saxon introduced and the lancet window prevails the most throughout the building.

It is very much to be regretted also that so interesting a city and county where so many Roman stations have been held and where so many Roman pavements and other antiquities have been found, should not as yet have had its historian to elucidate its antiquities, and give information to the curious traveller. But it is to be hoped in the present age, when topographical researches are so much encouraged that someone will undertake the history of a county so little known and so well-deserving of notice. I found in the waiter at the Angel Inn an antiquarian who possesses a large collection of coins found in the neighbourhood.

An old gateway leading into the Close opposite the western front of the Minster is now taking down. The Bishop's residence being at Bugden [*Buckden*] the upper part of the town bears a melancholy appearance; he comes only once in three years to hold a confirmation etc. The waiter informed me that under his house there were some considerable remains of Roman antiquity. . . . The remains of the castle are trifling.

Sunday 18th May.   High wind and stormy. . . . There is a curious piece of antiquity on that side of Lincoln where I left the town: a stone circular arch which has every appearance of Roman workmanship; it is annexed to the walls of which there are considerable remains.[5] On the right of it is a smaller and lower arch. It still serves as the gate of the town. The Roman road leads directly from this gate in as straight a line as possible to Spittle, and from thence pursues the same direct line to the River Humber. In this tract many Roman relicts and antiquities have been found. . . .

Gainsborough, a dull town, built of brick; the inns appear indifferent. . . . Roads and cultivation mend. At Bawtrey I was not sorry to meet the North Road again, for since I had left it at Newark I had met with indifferent inns and bad horses. Noble road to Doncaster, trifling inequalities of ground and good cultivation. They have a custom here of ripping the bark from the trees whilst standing. Fine raceground on the right. Handsome approach to the town. One long broad street, wide foot pavements. Angel Inn lower end of the town. The parish church is a handsome Gothic building, the ceiling painted in compartments with figures of the Apostles, birds, beasts etc. . . .

Monday 19th May.   Warm and fine weather. After breakfast rode to

Coningsborough [*Conisbrough*], five miles on the road leading to Sheffield.
. . . I first visited the church. The outward porch is Gothic, the inner
Saxon. . . . Many remains of old monuments, all in a shattered state. . . . I
next descended to the castle, finely situated on a well-wooded knoll looking
down on the river beneath.⁶ Little remains to interest the traveller and
antiquarian but the keep which is a lofty well-built structure and in good
preservation. Its form is circular with six projecting square towers [*sketch*].
The entrance to it was over a drawbridge on the western side surrounded
with a deep foss, now covered with fine forest trees. The keep (as is generally
the case) is not the center of the area but joins the rampart walls on the N.
East side. The walls are 15 feet thick. . . . Two large chimney pieces remain
and in the upper story on the south side is a vaulted room with a groined
roof made within the thickness of the walls, but it was so difficult and
dangerous of access that I did not venture into it. . . .

After dinner I left Doncaster crossing the River Don over a handsome
bridge. According to my map my route to Pontefract lay along the Roman
road. . . . Pontefract. From the ancient history of the castle I was led to expect
more than I found there; the remains of it are indeed very trifling, reduced
almost to the fragments of two round towers. The scite is converted into
garden grounds. . . . below it is the shell of a fine old Gothic church, a
melancholy sight to see a fine building in this situation, deserted by the
living yet frequented by the dead — for they continue to bury here. A group
of girls playing at skip rope upon the tombstones added to the desolation of
the scene. The inside of the church is full of tombstones. . . . A species of
cultivation new to me is practised here, the liquorice plant. It is planted in
ridges and is dug up once in three years. It is just now sprouting from the
ground and resembles the first shoots of a young ash plant. The town of
Pontefract is of a long extent but from its want of trade presents a
melancholy appearance. . . .

Tuesday 20th May.   Mild and rainy weather . . . to Wakefield . . . to Leeds.
Fine stone quarries — of a yellow tint. Coal mines. Canal. Road level, heavy
and sandy, cut up by coal carriages. Wakefield: a large, populous, cloathing
town, built of brick. Across the River Calder on the bridge is a rich Gothic
chapel built by King Edward IV to the memory of his father, now repairing.
To Leeds: heavy, dull road, very rough and much cut up by coal waggons.
Great fire engines. A long suburb to Leeds. Great population, dirty
appearance of the inhabitants. I have always found a commercial country
very unpleasant to travel through and uninteresting in point of landscape;
however gratifying it may be to see the very thriving condition of the
country and the good effects of diligence and trade. Enter Leeds by a
handsome broad street. King's Arms Inn in the principal street.

Wednesday 21st May.   Stormy, thunder and lightening. Passed the morning
amongst the ruins of Kirkstall Abbey three miles distant from Leeds; rough
carriage road and indeed (according to report and some experience) they all

are in the neighborhood. On descending to the village the ruins present themselves full to the view and perhaps they appear in no point to so much advantage as seen from this hill, where the fine east window faces the eye and the river is seen meandering through the vale on the left, and the whole ruins are backed by a fine wood of oaks. The east and west fronts totally differ in the style of their architecture, the latter mostly Saxon, the former Gothic. . . . On the south side is a square enclosure, converted into a garden, in which the Saxon architecture prevails; these are probably the remains of the cloysters. Joining to them and towards the river are the remains of a variety of other buildings, from which much of the original plan of the abbey might be traced. . . . The ivy is very happily mixed with the stonework of the building, not concealing too much of the architecture, which I have often had to lament when viewing the old castles and abbies in Wales. I was glad to find workmen repairing some of the walls. Much might be done to add to the beautiful appearance of this abbey by clearing out the rubbish from the inside and thereby rendering it neat. Many have con-demned the neat and trim changed appearance of Tintern Abbey, but I am sure no one with one grain of sentiment or feeling ever entered that building without strong sensations of pleasure and admiration. . . .

To anyone whose taste and pursuits do not lead him to examine into the mechanism and state of manufactures Leeds is an uninteresting town. I was however highly gratified in visiting the mixed cloth hall which is a most singular building. It has 39 large windows in length and 21 at the end; divided into four long streets and two at the ends with a large area or court in the middle where carts enter to load and unload the goods. [*Sketch*] [The building is in length 127½ yards, in breadth 66 yards. Each street contains two rows of stands, the freehold property of separate manufacturers. Each stand is 22 inches in front and the whole number is 1,770. . . .] There is another hall called the White Cloth Hall, 99 yards long and 70 broad, containing 1,210 stands. . . . The market days are Tuesday and Saturday for mixed cloths, and Tuesday only for white. The cloths are sold in a rough state, as they come from the fulling mills, and afterwards dressed, dyed etc by the merchants. The manufacturers who are generally men of small capital are dispersed in villages and houses over the whole face of the country; not a single manufacturer is to be found more than one mile east or two miles north of Leeds. The whole number of Broadcloth manufacturers in the West Riding of Yorkshire is estimated at 3,240.

After dinner I left Leeds and proceeded through Harewood to Harrogate. . . .

Environs of Harrogate.

Ripley. Three miles from Harrogate on the turnpike road leading to Rippon cross the River Nidd over a handsome stone bridge, picturesque scenery on the right. . . . The church is a plain Gothic building and contains nothing curious in its external appearance. . . .

Plumpton, three miles, good carriage road. This place from its singularity and commodious distance is much visited by parties from Harrogate. It belongs to Lord Harewood and when the family is in the countty is shown only on a Tuesday. In describing the grounds it appears to me that the scite of them was originally a stone quarry. The irregularities and excavations made in them partly by art and partly by nature have been happily improved and ornamented: walks have been cut out and made to lead through the windings, interstices and cavities of the rocks. The intervening spaces have been planted with forest trees and a great variety of flowering shrubs. The rocks are of a good tint as to coloring and are covered with heath and other wild plants. On one side they are perpendicular and bounded by a lake in which there is an islet among the rocks which has a good effect. The place is still capable of very great improvement: by continuing the plantations and walk on the opposite side of the lake from whence the rocks appear to greatest advantage. . . .

Spofford, [*Spofforth*] five miles from Harrogate, two beyond Plumpton. Here there are the ruins of an old mansion house belonging to the Percy family (now the property of Lord Egremont).[6] It is situated on a gentle eminence. Below the castle is a large piece of stagnant water. . . . There is a small octagon tower remaining with a stone roof in which was the staircase. The hall was a fine room and its dimensions according to the Knaresborough guide were 75 feet by 36. It makes a picturesque view when seen on the other side of the water. The parish church is a handsome stone building well fitted up within. . . .

Harewood, eight miles from Harrogate, the seat of Lascelles, Lord Harewood. Enter the park through a handsome gateway. The house has a handsome elevation; built of stone; architects Carr and Adams. The interior may be described in a few words: a mass of ill-judged expence, a fine suite of rooms fitted up in the most gaudy and expensive style imaginable. The ceilings by Adams are the richest I ever saw with paintings by Rebecca, Tucchi [*Zucchi*] etc. No pictures worth mentioning except one by Sir Joshua Reynolds over a door representing a small female portrait in the character of a Madonna and Child. Great care in the attitude of the woman and great nature in the child. . . . This place is still in its infancy; great plantations and a wall round the park are now making. The antiquarian will find a rich treat in the parish church, a neat Gothic structure finely covered with ivy. It contains many monuments of excellent sculpture. . . . The village of Harewood is remarkably neat and built with a certain degree of uniformity; all (even the turnpike houses) announce the riches of the landowner. . . . The castle is situated on an eminence near the village, and close to the turnpike road leading to Harrogate. It commands a fine view. . . . the building is by no means picturesque; it wants projections and turrets to make it so. . . .

Brimham Rocks ten miles from Harrogate; pass through Ripley and turn off to the left; follow the road leading to Pateley Bridge for five or six miles; go through a bar gate and turn off to the right which leads you to the rocks. On this eminence nature and time have formed the most curious assemblage of rocks I ever beheld — for to these and not to human art can I attribute the singular forms into which many of these rocks are moulded. A member of the Antiquarian Society, Mr Rooke. . . . endeavors to prove that this was a seat of the Druids. . . . The stone is a composition of sand which easily decomposes when exposed to rain and water of which I made a trial on a piece I brought home with me.[8] The strata are large and lye chiefly horizontally. The weather acts upon them by wearing away the lower part of the strata first so that many pieces are supported on a very small basis [*sketch*]. . . . Nothing can be more varied or fantastical than the shape of these rocks, which occupy a large space of ground. They are well worth the notice of the curious traveller. In the midst of these rocks is a house built by Lord Grantley for the accomodation of those who visit them. It is necessary to bring meat, wine, knives and forks with you. Plates and glasses are found there. Accomodation for five horses at a neighbouring farmhouse.

Knaresborough, a large market town three miles from Harrogate. I have seen few places whose situation and environs present a greater variety of pleasing scenery. The first appearance of it from Harrogate, when it unexpectedly breaks upon the sight, is very striking and I do not know any point of view from whence it appears to greater advantage than from this bridge. The town stands on an eminence; the houses built on the declivity of the hill, interspersed with terraces, gardens and perpendicular rock and the River Nidd at the bottom, have a very picturesque effect. . . . The principal objects of attention are the castle, church, dripping well and St. Robert's Cave. . . . The church is Gothic and has nothing particular worth notice in its architecture. . . . Little remains of the castle to attest its ancient strength or grandeur. . . . There are several detached masses of ruin but one only of any size. . . . The dripping well is a singular sport of nature; the water is of a petrifying quality. . . . St. Robert's chapel is a small room cut in the rock with a Gothic groined roof, an altar and other ornaments in the same style. On the outside the figure of a Knight Templar in the act of drawing his sword cut in relief. . . . A considerable linen manufactory is carried on and some cotton; a large corn market. As a proof of the healthiness of the place I will mention the ages of thirteen persons (who dined together on the King's birthday) which amounts to 1,115 years. . . . The scenery round Knaresborough is chiefly indebted for its beauty to the River Nidd whose banks are in general well-wooded. . . .

Harrogate, on the contrary, has not *one* beauty to recommend it: in point of situation it is bleak, exposed and cold; but I believe healthy to those who can bear so sharp an atmosphere. At a very short distance you feel quite a different climate. It abounds with springs of different qualities, calybeate sulphur, and the two united at the Crescent. The two last are at Lower Harrogate. Fashion, certainly not convenience, has made Upper Harrogate the general *rendez-vous* of the best company. The lower town is objectionable in hot weather from the strong smell of the waters, and perhaps the walk of a mile to the well may be beneficial, though as a daily task it is certainly not very pleasant. The upper town has three good lodging houses: the

Granby (W. Dinsley), nicknamed the "House of Peers', the Green Dragon (Thackeray), the 'House of Commons', and the Queen's Head (F. Hews). Of these the Dragon takes the lead in point of numbers and the Granby in point of good company. I had every reason to be pleased at having fixed on the latter as my residence. Our party was small and pleasant.

The method of living at these houses is well arranged and comfortable: about eight o'clock the company begin to make their appearance at the well, breakfast about ten, dine at four, tea at seven, supper at ten, retire at eleven. People generally breakfast at separate tables. Dine together; the last comer sits at [*the*] bottom and rises gradually to the top. Each person has his own bottle of wine with his name fixed on a label to it. If you invite a friend you pay for him. The house consists of two large rooms in one of which you dine, the other you sit morning and evening. Those who do not take a private parlor have no other place except their bedroom. The parlors are more in number and much better than at the Dragon. The walk to the well from the latter is much the best. . . . The Crown Inn at Lower Harrogate since its late improvements is perhaps superior to any of the houses in point of rooms. Much is still wanting to make this place complete, for nowithstanding its long establishment and the great resort of company, there is neither Pump room to shelter the company from the rain, or any building over the well to shelter the women who serve the water, of whom one attends from each house to attend their different guests. In bad weather you must either go down in a chaise or take the water at home, where it loses much of its spirit and good quality and is infinitely more nauseous. Such a composition surely can scarcely be found except sea-water which I think is still more disgusting. The usual dose is three glasses taken at intervals of ten minutes or quarter of an hour, but if the stomach can bear it they may be taken quicker and then they operate more. Two physicians attend, Dr Jaques and Dr Adair. The latter is a very sensible and well-informed young man.

The balls generally commence on the King's birthday and are continued every Monday and Friday at the Dragon, Granby and Queen's Head in the above course of rotation. Each person pays on entrance one shilling; those who dance pay more for the music etc. The company of these three houses are reciprocally invited by the company who give the ball. No supper for strangers unless invited by any of the company. The tables are well supplied: good fish from Hartlepool and good mutton. Vegetables backward and rather scarce. The trout in the Nidd are small; no good fishing as the river is much netted and poached. There are ? pike in it. Few walks about Harrogate and those bad in general. A sandy soil which dries soon. The heath on the borders of which the upper town is situated is very marshy and capable of great improvement by draining etc. . . . The rides are good, particularly in the environs of Knaresborough but the roads stoney. Tolerable horses are to be hired. A good circulating library and a small theatre. A man has collected a museum worth seeing of specimens of different woods. . . .

Thursday 13th [12th] June. Left Harrogate; breakfasted at Hopper

Lane. . . . Turn off to the right to see Bolton Abbey. . . . Like the generality
of monastic establishments it is situated in a rich vale surrounded with fine
wood and water; wood, water and retirement seem to have been thought
requisite to the monks and to these we owe the picturesque scenery which
these ruins often present. A part of this extensive building is still appropriated to a parish church; the greater and finer part is in a decayed state. This
priory of Augustine monks was founded about the year 1120. Of the
western front we know the exact date by the following inscription [*quoted*]. . . .

Saturday 14th June.   Having been prevented from drawing yesterday by
the badness of the weather I returned this morning to Bolton Abbey. I
fortunately met with the clergyman of the parish who, in the most obliging
and friendly manner *forced* me to accompany him through the park. Having
never heard it mentioned as an object particularly worth notice I was not
overanxious to see the grounds. I was however most agreeably surprised. All
here is nature, uncontaminated by the hand of art, wild at one time,
beautifully rich at another. The River Wharfe contributes much to the
beauty of the scenery. It runs through a fine valley in a rocky bed, its banks
covered with the most luxurious wood imaginable. The prospect is terminated with the distant hills which are covered [*with*] heath and from their
purple hue form a fine contrast with the rich foliage in the foreground. . . . I
am surprised that this place should have been so little noticed by travellers,
or so little visited by its owner, the Duke of Devonshire. The smallness of
his house may perhaps be one reason. This building which is fitted up for his
reception when he comes here to shoot grouse, of which there is a great
abundance on his moors, appears to have been the gateway to the priory. . . .
    The road from hence to Skipton is good but hilly; rich sheep pasture,
enclosed with stone walls; a wide valley and others at a distance with
mountains beyond them. [The sheep here have black legs and face, resembling South Downs with the exception of their horns. Cattle chiefly light-
coloured, handsomely spotted].
    Skipton: the capital of Craven, situated in a fine vale surrounded by hills
cultivated nearly to their summits. The town consists chiefly of one wide
street, at the upper end of which is the church and castle, the property of
Lord Thanet. On this side it must have depended on its walls for defence;
the back part of it rises from a steep perpendicular rock and is sufficiently
fortified by nature. Having been the residence of the Clifford family it bears
more the appearance of a castellated mansion than a fortress. It is at present
in a most ruinous condition. . . . The church is a handsome Gothic building;
has seven Gothic arches to each ile supported by octagonal clustered
columns. . . . The situation of Skipton is very pleasant. Near it are extensive
lime quarries and iron mines [? *the ores of*] which are brought on a rail road
to a canal behind the castle . . . there are extensive cotton works. No building
so little picturesque as these; generally are very lofty and full of windows. . .

Sunday 15th.   Left Skipton and rode to Settle, 16 miles. . . .

Monday 16th June. After breakfast rode to see two natural curiosities in the neighborhood of Settle: Malham, vulgarly called Maum Cove and Gordall Scar. A long and steep ascent; rough, stoney road; many loose stones and the rock being limestone is often slippery. Fine pasture for sheep and cattle amongst these mountains. No trees.

Malham Cove is a perpendicular mass of limestone rock, remarkable only for its great height and perpendicular form. It has no accompaniments of wood; a stream issues from under it; supposed to come from a lake above called Maum Tarn. This object is certainly not worth the journey to it over a bad road, but the second curiosity, Gordale Scar, will repay the traveller a hundredfold for his trouble. It is one of those grand and sublime works of nature which neither pen can describe or pencil delineate in adequate terms. Our poet Gray visited this spot in October 1769 and has given the following account of it in his journal:

> "October 13. From Malham I was to walk a mile over very rough ground, a torrent rattling along on the left hand: on the cliffs above hung a few goats; one of them danced and scratched an ear with its hind foot in a place where I would not have stood stock still
>
> *For all beneath the Moon —*
>
> As I advanced the crags seemed to close in but discovered a narrow entrance turning to the left between them . . . the rock on the left rises perpendicular with stubbed yew trees and shrubs starting from its sides to the height of at least 300 feet; but these are not the things; it is the rock to the right under which you stand to see the fall that forms the principal horror of the place. From its very base it begins to slope forward over you in one black or solid mass without any crevice in its surfaces and overshadows half the area below with its dreadful canopy: when I stood at (I believe) four yards distant from its foot, the drops which perpetually distil from its brow fell on my head. . .".[9]

The masses of rocks are of the finest forms imaginable, their tints rich and beautifully varied, the effects of light and shade grand and striking. With such a scene every painter must be enraptured, and regret that it is beyond the reach of human talents to do more than humbly imitate it. He may [*try*] and give the general form of the rocks, the situation of the waterfall etc etc, but, as I before said, no pencil or words can convey to the eye or the imagination an idea adequate to the sublimity and grandeur of Gordale Scar. Yet strange to say I have heard that some people have visited it without expressing signs of wonder or admiration. I can only say to them — I pity your insensibility. . . .

The village of Settle is situated under a lofty perpendicular rock which overhangs it and bears an Alpine appearance. It has no parish church though a largish village[10] and having many neat gentlmen's houses. There is a curious old mansion house in the upper part of it.

Tuesday 17th June. Fished Maum Tarn, 7 miles from Settle. . . . this water belongs to Lord Ribblesdale, who has built a comfortable house on its banks[11] and made considerable plantations adjoining it. It abounds with trout and perch of a large size. The former are of a goodsize and rise very freely at a fly. We caught 17 fish weighing 17 lb. . . . You fish out of a boat.

Wednesday 18th June. Left Settle, rode to Ingleton. Ascend a long hill. Ridge of limestone rocks; a curious spring by the road which ebbs and flows. . . . Proceeded to Kirby Lonsdale. Stopt to see a curious bridge over the River Lune.[12] It is of great height and the underpart of the arches is ribbed. As I was examining the bridge two chimney sweepers who had sheltered themselves under it from the rain told me with grave faces that the Devil was the builder of it. . . . Proceeded to Dallam Tower, seat of Mr Wilson. Country becomes more wooded and fewer stone walls. Dallam Tower is situated near the village of Milnthorpe. It is backed by a beautiful grove of oak and other trees which cover a large hill above it. Behind it an immense tract of sands extends as far as Lancaster and the Spring tides come up the river close to the house. The county rich and fine. I have seen few places which have given me the idea of comfort on first sight, and I found these ideas completely realised.

Friday 20th. . . . Nothing interesting on the road to Kendal. A large town. Stop at the bridge and go up to the castle, built on a circular mount with a deep foss round it. The outward walls remain and some round towers. . . . The country round Kendal is thinly wooded and is still deformed by stone walls. The church is a large Gothic building with two side isles containing nothing curious with respect to monuments. . . . From Kendal to Bowness on Windermere Lake, a fine valley, well cultivated, on the right. Leave it together with the main road and turn off to the left . . . descend to Bowness having a fine view of the lake beneath.

Bowness inn: White Lion, situated about the middle of the lake; one large parlor, one smaller and good bedrooms. In the evening took a boat and rowed round the large island, to the ferry, and from thence ascended to a summerhouse built on an eminence and commanding a very advantageous view of the lake on each side.

Saturday 21st. . . . West[13] in his guide has pointed out a variety of stations from which the lake may be seen to advantage and marked them down in his map. They are also marked on Crossthwaite's maps. These may be [of] use to the traveller who cannot devote much time to viewing the environs but the man of taste, who makes any residence on the spot, may find points of view equally fine by mounting the different hills in search of them. The view from the opposite ferry on the eminence where the summerhouse is built and another from a cleft rock on the left of the road leading to Kendal will give very good ideas of the extent of the lake. I would also recommend a ride on the east side of the lake for about three miles. Here the lake presents a fine sheet of water and the opposite banks are finely covered with copse wood, and the tranquillity of the scene uninterrupted by those staring white houses with which the eastern banks of the lake, and particularly the upper end of it, are crowded. . . . This lower part of the lake is much the tamest in point of mountains; those at the upper end have very grand features and fix a noble finish to this piece of water. . . .

There are nine or ten islands in this center part of the lake, some very small only appearing like spots. They are most of them thickly covered with wood. I doubt whether they are an ornament to the lake or not, as they appear like spots and in some measure detract from the grandeur of the lake. The large island consists of near thirty acres. The first improver of this island was Mr English . . . it is no easy matter to form a plan for a house and dispose grounds conformable to the nature of the scenery around this island. . . . The original house built by Mr English was exactly the form of a large tea canister, which we often see exposed at the outside of a grocer's shop, the chimneys forming the mouth of it. [*sketch*] Mr Curwen, the present proprietor added an Ionic portico to the front of this building facing Bowness. He has also planted the island so thickly that its form cannot be seen; I wish it had been done with taste, but weeping willows, Lombardy poplars, trim flower beds etc, etc but ill accord with the fine rude scenery of Windermere Lake.

Dined at Calgarth where the Bishop of Llandaff (Watson)[13] had built a comfortable house and made considerable improvements in planting, agriculture etc Near his house on a little eminence where there are some fine sycamore trees there is a good view of the lake. . . .

To a person wishing to explore the views of the lake I should certainly prefer Bowness to any other situation though the house commands no prospect of the lake; nor are there any good walks on its banks. Lowood Inn is delightful in the last respect, being close to the borders of the lake, but here it is so near its termination or rather beginning that its magnitude is not perceived; Bowness presents a grand, Lowood a quiet scene. We found good accomodations at the Salutation Inn at Ambleside.

Sunday 22nd. June. Ambleside is prettily situated in a valley surrounded by mountains about a mile distant from the lake. After breakfast we took a ride which for its extent (about ten miles) presented such a variety of natural beauties as I believe can scarcely be equalled in any ride of the same distance. From Ambleside to Rydale, cross the river, turn up a rough road to the right. Rydale Water, a pretty little lake on which are two islands; on the right of it rises a lofty mountain from the summit of which our guide told us that he could see eight lakes. Descend to the borders of the lake and ascend again. On the summit of the hill Grasmere Lake breaks upon the sight in the most pleasing and unexpected way.[14] A conical mountain on the left of the lake forms a fine feature. The village of Grasmere appears to advantage, surrounded by a fertile and well-cultivated vale. Beyond it is another fine valley leading to Keswick, terminated with a part of Skiddaw

Mountain. . . . There is a pretty little green island, chiefly pasture, with a small patch of trees and a cottage. Leaving the view of Grasmere behind a prospect of a very different sort presents itself: three lakes surrounded with woody hills and more distant mountains; Langdale Chapel, a picturesque little building; further on some large slate quarries; masses of fern very fine, as are the tints of the rocks — a striking scene. A little above them see Langdale Pike, two noble mountains of the most rugged form. The scenery there is particularly wild. This was the extent of my ride. . . .

[1. Windermere Lake has pike, perch, trout and char; the trout rise best at the May fly; the fishing not very good.
2. Rydale Water. Pike, perch and a few trout.
3. Grasmere Water. The same.
4. Elter Water. Small trout of good colour].

In October when the fish spawn the char frequent the Brathy, the trout the Rydale river, and in the latter they are caught of the enormous weight of 20lb. The way of catching these large trout is this: they always come out of the lakes to spawn in the smaller rivers where they are easily seen, and a man takes his spear and kills him. It is often done by night with a candle or lantern.

Sunday evening. Drink tea at Rydale Hall with Lady Diana Fleming; nothing particular in the house, two good rooms and a charming view from the front windows. . . . A winding path through a grove of the only large oaks I have yet seen in Westmoreland. A rustic bridge over a rapid mountain torrent. Ascend the hill by a path cut through a natural copse wood. First station from which you view the upper cascade: it forms from this point of view two falls, through a narrow chasm amongst the rocks. The sides are finely wooded, all in the state of nature; the hand of art has here never been employed. . . . The path conducts him [*the traveller*] to a rustic building, on opening the doors of which the most beautiful little picture imaginable bursts suddenly upon his sight. It is not the magnitude of this cascade but its character and accompaniments which render it so interesting and so deservedly admired. Figure to yourself a semi-circle, the sides of rock covered with a variety of mosses, ferns and other wild plants. In the center a fall of water dividing itself into two channels throws itself into a clear nd transparent bason below, which forms the foreground of the picture. In the background and immediately above the cascade is a rustic stone bridge (Gothic) of one arch (over which the passengers and cattle passing occasionally add an additional good effect to the scenery), the whole overhung with a rich canopy of natural wood so thick as to admit very partially the rays of the light and sun. . . .

Monday 23 June. Very fine. After breakfast visted a waterfall at a short distance from Ambleside. . . . Proceeded on my way to Paterdale [four horses required to pull up a chaise, if laden, uphill. . .] a very long and

tedious ascent, not a tree or bush to be seen for some miles after quitting the
rich and beautiful environs of Ambleside. As tedious a descent to Broader
[*Brother's*] Water, a small lake, where cultivation again appears. . . . [The
character of this morning's ride is wild mountain scenery. An immense flock
of sheep attended by a numerous pack of dogs and herd of shepherds, who
had just driven the mountains in order to collect the sheep to be washed and
shorn, added to the effect of the pastoral scenery].

The addition of a parlour and two bed rooms has made the little inn at
Paterdale very comfortable.

The first appearance of Ullswater has nothing in the least striking when
seen from this point of view. In the evening we took a boat on the lake and
rowed along with our fishing rods towards the middle of it, to a rocky
island. There on looking back we were most agreeably surprised, or rather
astonished at the beauty of the scenery behind us. The rocky island before us
as a foreground, the fine woods of oak on the right added to a noble range of
mountains in the center amongst which the Dod is the most prominent
feature, form a *tout ensemble* in point of grandeur and beauty which I have
rarely seen.

Tuesday 24 June.   Our guide conducted us to Hays [*Hawes*] Water. Follow
the great road to Ambleside, turn off to the left. . . . In the evening I
surveyed the environs of Paterdale. No spot can be more sequestered. The
ground and fields around this small, scattered and retired village, are
beautifully varied with many picturesque patches of wood and rock. . . .

Wednesday 25th.   A hard rainfall in the night which prevented my pursuing
my route to Penrith on horseback. We were obliged to send for posthorses
from Penrith. The carriage road leads on the N. West side of the lake which
is of a very irregular form. Pass through some beautiful woods where the
masses of rock are happily intermixed. . . . At Penrith we found ourselves in
a largish town and handsome inn, and away from all wild and mountain
scenery. As I mean to return to Penrith I will say nothing about it at present.

Thursday 26th.   Day fine. Rode to Keswick 18 M. Large inclosures with
stone walls and little wood. Cross a wild moor. Continual ascent and
descent. On approaching Keswick is a fine range of mountains to the right
and left, a chasm in them to the vale of St John on the left. A perfect
Druidical circle on an eminence in a field to the left of the roadside.

Friday 27th June.   Very Fine. Breakfasted at Wythburn, a little public
house 7½ miles from Keswick on the direct road to Ambleside, and a short
distance from Thirlmere Water. After breakfast took a guide and ascended a
steep mountain opposite the inn to a tarn called Harrap in which we had been
informed, there were a great many large trout but on this (as well as on many
prior occasions), we were deceived. . . . From this place we proceeded to
another tarn in a westerly direction over a wild moor and steep ascent. This

is called Blair [*Blea*] Tarn and is somewhat similar to Hayswater and I think nearly as large. The sides rather wet and spongy but here deep and good for fishing. The day was rather unfavorable to our sport, being too bright and insufficiently windy. I caught five trout here, about half a pound each. Outside blackish, flesh white and not good. . . . From hence I directed my course back to Thirlmere. In my way found a tarn still smaller than Harrap. . . .

Sunday 29th June.   Left Keswick on an excursion to Buttermere. The road leads on the left banks of the lake through some flourishing young woods, formerly a part of the Derwentwater Eastate, now belonging to Greenwich Hospital. Pass the house now inhabited by Mr Pocklington, less grotesque in its architecture than the two others built by him. Here there is a cascade but far inferior to Lodore. As the beauty of this waterfall entirely depends on the quantity of water with which it is supplied and, as the season has of late been very dry I saw it to great disadvantage. It falls in a deep chasm between two high towering rocks, well wooded, and when full must have fine effect. A range of high crags on the left and immense fragments which have fallen down and lay scattered in the most confused and picturesque manner. They are happily described by Gray in his Tour: "The whole way down, and the road on both sides is strewed with piles of fragments, strangely thrown across each other, and of a dreadful bulk etc. The place reminds me of those passes in the Alps where the guides tell you to move with speed and say nothing lest the agitation of the air should loosen the snows above and bring down a mass that would overwhelm a caravan".[14]

At about 4¼ miles from Keswick enter Borrowdale where the little village of Grange with its bridge etc have a very picturesque appearance. Pass under Castle Crag, a boldly towering rock rising in the center of the valley, once its proud guardian [On this formerly stood a castle . . . completely demolished by the slate works which have undermined it]. Bowder Stone, an immense fragment of rock which has fallen from the mountain into the plain close to the roadside, and is balanced on its side in a very curious and picturesque manner. . . . Ascend by the village of Seaton on the right. Bad, rough and steep road. Descent equally bad under the lofty crag called Honister on which slate quarries are worked. Frightful to behold from the great height and dangerous situation. I was told that this quarry was the first worked in England. There are others on the opposite hill. Immense fragments of rock lye scattered on the plain beneath. Follow the banks of a clear mountain torrent to the Lake of Buttermere. In a cleft of rock on the opposite side of the lake my guide showed me the place where the Golden Eagle used to build their nests, but they have also disappeared. [The damage done by the eagles was calculated at a lamb a day at least, besides their other food; no wonder they were destroyed. . . .]

We found at Buttermere a small inn; what was wanting in show was amply made up to us in the cleanliness and civility of the landlords. This little inn is kept by two old people who have now one only daughter left, their sons having followed the sea service and there lost their lives. Tourists have proclaimed aloud the beauty and form of the Fair Maid of Buttermere, and with justice, for such a form, and such a face, and such a head of hair are rarely to be found even in more cultivated and civilised spots. Her face is truly Graecian, her hair of a fine dark brown, of an extraordinary length done up with great taste. She reminded me of a fine Italian beauty, both as to the form of her features and the method of dressing her hair. This little inn furnishes one double-bedded, and one single room, and one small parlor. They have no wine. We could procure no straw to litter our horses with. Notwithstanding these inconveniences we spent the night here; otherwise we should not have had sufficient time to view the various beauties of this sequestered spot.

The village of Buttermere is situated exactly between the lake of the same name and that of Crummock. It does not consist of twenty families; a little vale, well wooded and watered, surrounded by lofty mountains. All seems here peaceful and tranquil but even here the grotesque forms of architecture have been exercised in a whimsical house lately built at the upper end of Buttermere Lake by an attorney from Cockermouth, but fortunately it is so placed as not to offend the eye in the general view of the lake and country.

In the evening we walked about two miles over stoney and wet moor to see a cascade situated under the lofty Mountain Mellbreak on the left side of Crummock Lake. . . . It is far superior to any others that I have yet seen, and one of those pleasing objects which, like Gordale Scar, take the traveller by surprize and wrap him up in wonder and admiration. . . . It is however difficult of access; the easiest mode is certainly by a boat from the lower end of Crummock Lake. . . . About half a mile from Buttermere on the left of the road to Crummock on a rocky knoll covered with copse wood is a very advantageous station for viewing the two lakes and their surrounding mountains. . . . High Stile, Red Pike and Melbreak on one side with Grasmere on the other produce as fine an amphitheatre of mountains as any in Cumberland and together with the general tranquillity and solitude of this little vale, the want of numerous habitations with which many of the other lakes are crowded, so render these lakes as interesting as anything I have yet seen.

Monday 30th June.   Left Buttermere and proceeded on the right bank of Crummock Lake. This lake is about four miles long. The mountains around it are more barren than about Buttermere. . . . I again crossed the Cocker and entered the beautiful Vale of Lorton. What a sudden change of scenery! Adieu to craggs, torrents, lakes and precipices. An extensive well-wooded and cultivated valley watered by [the] R. Crocker with several neat farmhouses happily interspersed, now presents itself. . . . Pass through the Vale of Embledon which after that of Lorton does not deserve notice. First view of Bassenthwaite Water not striking, more so on descending to its shores. . . . As a sheet of water I have seen none equal to Bassenthwaite — being of a straighter form and less intersected with promontories etc.

[As nearly as I could guess I think this morning's ride must have been about 14 miles, the whole road good. Very little wheat is grown in this country. Instead of barley they cultivate a grain called bigg; it differs from barley in having four rows of spikes instead of two. A fine sort of oat is also sown called the potatoe oat. . . . They also have a singular method of sowing their turnips in drills or ridges which are howed and earthed up like peas or potatoes. . . .]

In the evening I had a most delicious ride back to Keswick on the western banks of the lake. On the opposite side you see lofty Skiddaw, illumined with the western sun. The shores neatly cultivated and ornamented with several good houses etc. In short the whole presents a most pleasing scene of wild and cultivated nature. A valley of about 4 miles separates the lakes of Bassenthwaite and Derwent Water and in high floods they are completely united, leaving the higher ground as islands. . . .

It now remains for me to give some description of Keswick and its lake which takes the name Derwentwater from the unhappy family who formerly lived here and whose estates were forfeited to the Crown.[15] This water is of a rounder shape than Windermere or Ullswater and on that account gives you more the idea of a lake. It is of such a size that you can command it all with the eye. Its length is about 3½ miles; its banks are more equally beautiful and varied than any I have yet seen. In Windermere, Ullswater, Bassenthwaite and Crummock the lower ends of their lakes fall off much in point of beauty; the mountains sink, the views become tame when compared with those which the upper ends present. But Derwentwater being backed by the noble mountains, Skiddaw and Saddleback, has not this defect. A variety of good stations have been mentioned by Mr West in his Guide and by Mr Crossthwaite in his maps. Indeed they are so many and so varied that on following the windings of the lake you cannot go amiss. . . . There are several islands in this lake. . . . [A curious phenomenon makes its appearance at times in this lake: floating islands which without any apparent cause suddenly make their appearance and as suddenly depart. One of these islands measured 180 yard square. . . .]

The appearance of this beautiful lake has been much hurt by the variety of uncouth buildings which Mr Pocklington has erected in different parts of it: no less than three houses, two of which are placed in the most conspicuous situations on high ground and being high themselves have still a worse effect. The one he now inhabits near Loudore being lower and backed with wood is less bad. There is a great contrast between these and the little retired villa of Lord William Gordon which is built on the ground with one storey only, in a sequestered bay and so much enveloped with wood than you can scarcely discern it.[16] To him belong all the fine woods on this side of the lake. It commands a delicious view of the lake without itself being commanded. In St Herberts Island a rustic summerhouse has been built and a walk made round it, but the trees are here too thick and too many firs. It is impossible to be tired with the beauties of this lake, and the environs of Keswick are chearful and afford a great variety of fine rides and walks.

In short Keswick is a place where every tourist to the lakes should fix his headquarters for some days. The inns are good; there are good horses, intelligent guides, safe boats, and the lake affords ample amusement to those who are fond of fishing in all its branches. In a wet day the museum kept by Crossthwaite and the guide Hutton will fill up some of the traveller's time, where he will see collected good specimens of the different mineral and natural productions of this country besides other antiquities and rare curiosities. In short I know of no place where a few days or even weeks may be spent more pleasantly.

Wednesday 2nd July.   In the evening left Keswick and returned by the same road I came to Penrith; there are many things at Penrith and in the neighborhood to arrest the attention of the curious traveller, and the excellent accomodations he will meet with at Buchanan's House will make amends for the dullness of the town and its immediate environs.

Thursday 3rd July.   The first object of my curiosity was Brougham Castle. . . . It is a large, massive ruin built generally with the red stone of the country, but some of the walls have been faced with one of a greyer tint. Its architecture bears the marks of its having been repaired at several different times — of the strong fort and of the fortified mansion.
     Return to Emont [*Eamont*] Bridge by Brougham Hall, an old-fashioned house on an eminence commanding a fine view. A fine avenue of oak trees. On the left hand of this road, between the bridge and the village, are the remains of two ancient circles. A great part of the first has been destroyed by digging gravel; the rampart of this is very low. Nearer the village is another circular intrenchment, vulgarly called Arthur's Round Table.[17] Here the ditch is deeper and the area or platform is raised higher. Instead of going back to Penrith through the village turn off to the left, and at a short distance from the common on the right you will see a gentle eminence covered with wood. Here you find another antiquity much more curious then either of the other two circles. It goes by the name of Mayborough and is also a circle but much larger than either of the other two and different in its con-struction. The spot is naturally an eminence of a round form. The inside area has been enclosed apparently by an immense quantity of stones collected and heaped up, for there is no appearance of cement or mortar being used. Besides, the stones from their circular and even appearance appear to have been brought there from the bed of the river. In the center stands a large block of unhewn stone.
     To what purpose these circular areas were appropriated antiquaries have not been able to determine. They may probably be the works of the Romans as we know they had stations at old Penrith and a supposed one at Brougham Castle; and these may have been used for their games. By the stones at Mayborough we might also be led to suppose that this monument belonged to the Druids, but I do not remember any instance of their circles having been fenced in. Perhaps it might have been used as a circus for chariot races and the stones were the *metae* or goals. . . .

Thursday 4th July. The objects of this morning's excursion were the Nunnery and the Druidical circle at Little Salkeld. . . . The Nunnery is about two miles distant; it belongs to Mr Bamber who married the lady who was the owner of this place. Its beauty arises from the singularity of its grounds. The first walk called the Upper leads through a thick and natural wood to the banks of the River Eden which here has a rapid course over a rocky bed of stone. The rocks, fine birch trees, fern etc are quite in character with the river etc., etc. . . . The walks have been ingeniously turned along this narrow pass by numerous flights of steps, by excavating the rocks etc., etc. There are many fine masses of rock, the whole wooded and left judiciously in a state of nature. It derived its name probably from having been formerly the scite of a convent and surely no place was better adapted for solitude and retirement. [On asking a young raw Irish gardener how long it had had the name of Nunnery he told me that *nuns* had been *kept* there in former times]. . . .

I returned to Kirkoswald, refreshed my horses and proceeded to Little Salkeld. Here on a lofty eminence, commanding an extensive view, are the remains of a very large Druidical circle, vulgarly called Long Meg and her Daughters. According to Hutchinson its circumference forms a circle of 350 paces and the number of stones 67. On walking round once only I counted them — 69. Many are quite flat. They are different sizes, all unhewn and in a state of nature. On taking the point of it with my compass I found Hutchinson incorrect in placing the single stone to the south, whereas it stands nearly west. Two other stones project also beyond the circle. I wonder it has so long remained unhurt as half of it is in a piece of cultivated corn land and intersected by a fence wall, the other half on a common. This is certainly is a very curious piece of antiquity and deserves notice. Its size appears to me more considerable than Stonehenge. It can be seen without inconvenience as a chaise can go up close to it. . . .

Saturday 5th July. This morning I rode to Shap, 11 miles . . . to Lowther, the seat of Lord Lonsdale. Grounds laid out in the old-fashioned style, finely wooded. The old seat was burnt down; one small wing of red stone remains. Great preparations have been made of timber and other materials to rebuild it, but it is not yet begun. Lord Lonsdale has shown great public spirit in erecting extensive buildings for manufactories etc, etc. Has built a whole village on a neat and regular plan, but either for want of population, present encouragement or some other cause these new buildings are mostly uninhabited and bear a most melancholy appearance. The carpet manufactory has now only one hand employed in it. It deserves the notice of the traveller from the extreme beauty of the workmanship; the colors vye with the celebrated Gobelin tapestry. An immense number of these carpets remain packed up in boxes intended for the new house which the new owner will probably never build.[18] They are all worked by hand and in one piece. One loom is supposed to be the largest in England. . . .

Shap is a long village of one street, houses dispersed intermixed with trees

. . . on the left of the great road leading to Kendall over the moors is a most curious and singular piece of antiquity. It consists of a long avenue of large stones, placed at different intervals and extending near two miles. One end seems to have terminated in this common, as the avenue closes with a row of stones placed in semi-circular form. This end stands nearly south and from thence the avenue takes a curve inclining to the west. The line of these stones may be traced to the village of Rasgill where I saw one of them. Many of those lying in corn and meadow lands have been blown up and removed. Enough however are left to ascertain the direction they took. The stone resembles red granite. They are all unhewn. I have not as yet heard any account given of this singular piece of antiquity.[19]

Sunday 6 July.   After breakfast visited Hawes Water, distant six or seven miles from Shap. . . . The upper part is shut in with bold and lofty mountains as is the case with the generality of lakes I have seen is by far the most picturesque part. This lake will well bear seeing after the others, although its beauties are less talked of because less known. The farmhouses are dispersed about in a very picturesque manner sheltered mostly with some fine trees around them. The two opposite banks of the lake are well contrasted: that on the left has a fine natural wood, that on the right patches of cultivation. A picturesque waterfall on the right. . . . Descended into another vale watered by the Lowther river. Here was situated the Abbey of Shap, the greatest part of which is gone to decay.[20] One large square, high tower remains with the western window, tall Gothic. On the side of this tower are windows *temp*. Henry 8, and no part of it denotes high antiquity. This abbey is situated on the banks of the Lowther and from the ruins of its foundations must have been a considerable building. . . .

Monday 7th July.   After breakfast rode to the foot of Ullswater, to Dacre, and back to Penrith. Passed by the old mansion house belonging to Lord Lonsdale called Stockbridge Hall, remains of a tower and a large bow window. . . . The castle at Penrith[21] stands on an eminence at a short distance from town. Is a square building of a stone as red as brick which gives it a very heavy appearance. Its architecture is equally heavy with its color and by no means an interesting ruin. . . .

    In the evening proceeded on my journey to Appleby; road good, country very dull. . . . The usual post-stage is at Crackenthorp, a single retired inn on the right of the road, two miles short of Appleby which, though the county town, does not furnish post horses. Having nothing to see at Crackenthorp and much at Appleby I went there and found very good accommodations at the Kings Head Inn [the innkeeper means to take out a licence for post horses] where Lord Lonsdale has lately added much to the house. Appleby has a singular and novel appearance: it consists chiefly of one long and wide street. The church at the bottom closes the perspective and the castle at the summit. The ascent is rather steep. Near the top and also near the bottom are two stone columns. On the base of the former is the inscription: 'Retain your loyalty-preserve your rights.'[22] The appearance of the street is much injured by a wretched town hall and some dirty shambles erected in the middle of it. The castle presents a mixture of ancient and modern architecture; I could observe only one old round tower annexed to it. . . . Adjoining the inhabited part of the castle is an ancient square building with four low turrets at each end, vulgarly called Caesar's Tower. It is built on an eminence, partly surrounded by a deep foss. It bears the marks of great antiquity. . . . The church is a Gothic building and contains two monuments of the Clifford family. . . . In a wall opposite to the grammar school are preserved several Roman inscriptions found in the neighborhood, but amongst them are several of a modern date, the invention and handi-work of one Reginald Bambrigg, a quondam schoolmaster here. Appleby is supposed to have been a Roman station.[23] The banks immediately round the River Eden are well wooded [We drew a net in the river and caught several trout, all white but of a bright color outwardly. One of 7 lb. had been lately caught in this river].

Tuesday 8 July. In the evening rode to Brough. . . . Turned off on the right before I came to Brough to see the ruins of the castle. . . .[24] Towards the west a square tower, apparently of higher antiquity than the other part of the building and very similar to that at Appleby. Some parts of it, particularly a window on the southern side bear the marks of Norman architecture. There was formerly an inscription over the southern entrance ('. . . repaired by Lady Ann Clifford . . . 1659').

Wednsday 9th July. Rode to Barnard Castle, 17 miles, a most melancholy ride indeed over a most bleak and barren country. Still, however, it was not void of interest and the road was excellent. Brough was supposed to have been a Roman station.[25] There was another beyond it on the road to B' Castle, called Maiden Castle. At Mile VI there is another encampment called Roy Cross. . . . Bowes, a village 4 miles from Barnard Castle; remains of a square castle somewhat similar to those at Appleby and Brough, but I think it is older; well cased with hewn stone, much of which has been removed; the windows are round, and eyelight holes.[26] All calculated for strength and defence; the walls are very thick. This place was supposed to have been situated on the Roman road and to have been a station of which there are marks in a field on the south side of the castle. Several Roman antiquities have been found here.

The two roads separate at Bowes: the great northern road going straight to Greta Bridge, that to Barnard Castle turning off to the left. The latter road I took and proceeded to Barnard Castle, 4 miles. I found much noise and bustle in the town, it being market day, and the same in the inn where I took up my quarters, the Rose and Crown.

Northern Tour, 1800. Part Second.

Thursday 10th July. Yesterday being market day the town was all noise, hurry and confusion; today all tranquillity and dullness. The town is situated on the declivity of a hill. Consists chiefly of one long and wide street to which you gradually ascend from the bridge. This street, like that at Appleby and many other places, is disgraced by the shambles and market placed put in the center the best part of it. There are several good houses in the town built of a good stone of a yellow color. The castle is situated at the upper end of the town and is very extensive; the area enclosed by its walls is large.[27] In many points of view it is a most picturesque object but particularly so from the west. There is a delightful walk through a fine wood on the right hand banks of the River Tees (to which you descend from the upper end of the town), where the castle, bridge and part of the town present themselves in a variety of different points of view, all beautiful. I have as yet during my tour seen nothing so picturesque or perfect in all its parts as a composition for a picture.

   After breakfast took a ride in the environs . . . you come to Eggleston Abbey.[28] Hutchinson in his *Tour* mentions the above under the name of Athelstan, but they are generally called Eggleston. The remains are considerable, well-situated on rising ground on the well-wooded banks of the River Tees. The style of architecture is early Gothic, but as in all old abbeys and cathedrals the different style of architecture marks the different aera at which they have undergone repairs. Underneath the abbey there is a small bridge over a brook which appears coeval with the abbey, and from the banks of the river you have a good view of the handsome stone bridge built over the Tees by Mr Morritt. It appears to advantage from hence well backed up with wood. . . . Continued my ride to Greta Bridge where there are two good inns. . . . A handsome stone bridge was built over the Greta at the expence of the County. . . . I returned to B'Castle on the Durham side, the River Tees dividing the counties of Durham and York.

Friday 11th July. Having been informed of a singular fall of the River Tees about seventeen miles distant from Barnard Castle I resolved on seeing it. . . . At mile III turn off by a farmhouse to the left to see a singularly constructed bridge over the river. Some strong chains are fastened to the rocks on each side of the river and drawn as straight as possible. Upon these a narrow wooden bridge is placed with a balustrade on each side and fastened to the chains which support it. It is balanced by other chains, two on each side, which are fastened on the rocks. The tremulous and unsteady motion of it on crossing gives you an unpleasant sensation as there is a tremendous gulph at a considerable depth beneath you, and it has still more aweful an effect when you see some people crossing it and giving it purposely a swinging motion. It then resembles the slack rope. This country is mostly inhabited by the miners who work in the lead mines which lie in the mountains on each side of the river. Those in Yorkshire belong to Lord Strathmore, those in

Durham to Ld. Darlington. Both their moors abound with grouse.

Turn off to the left by the side of the wall and a belt of trees and at a distance see a declivity covered with brush wood. Here is situated the waterfall; owing to the openness of the country it shows itself sooner than it ought. All similar objects have a stronger effect when they take you by surprize. I first viewed it from the summit of the rocks, looking down into the dreadful chasm beneath. . . . It is not in the power of the pen to do justice to the description of similar scenes. Words cannot convey to the mind's eye the happy mixture of colors, forms, light and shade on which their principal beauty depends. The forms of these rocks are very grand; being quite perpendicular their summits are covered with brushwood, and in the strata of the rock the tints are varied by the wild plants which have crept up between them. Below all is dark. . . . The rocks on this side are well covered with copse wood to their summits. Large masses of rock which from time to time have fallen down from the mountain above lye dispersed in the most picturesque confusion on the banks of the river. These intermixed with the copse wood, wild plants, weeds etc etc form an excellent foreground. . . .

I returned to Barnard Castle on the Yorkshire side of the river. . . . This side of the river is much more inhabited, and the ride more sheltered, than the Durham side. At Lastington there is a seat of Mr Maire and several other good houses on the road. I paid for my trip into the mountains on my return to Barnard Castle having caught a violent cold which attacked my bowels and confined me to the house till

Monday 14th July.   . . . Proceeded on my journey to Staindrop, 5 miles, a long village consisting of one wide street. A decent looking inn opposite the church, but no posthorses kept. Saw the church, a handsome Gothic building without. The arches which divide each isle are Saxon with varied capitals, those into the chancel and nave are Gothic. . . .

The first approach to Raby Castle on this road is on the most unfavorable side, that which has undergone much modern innovation. On turning round the angle of the building you approach the Porter's lodge, picturesque and characteristic: the portcullis, large grated folding doors; two knights in armor standing on the battlement's recall to one's imagination the ancient days of chivalry. This idea is still maintained and perhaps increased on entering the inner court, and from thence a grand hall in the center of which two flights of steps lead to the apartments on the right and left. [In this hall chandeliers are hung and on any grand fete given at the castle they are lighted, and carriages drive thus absolutely into the house. This is novel and I believe unique.] The interior of the house does not correspond with the exterior. The habitable rooms are few in number and fitted up in the modern style. There are but few family portraits. On viewing the outside of these great old castles we are led to expect much room within but this is seldom the case; they were erected more for the purposes of defence than luxury. Of course the walls were thick, the windows small and the rooms gloomy. Raby Castle is an immense pile of building still very characteristic of its ancient destination, being little hurt by modern improvement. Its situation on flat ground is not very advantageous to it. The best view of it is from the north where little of the modern part appears. The parts are finely broken and it forms a very picturesque subject for a drawing, as so few of the old baronial castles remain inhabited in modern times. It is peculiarly interesting to every Englishman and antiquarian.

The grounds and park have not much to boast of in point of situation. The plantations (of which there are many) are rather formal in their shapes, as is the water. Fine stables and kitchen garden. The breed of cows and cattle seems also very fine. Many detached and whitened buildings about the park are hurtful to the general view.

The country from hence to Bishops Auckland like that from Barnard Castle to Raby is enclosed, a mixture of corn and pasture lands, little woods, turnips cultivated in drills and ridges as in Cumberland. The general appearance of the country much defaced by a number of staring red tiled houses and villages.

Dined at Bishops Auckland — Talbot Inn, good. One wide principal street terminated by the gateway leading to the Bishop's Palace. On the left is a new Gothic building lately erected by the present bishop (Barrington): a medley of the different styles of architecture, broad, pointed etc. It is applied also to a medley of different purposes; it is at once a school, a market shop, a chapel. The old infirm however are much indebted to the bishop for having applied it to the last purpose as the church belonging to Bishops Auckland is too far distant for them to attend. This town is very dull except during the residence of the bishop who lives here quite *en prince*; has his public days weekly, his park, hothouses, and every luxury.

His palace is an irregular pile of Gothic architecture of different aera. He has lately fitted up some of the rooms in a handsome and appropriate style, particularly the hall and audience room. Many of the other rooms remain in their old state with the addition of new furniture. The chapel is a beautiful Gothic building, and contains a fine whole-length figure of Bishop Trevor in a sitting attitude, finely executed by Noleekens. I do not much admire the new stone Gothic skreen lately put up in front of the Palace; a colonnade of open arches or of columns (as at Carlton House) supporting *nothing* have no meaning, neither are these slender towers well adapted. They have a good effect when rising out of larger ones as at Conway and Carnarvon castles, but here they are too slight for defence and too insubstantial. I should have preferred a plain iron railing which would not have hid the handsome front of the palace, which this skreen now does in a great measure. . . .

Binchester (a large white house) on the left — here was a Roman station [*Vinovia*]. Fine wide road to Durham, the country better, wooded, particularly near the sides of the road. . . . The first approach to Durham is indeed very striking: the cathedral proudly seated on an eminence, rearing aloft its turrets and pinnacles above the town. The whole forms a noble mass of wood, water and building. At the Red Lyon found a very good, quite and pleasant inn, the windows commanding a view of the river etc.

Tuesday 15th July.   The early part of the morning was taken up in making some views of Durham Cathedral, a difficult and laborious task, the cathedral being richly ornamented and much delicate work in it, and the whole scenery very rich and full of objects. I afterwards visited the interior of the cathedral. Its character is Saxon and wonderfully grand in its architecture. On entering by the northern door and traversing the nave to the right aisle the Lady Chapel is the first object which arrests the attention, a most beautiful specimen of Saxon workmanship and unlike anything I have yet seen. It has three arcades of light Saxon arches, ornamented with Saxon mouldings, supported on four clustered columns. This chapel is called the Galilee, as well as Lady's Chapel. . . . At the end of this ile enter a place called the nine altars, the space between the screen and the eastern extremity of the church. The character of this part of the building is light Gothic: lancet windows, light clustered columns with capitals of foliage, blank arches with trefoils, supported on a slender pillar. . . .

Let us now go back again to the western end. This window as well as the eastern are both Gothic. Underneath it is a Saxon arch with zig-zag ornaments filled up and a row of intersected Saxon arches. *Quere*, if there ever was an entrance here? In the centre is a handsome font of carved wood. The nave consists of eight Saxon arches supported by massive columns of the same order with Saxon capitals. . . . The grand tower is supported by four grand Saxon arches in clustered columns of the same order. . . . The screen over which the organ stands is of carved oak. The choir has handsome stalls of carved oak. . . . The skreen is a beautiful specimen of the lightest Gothic architecture. It is composed of niches, pinnacles etc. and has a fine effect from being so constructed as to see through parts of it into the church behind it. Near this skreen the Gothic architecture commences and the Saxon terminates. The roof is groined with zig-zag ormanent till it approaches the choir. . . . There is a curious old building called the dormitory which seems to have been left in its primitive state, also another small room with Saxon arches where the choiristers dress.

The northern front is the one most exposed to the public view, there being a large open area before it. There is a great variety of Saxon and Gothic in this front. Much of it has been so scraped over and repaired as to appear new. There are several *bas reliefs* in circles and Gothic niches on this side of the building. The main tower still remains untouched in its ancient state and unrepaired. Its architecture is Gothic. In the buttresses are niches with statues which give it great lightness.

Such are the leading features of this venerable structure. I have as yet seen no building of such grand and perfect Saxon architecture. Much however of its effect is lost by the modern alterations and improvements (as the Bishop and his architect, Mr Wyatt, would wish them to be called); I wish I could think them so. Repairs if they are necessary should certainly be done but not in the manner they are here done. In entering these grand Gothic structures the mind should be impressed with religious awe suited to the place. Here no such effect, no such sensation, no fine mellow tints on the columns, no effect of light and shade, no relief to the eye — one general glare; and one general yellow wash has been unmercifully smeared over the walls, cieling and every part of this reverend building. Even the marble monuments have not been spared. . . . This put me in mind when at Milan, going to see the celebrated fresco painting of Leonardo da Vinci in the refectory of a convent, which in cleaning up the convent had been covered with white wash, but luckily for lovers of the fine arts has been since uncovered: the same bad taste in both cases. In many things the *lucidus ordo* may be pleasing but I shall never think it applicable to an old cathedral like that at Durham. Neither do I approve of the scraping system without. If stones are wanting they might be replaced and, if they do not soon gain the color of the old, they never would look half as bad as the new *in toto*. Everything should be in character. The Cathedral of Durham should both in its outside and inside appearance bear the character of the aera in which it was built. It would be just as ridiculous for a collector of medals to clean and brighten those of Syracuse or Rome. And in my opinion it is just as great presumption in Mr Wyatt to attempt the restoration and improvement of a fine old Saxon and Gothic cathedral as it would be in any modern painter to retouch (with an idea of amendment) a picture of Raphael or Claude Lorraine.

[The ancient chapter house is no more. I have heard it mentioned as a beautiful piece of architecture in the ancient style of the cathedral. A modern room supplies its place built on the same scite and from its furniture, an inlaid mahogany table covered with newspapers, bears more the appearance of a coffee house than a chapter house. The cloysters have been modernised some time ago. They are a poor meagre Gothic].

The Bishop's Palace, Castle etc are on the opposite side of the area to the north of the cathedral, and form a large irregular mass of Gothic architecture and a mixture of modern Saxon. The walks on the banks of the river here are very beautiful; from thence the cathedral towering above the town is seen to the greatest advantage. . . . The City is built on very irregular ground and the river winds in a great part round it. There are three bridges over it. At this time of year it is rather dull, in winter less so as many of the prebends etc then reside there.

Wednesday 16 July.   After breakfast rode to see the ruins of Finchale Abbey, about four miles or five from Durham[29]. . . . This abbey is situated on a little eminence above the river in a valley well-watered and wooded, though the latter has of late been much cut down. Here the River Ware takes a more rapid course than it does at Durham, but equally circuitous. The ruins are extensive but not very picturesque, having no tower or high point to give them consequence. Their character is Gothic. In the body of the church are several massive round columns formed of layers of stone. Many of the vaulted apartments with groined ceilings remain, but upon the whole I was not much pleased with these ruins, as I could find no point of view in which they appear to advantage. Perhaps they might look better on the opposite side of the river which would give a good foreground.

I wished to have visited some walks which were laid out on the side of the river by Mr Carr but had not time. . . .

In the evening proceeded from Durham to Rushy Ford, a good single house — to Darlington, a town built of brick. [I have somehow or other a violent prejudice against towns built with brick, perhaps from judging of them in a picturesque point of view].

Thursday 17th.   The town [*Richmond*] is built on the most uneven ground imaginable, from the summit of the hill and on the declivities to the bottom where the River Swale runs. At the summit is the castle;[30] the area contains about two acres, and from this little property the Duke takes the title of Richmond. The circle of the walls may be traced, many of the buildings around them still remaining though in a very dilapidated state. One however of them, the Citadel, remains nearly entire and from the strength of its walls and goodness of its construction seems to defy the ravages of time. It resembles in some degree those at Appleby, Brough and Bowes and bears I think stronger marks of Norman origin than any of them. It is a lofty square building, on one side ninety-nine feet, strengthened on each side by slight projecting pilasters, between which there are in some places small round Norman windows supported on Norman or Saxon pillars and small eyelight-hole windows. The principal entrance seems to have been in the south by a round Norman archway which is now stopt up. I entered the building however by means of a ladder and found the interior part worthy of observation. . . . In the centre of the upper apartment rises a round pillar supported on the foundation of the octagon pillar below. Strength alone seems to have been considered in the construction of this building; the walls are of great thickness. Opposite to this southern part of the citadel is an oblong building apparently of great antiquity by the form of its windows, doors etc. The windows are formed of two narrow arches supported by thin Saxon columns. On two sides this castle was strongly defended by the nature of the ground, which descends very abruptly to the river below.

Where in ancient times there were castles we generally may trace monasteries and abbeys in their neighborhood. Near Richmond the remains of several exist, but none so considerable as that of St Agatha, better known by the common people under the title of Easeby Abbey.[31] A pleasant walk on the banks of the river leads you to it. Its remains are considerable but not very picturesque; some grand projecting tower or steeple is wanting to make them so. It appears to have been an abbey of very considerable extent, the architecture Gothic of which one rich window still remains. The entrance to the east is by a broad Gothic arch. . . . The whole plan of this large abbey might still be traced from the existing walls. Its situation was similar to those generally chosen for monastic institutions, and so well adapted to them, in a rich and retired valley. . . .

The situation of the town of Richmond is such as must afford amusement to every traveller who has an eye for its picturesque beauty and occupation for the artist's pencil. The town and castle appear to great advantage from many points on the opposite side of the river, and the bridge forms an excellent object in the general picture. The best inn is the King's Head — Martin, in the Market Place.

Thursday 18th July.   Left Richmond and went to Leyburn where I dined and slept. Hilly and stony road, a great part of it over a barren and heathy moor. The roads in many parts of Yorkshire are very bad for horses, being full of loose stones. In making them they do not give themselves the trouble of breaking the stones. I have often wondered how the post-horses go on them so safely. Practice (they say) makes perfect. Leyburn is a small market town in a pretty vale, well wooded and watered by the River Ure. The lands are chiefly pasture. I found a clean little inn at the Blue Bell. After dinner I rode to Bolton Castle, five miles, good horse road. A large pile of a bulding, partly modernised. It has four square towers at each end, one of which has fallen down. The entrance into the inner court is (I think) from the east. When viewed from the present habitable part of it it has a grand appearance. There is a grove of fine trees adjoining on this side. The village adjoining is picturesque from its miserable appearance, with thatched roofs, covered with weeds, flowers etc. . . .

Saturday 19th July.   After breakfast left Leyburn, forded the river to Middleham. . . . Having ordered dinner at Middleham I proceeded to Coverham Abbey, about two miles distant. Little remains now of this once large abbey, if we may judge from the appearance of the foundations. A few arches remain entire of the isle of the church and the gateway or porter's lodge leading to it from the west. A great number of scattered inscriptions, escutcheons etc, etc are dispersed in the walls of the adjacent houses which have [*been*] built out of the ruins of the abbey. Two curious old effigies of men in armour have changed their ancient *recumbent* posture and are placed upright as *careatides* in the portals of a gentlemen's house adjoining. . . .

   Middleham is a small market town. I found a clean bed and sitting room at the Swan Inn (Burton), where posthorses are kept. In the upper part of the town there are the remains of a very spacious castle.[32] Its form [*sketch*] is a square flanked at each angle with towers. . . . The east side is the least entire. The keep is here connected with the other buildings; on every other side it is insulated. The ruins of the two rooms in the keep are grand and massive. They reminded me of some of the large ruins at Rome. It was vaulted and had two stories. Round windows in general prevail in this castle. Towards the south it appears to have been moated round. On the whole these ruins are grand rather than picturesque; they command no beauty of situation about them, being situated in a bare field adjoining the town. On an eminence to the south there are the remains of an intrenchment, one circular and another annexed to it in the form of a crescent [*sketch*]. . . .

Sunday 20th July.   After breakfast left Middleham. About half way stopt to see the ruins of Jervoise [*Jervaulx*] Abbey. From the ruins it appears to have been of a considerable extent, but in their present state so little interesting in point of picturesque beauty that I did not attempt to make a drawing of them. Two farmhouses are built on the spot and many of the neighboring fence walls have been made out of the materials of the abbey. The situation is good, an agreeable eminence looking over a very fine vale. They belong (as I was informed) to Lord Aylesbury.

Proceeded to Masham, a neat-looking town with a handsome church. . . . Proceed to Rippon, fine rich country. The three different sorts of grain which I now saw for the first time in ear reminded me of having reached a warmer climate. . . . The first approach to Rippon is picturesque; the Minster and town form a good mass. A good inn in the market place.

My pencil has at last had a day of rest. Castles and abbies have furnished it with employment, and in such a rapid succession, ever since I left the mountains in Cumberland, that it has almost been surfeited. Still I have some very capital objects in view before I conclude my tour. These ancient buildings may be called the guides and lankmarks of history. They animate the artist's picture and often induce the tourist to trace their origin, their architecture, their history; by them he by degrees gains a daily knowledge of his country. Independent of the amusement and resources it affords, the love of drawing has many more essential advantages. The Man of Taste, gifted with a picturesque eye, views every object with a double pleasure: every tint, every shadow, in short every object in nature affords employment to his mind. Nothing remains to him unobserved for even in the dullest of countries something may be learnt by the steady observance of nature.

Monday 21st July.   The weather was so sultry that I remainded at home the greatest part of the morning. Visited the Minster, an elegant light Gothic building with a turret (square) in the center and two others in the west front. The character of the architecture is narrow pointed Gothic. There are a few round arches. Having suffered great damages at different periods it has of course undergone many repairs which will account for some irregularities in the architecture, such as the columns which divide the nave from the transept. On standing in the center of the church at the western door you will observe that the arch over the choir stands crooked and not centrical. The great steeple is called St Wilfrid's. It formerly supported a spire which was blown down A.D. 1660. There is a curious subterraneous passage under the pavement of the choir called St Wilfrid's needle. To what purpose it was formerly appropriated is not well known.[33] It leads to a little chapel in which there are niches, in one of which probably stood an image. The chapter house is said to be one of the oldest parts of the building. It is a plain low room with a groined roof. In it are preserved some curious figures cut in *bas relief* in oak which formerly stood in the ceiling of the old church. There is also another curious old building similar in its architecture to the chapter house called the charnel house in which an immense number of human bones and skulls are piled up. The church contains some old monuments and many of a modern date. . . . The screen over which the organ stands is a handsome piece of stone carve work. The stalls are of oak, well executed. One of them bears a date. The whole church is kept in a neat and clean order. It is collegiate and has dean, prebends etc etc. It is an elegant piece of light Gothic architecture, but I think the height of the columns is too great for the arches that spring from them; they certainly do not appear well proportioned.

In the evening I visited Studley Park and Gardens situated at a short distance from Rippon. The approach to the gardens from the park is by [*a*] long irregular avenue of trees, terminated at one end by an obelisk on a hill and at the other by Rippon Minster. . . . On the right is the house, a modern handsome stone building.[34] Landscape is composed of ground, wood, water and buildings, and by a happy mixture and harmonization of these, its beauties, nay even those of nature, entirely depend. At Studley the situation of the grounds is good and well varied with hill and dale. The woods [*which* are extensive consist of a judicious mixture of a variety of evergreen and deciduous trees, and may be looked upon as the most leading and beautiful feature of the place. The water in all its parts is detestable; narrow, round, oval canals, bedecked with little islands, and staring white painted statues ill accord with the beautiful woods on their banks. The buildings also are in general bad. The temple of Piety, if well placed amongst the woods and not on the borders of the most formal of all the pieces of water, would appear to advantage as it is in itself a handsome building. The color of its stone is of a good color and its Doric portico, if embosomed in wood, or rather if it had a better foreground (for it is well backed) would have a good effect.

Amongst the buildings I do not mean to include the venerable ruins of Fountains Abbey which constitute the most interesting part of the place. They are however at first sight introduced to you with every disadvantage. They surprize and at the same time please, I will allow, but the eye and mind, when satiated with the first *coup d'oeuil*, cannot but criticize and blame the arrangement of the grounds about them. A variety of formal lines hurt the eye. A staring gravel walk, adjoining it a trim, mown, sloping bank, then a straight narrow piece of water — all forming so many stripes and detracting from the general beauty of the scenery. The lawn beyond is also too smooth and intersected by an uncouth road, forming another unpleasant line. In short all this scenery wants the assistance of the hand of taste. Here nature should be seen in her own attire; all should be in character with the majestic ruins which are so essential an ornament to the scene. Art should not have been suffered to alter this solitary and peaceful vale and violate the venerable sanctuary of Fountains Abbey.[35]

On entering its doors I felt a similar, but not I think equal, sensation to that I experienced on entering Tintern. A neat mown turf now supplies the place of the ancient pavement. The grandeur of the building and the beauty of many of its parts is much injured by the number of trees and bushes which are suffered to grow within its walls. Many of the trees (particularly in the part behind the altar) are so high that they reach the summit of the building and totally hide a very beautiful part of it. The architecture is a mixture of Saxon and Gothic. The columns in the nave are round and massive with Saxon capitals, supporting Gothic arches; those over the side isle are round. The nave struck me as being rather narrow in proportion to its length. Its proportions are injured (as I said before) by the number of trees which are suffered to grow up within the walls. The old pavement before the high altar has been uncovered. In the part behind the altar I again remarked some of those arches with a small span and long column, as at Rippon, but here more out of proportion. In many parts of this building I could trace a similarity of architecture with Rippon.

Tuesday 22nd. Went in a chaise to Hackfell — pay for nine miles though the distance is only seven. This place has been justly celebrated for its romantic beauties. The nature of the country around does not lead you to expect a similar situation. I shall not attempt a minute description of these grounds, as it is impossible to convey by words a proper idea of the beautiful disposition of wood, rock and water, which nature has here so happily displayed. The ground is unequal without which attribute no place, in my opinion, can be perfect. The highest point commands a distant prospect as far as York, and overlooks the river and fine woods immediately beneath. The lowest point leads you on the banks of the rapid and rocky River Ure, on all sides feathered with fine wood down to the water's edge. . . . The artist and man of picturesque taste will observe how happy an effect, what a relief to the large mass of green, is produced by the few rocks which shew themselves amongst the copse wood on the right of the picture. He will remark also the good general effect produced by seeing the more distant scenery through the oaks which are left in the foreground. I seldom have seen so delightful and pleasing a scene, never, I think, in a garden and seldom in nature. After this superb view every other must appear tame. In seeing places we like to take the usual round prescribed by our guides, fearing to omit some principal view, but were I to revisit Hackfell I should content myself with this one view. . . . A variety of modern buildings have been erected here, as well as at Studley. . . . They are not principal enough to catch and offend the eye. These places were laid out about forty or fifty years ago by Mr Aislabie. . . .

In the evening I visited Newby. . . . A modern brick house. Here art has been applied with great taste and prevails over nature. . . . The interior of this house has been fitted up with great elegance and taste united — not like Harewood, gaudy, expensive and tasteless. The drawing room is fitted up with beautiful Gobelin tapestry which will preserve the great brilliancy of colour for which this manufacture is so justly celebrated. . . . But the room most worthy of notice is the statue gallery, containing (for an English collection) many good specimens of ancient sculpture in statues, busts, *bas-reliefs*, urns, tripods, etc, etc.

Wednesday 23rd. After breakfast I returned with my portfolio to the ruins of Fountains Abbey. Took two views of them from east and west, and surveyed the fine monastic remains with more attention. The view from the south-west appears to me the most advantageous point, where the cloysters form a noble line and the west front is well broken with ivy. In every circumstance this side of the abbey is the best; all is here in character, wood, rock and building, uninjured by the hand of art. So similar in many respects are the situations of these ancient religious establishments that wherever we find their remains we may naturally expect to find a sequestered spot, fine woods and abundance of water. Such was the scite chosen by the monks of Fountains. A fine quarry of stone supplied them with materials on the spot to erect their stately edifice. The different styles of architecture shew the reparations it has undergone at different aera.

The east front is composed of one fine Gothic window, three narrow lancet Gothic windows with buttresses between them form the whole of this front. The architecture is not much enriched, plain and chaste. . . . The same lancet windows are continued round the north side of the choir from which the great tower projects. The nave on the outside presents a double row of narrow Saxon windows (two Gothic excepted) with buttresses between them. This side reminded me much of the northern front of Llanthoney Abbey. The entrance into the abbey from the west is through a Saxon doorway. . . . The cloysters are on this side very singular in their construction and in fine preservation. Their exterior is Saxon round arches between buttresses or rather pilastes. The columns are formed by the groins or ribs which support the roof. I do not recollect to have seen anything like them before. They are three hundred feet long and are entirely covered in, these arcades forming a very grand and gloomy walk. There is a large octagon stone cistern lying there. The river runs under them. All the differnt rooms of this extensive building may still be traced, as they remain in a good state of preservation. . . . I must not in my description of this abbey omit the principal tower which is a fine pile of building and of a great height. On each side it bears a variety of inscriptions. . . . The tower by the style of its architecture appears of a more modern date than many parts of the church. Some appears as late as the time of Henry viii in whose reign it was dissolved.[36]

Upon general reveiw it certainly is a most noble and interesting pile of building such as few individuals can boast of possessing within their grounds and gardens. I have often regretted that the generality of fine old castles and abbies of which we have so many specimens left in different parts of England are so often situated in places where they are seen to every disadvantage, often blocked up with farmhouses, and but too often, owing to such a situation, furnishing materials for them and even for the repair of the roads, their beauties (as at Tinterne) concealed by orchards and some miserable hovels. Had their fate placed them in the gardens of their owners, many more which have now been destroyed would still exist. Their beauty as objects and their history as specimens of ancient architecture would have rendered them doubly interesting and ensured their protection.

Having finished my drawings and satiated my curiosity with another view of the ruins I rambled amongst the wood behind the abbey, and there found a most picturesque mill deeply embosomed in the wood overgrown with wild plants etc. A rustic wooden bridge thrown over the rivulet and, at a little distance from it, the ancient Gothic bridge coeval with the abbey added to the scenery, which is here solitary, picturesque and characteristic. I cannot say so much for the adjoining building of Fountains Hall . . . a sad medley of Italian and English architecture. . . . Having an hour to spare, on my way home I rambled over Studley Park. Chance led me to a little retired vale on the opposite side of the round pond, which you pass on going to the garden gates. This little vale for its extent possesses as many natural beauties as any spot of its size I ever beheld. I am quite surprised that it has not been taken more notice of and introduced into the garden. Improved it cannot be; nature has here done everything one could wish. . . . Nothing more is necessary, not a tree, bush or stone should be touched.

In the evening I left Rippon and proceeded to Boroughbridge where I slept. Crown Inn, good. At a little distance from the village are some curious remains of antiquity. The history and original intent of them is not known. They are three large masses of stone, of rather a pyramidical form, placed at some distance from each other in a direction from N.W. to S.E.[37] They have been evidently placed there. The lowest is said to be 18 feet and the largest 22 feet in height. As the Romans were established in the neighborhood I do not think it improbable that these stones were originally the *metae* or goals of a circus, as obelisks were used for that purpose at Rome.

The modern village of Aldborough adjoining to Boroughbridge now occupies the centre of ancient *Isurium*, the capital of the Brigantes. Many Roman antiquities have been found here and two mosaic tesselated pavements are to be seen in the village. Boards are fixed to each house. The one at the upper end nearest the church is the most worthy of notice. It was above a yard under the surface of the earth when discovered. . . .

Thursday 24th July. Pursued my journey to York. The whole road from Rippon there is mostly flat and uninteresting in point of prospects, finely cultivated however, and rendered interesting to the traveller at present by the very promising appearance which every sort of grain, turnips etc seem to bear. I arrived at York in an unfortunate time to get good accomodations. I applied to the Tavern but in vain. The rooms were engaged by the Sheriff, but by this refusal I was a gainer, having got comfortable rooms in a much quieter inn, Ringroses, late Bluetts. But my time is limited as on Sunday I must depart or be turned out. The inns at York are not equal, nor indeed is the city itself equal to the ideas formed of it by the report of its size, antiquity etc. The Tavern and Ringroses Inn are reckoned the best. There are two others in the principal street, Coney Street. One of them, the George, bears a very antique, yet a comfortable, appearance, but to those who require quiet and civil treatment I could recommend Ringroses.

So much for inns and accomodations, the first to be noticed, being the first object which every traveller looks to on first coming to a halting place.

The second object, and to many enthusiasts perhaps the *first* will be the Minster which is at a very short distance from the principal inns, nearest to Ringroses and then the Tavern. To describe the different parts of this beautiful building would require much more time and many more pages than I can spare, and could I allow time I should fail in doing it justice. To judge properly of the elegant symmetry and just proportions of its different parts *it must be seen* and seen with an eye of taste.

No two buildings can vary more in their styles than the cathedral I last visited (Durham) and York. The one solid, massive, grand and in the oldest national style of architecture; the other light, elegant and equally to be admired in its way. The antiquarian may perhaps prefer the former but the generality of people will be more captivated with the latter. If any comparison is made it must be between York and Lincoln, there being much more similarity between them. Indeed a comparison has been made between them and printed by an old traveller, Daniel Defoe,[38] in which he gives the decided preference to York. I must own that I was the most struck with the external appearance of Lincoln. Those very parts which appeared to him defects appeared to me as beauties adding much to the picturesque effect of the building. I mean the different chapels, projections, irregularities etc. The fact is he looked on the two cathedrals with the critical eye of an architect who by his profession must be [a] lover of regularity and precision. I viewed them with the eye of a painter. I am far however from blaming the regularity of this cathedral, for on the contrary I derived great pleasure from beholding so fine a building, so wonderfully and carefully preserved from the injuries of time.

History informs that different parts of it were built at different periods which is the case of most of our cathedrals (Salisbury excepted which was built in one uniform plan). The transepts are esteemed the most ancient part of the building and are supposed to have been erected under the orders of Walter Grey who lies buried in the southern transept. To him is also attributed the erection of the chapter house which is perhaps the most striking part of the whole building. This building with the approach to it, forms one of the most captivating sights imaginable to a lover of Gothic architecture. Still in these, as well as in the body of the church, all is Gothic. The four windows are each so beautiful and varied that I know not to which to give the preference. The eastern window for size may boast its superiority over every window in England. The masonry of the tracery work of the western window is I think finer. There is a wonderful simplicity in the northern window called the Five Sisters, and the opposite one to the south, called the Marygold window, has, I think, more variety and elegance than all the others. This cathedral derives a great part of its fine effect from the immense quantity of painted glass, almost every window in it being fitted with the old glass —

  'Casting a dim religious light'[39]

Some little modern glass has been introduced by that old artist, Pickett of York, which tends to show how much finer the effect is produced by the sober tints of the old than the more gaudy colors of the new. . . . The two screens which inclose the choir are beautiful and different from each other. That behind the altar is light Gothic. . . . The other over which stands the organ is more massive, fitted up with niches in which are effigies of the British kings from William the Conqueror to King James. . . .

Ouse Bridge itself deserves notice from the boldness of the arch and its antiquity. The different bars and gates have a very picturesque appearance unlike anything that I have met in England. They in some degree resemble the portal gates to the fortified towns abroad. The ruins of St Mary's out of Bootham Bar, a little way from the Ringroses Inn, should be seen. They are picturesque and extensive. The character of their architecture is pointed Gothic. The entrance lodge and a round tower near the river seem of a prior date.[40]

The City of York has rather a mean appearance: no squares; narrow streets and few handsome churches. Its chief ornament is the Minster, and such an ornament few cities can boast of. There is a pleasant walk called the New Walk on the banks of the river. Near this walk lived Pickett who brought the colors in stained glass to greater perfection than any other artist. He is dead; his widow wishes to dispose of his manuscripts. . . . The castle and inns of court deserve also to be visited. The former is a handsome court: in the center are the prisons, on the right the courts of justice which are of a circular form, both handsome and convenient. The turnkey showed me a most dreadful magazine of various implements of death, which had been taken from condemned prisoners. The irons of Nevison and Turpin are of such a size and weight that one wonders that human strength did not sink under them. Near the castle is an antique tower called Clifford's Tower, situated on a tumulus with a fosse round it.[35]

The Assembly Rooms have been mentioned as the handsomest in England. Their architecture is certainly grand but I think heavy. They were re-designed by Lord Burligton. Their dimensions are 112 feet long, 40 wide and 40 high [*plan*]. A rich frieze and cornice are supported by Corynthian columns. Above is an order of pilasters. The seats are in front of the columns, a double row, behind a vacuum for people to walk. This colonnade takes off much from the width of the room, and I think makes it too narrow in its proportions. It is lighted by old-fashioned glass chandeliers.

I was much disappointed in the general appearance of York, I mean the city; the cathedral amply repays the traveller for the trouble and expence of the journey. Durham and York should be visited soon after each other in order to compare the different beauties of these two fine specimens of old national architecture.

Sunday 27. I left York after breakfast. Pursued the road to Tadcaster, a long village with a bridge over the River Wharfe (White Horse Inn). Passed by the race course on the left a little way from York where there is a magnificent stand. Fine corn country, well cultivated. Proceeded to Leeds. Corn country. Several new inclosures. Bramham Park, seat of Mr Fox on the right. Road good, not very hilly. Dined at Leeds. Continued my journey to Bradford, a great manufacturing town. . . . The town is large, built on unequal ground of a yellowish stone. Handsome turret church. With difficulty I procured post horses on account of the York Assizes and was obliged to take four horses, having learnt to my sorrow that the roads for some miles were very hilly and bad. And such indeed I afterwards found them.

The road is such from Bradford to Halifax. Finely cultivated vales on each side. Great population and in this short stage I saw *more pretty faces* than in *all* my preceding tour. Fair complexions and a general appearance of good health. Continued for some time on the ridge of a hill having a complete bird's eye view of the town of Halifax beneath you, a most rich and gratifying scene of commerce, riches and cultivations. I found a decent inn at the Talbot. The day had been so sultry that I had no desire to stir out in the evening.

Monday 28th.   Before my departure from Halifax I visited a few of the objects most worthy [of] the traveller's attention. The Piece Hall claims the first place; it is such a building as does not find its equal in England. A large area is inclosed and built round; the form is square. The architecture consists of three rows of colonnades. Owing to the inequality of the ground there are only two rows on one side. In these colonnades there are upwards of three hundred shops, the property of the different manufacturers who subscribed to the building. It differs from Leeds in the manner of dealing as well as in the produce. At Leeds it is all woollen, here calimancoes, worsteds. There all business is transacted in an open hall, here each manufacturer has a little shop wherein his goods are deposited and a table to display them upon. One dealer only enters at a time to look at his goods. This open colonnade extends around the whole square and has a most handsome and unique appearance.

I next visited the baths which are the most commodious I have seen and of great variety. Two large cold baths, one under cover, the other in the open air, for men; two under cover for women. Two other hot baths besides are kept constantly to the temperature of the Buxton and Matlock baths. The gardens around the baths are very neat.

In my return to the inn I went to the church where there is nothing very remarkable either in its architecture or monuments. I called on an old acquaintance, Mr Edwards, the bookseller, and father of Mr Edwards, the well known bookseller in Pall Mall. Few country towns can boast of so elegant [a] collection as he has. I saw a most curious missal beautifully illuminated in the best taste, which is not to be wondered, being executed for a man of taste, Francis the First, and at a time when the arts were in a high state of perfection. He showed me also Watson's original manuscript for his History of Halifax.[41]

The situation of Halifax reminded me much of Bath; built in the same colored stone, hills around it and fine valley. Not the seat of luxury and dissipation but of industry and commerce and in this respect widely different.

Leave Halifax. A pretty country, fully inhabited. Many good houses etc Roads detestable but now mending. There is a new road to Manchester by way of Oldham. It appears to go through a picturesque passage of the hills on the left of the old road. The postmasters and postilions prefer the latter. From a scene of the highest population, and from the busy scene of commerce you at once enter a country as barren and desert as the wilds of America. On this heath is the boundary stone between the counties of York and Lancaster; it stands between miles VI and VII. Descend into another vale, less beautiful and hilly than the preceding one, in which the town of Rochdale is situated. A nasty town built of brick and rendered more unpleasant to me from being market day. In many places in the north the traveller finds much inconvenience on these days; he finds the inns full, people busy and his wants unsupplied. [The tolls in this country are immoderately high, yet the roads bad. Between Halifax and Rochdale I paid 6/9 for four horses and chaise. More attention has been paid to the canals than to the turnpikes]. . . .

. . . I proceeded on my journey to Manchester on which road nothing interesting occurs. Too much peopled to be picturesque. . . . Bridgewater Arms, Manchester, the newest and most frequented inn at Manchester, the *rendez-vous* of coaches, travellers, merchants etc — of course the noisest; such I found it. Bad attendance, little attention to cleanliness, much noise and bustle both by day and night. I have in general found large manufacturing towns the most unpleasant halting places. You find less attention, less urbanity of manners; self-interest and business occupy the minds of the inhabitants and prevent that polish which the inhabitants of other towns, where dissipation takes the lead of trade, more frequently have in their manners. But however more unpleasant these towns may be to the tourist who travels for his amusement the country profits; and as well-wisher to the interest of my country I by no means wish to see the honest blunt tradesman transformed into the modern fine gentleman.

To those who have not a turn for mechanics and the *minutiae* of manufactories Manchester will afford but little amusement. I wished however to see some of the processes, two of which appeared to me remarkably curious: the passing the velvets, calicoes and even muslins of the finest silk handkerchiefs over a red-hot cylinder to give them a gloss and take off the rough outside nap; the other, cutting the ribbs in velvet, plush, corderoy etc which is performed by a long narrow instrument resembling a sword and performed with the greatest rapidity and dexterity. The cylinders made use of are of cast-iron, semi-circular and hollow within, from which part they are heated and kept constantly hot. One of these will last about a week. This is one of the most curious operations I ever beheld and many who did not see it would disbelieve it.

There is a college for Bluecoat boys to the number of eighty, and a library worth visiting, the endowment of Mr Chatham. The building is ancient, the library of the style of those in colleges with so many private boxes for those who wish to read. It is open every day for the use of the inhabitants, but in a town where trade engrosses the minds of man, woman and child the library cannot be much frequented. . . . The town of Manchester is built of brick; has many good streets and a handsome square where the infirmary is built; is very populous.

The Bridgewater Arms is reckoned the best inn, but, when its owner in describing the excellent accomodations it affords, boasts of its supplying a hundred and twenty good beds, a traveller cannot expect much rest or sleep there. Such was my lot. The noise of people continually running up and down stairs during the greater part of the night effectually prevented sleep. Fortunately the objects of my researches did not detain me a second night at Manchester.

Tuesday Evening 29 July. Left Manchester, passed through Stockport, 7 miles, a large commercial town [cotton trade], built of brick on the declivity of a hill. Much ground on this road is in a bad state of cultivation. At Disley, or not much before, you begin to emerge from the smoke and bustle of the commercial country in which I had been travelling so many miles from Leeds hither. You also bid adieu to the rattling pavement and breathe a purer and keener air. . . .

Wednesday 30th July. I found a decent little inn at Chapel in the Frith, a perfect contrast to the one I had left at Manchester, the latter all noise and bustle, the former small and quiet. Proceeded after breakfast first to Castleton, 9 miles. A wild hilly country, stone walls and few trees. Fine low pastures on the hills. Limestone country. Fine road. A most picturesque descent to Castleton through a narrow passage in the mountains. The rocks around are of the most grotesque and majestic forms; one can almost fancy them the mighty ruins of some huge fortress erected for the purpose of guarding the pass. On the right the rocks resemble towers and on the left there is a shelving rock exactly like the wall of a fort.

At the bottom of the hill I stopt to see a cavern which is said to communicate with the one at the Peak. A man pays a rent of £10 per annum for it. I had not sufficient number of candles to distinguish well the different parts of this cavern. . . . It was made in search of lead ore, which, when found, did not answer the working and is therefore now neglected. I found a great draught of cold air in going but none in coming back. The subterraneous passage is dry and but few drops descend from the rock. A greatcoat will be useful.

From this cavern I walked to Castleton, about a quarter of a mile, prettily situated in a fertile valley. Visited the Peak. The entrance is particularly romantic through an unnatural arch of an immense span, supporting a high and perpendicular mass of rock over which hang the ruins of an old castle, most appropriately situated and accessible only on one side. The picturesque effect is much encreased by the miserable hovels and inhabitants with their implements for rope-making, all of which are seen at the mouth of the cavern. From the first cavern you go into various others of different shapes and in one place you are obliged to ford the river, lying yourself flat in a little boat, which the guide, going into the water, pushes through an opening in the rock just high enough to admit it. You are then led into a part of the cavern called the 'Chancel' which has a fine effect when properly illuminated and still more striking when a band of music and chorus of singers strike up unexpectedly. But the beauty of all these subterraneous caverns in a great measure depends on the quantity of candles expended in illuminating them. The return from these dark recesses, with the sudden reappearance of daylight, is by far the most striking and pleasing part of the whole.

At a short distance on one side [*of*] the entrance to the Peak are some lead mines, which, to those who wish to see the nature of finding and taking that ore, are worth visiting, as you enter on a level with the surface of the ground and go into the rock but a few paces.

After dinner I left Castleton. A steep ascent. Quit the vale and enter a dreary wild country. Stone walls, few trees. Many lead mines, known by the light yellow earth thrown out of the shafts. A great many gates to open. . . . Many limekilns. Cross the River Derwent at Corber Bridge. Cotton works. Vale more fertile. See Chatsworth woods at a distance. On a nearer approach the mansion house appears deeply embosomed in a thick wood. Good inn about half a mile distant. Found every room full with company from Matlock. Excellent roads from Castleton to Chatsworth.

Chatsworth, the seats of the Dukes of Devonshire, has a grand and princely appearance. The fine and rich west front is seen to advantage from the approach to it from the inn through the park over a handsome stone bridge, broken by a grove of fine old trees in the foreground and backed by the thick wood rising high above it. Enter the house by a handsome quadrangle. It is chiefly to be admired for the size of its rooms, its fine carve work by Gibbons. It contains but few pictures: one room of whole length portraits and a fine cartoon by Holbein of King Henry viii and K. Henry vii. The state apartments are grand but inconveniently situated at the top of the house. . . .

The gardens still exhibit a specimen of the old English taste which certainly has merits in its way, and has, I think, been rather too much exploded in the present mode of laying-out grounds. The waterworks are remarkably fine. The fountain in front of the house throws water up above ninety feet in height; the explosion of the air before the water has singular effect and noise. There are many fine trees of all sorts on the lawn which in many parts have been judiciously thinned. The whole place has indeed been improved by the present Duke. The public road formerly went close to the house; two rich pedestals which still remain mark its situation. The plantations have also been much increased. The water is formed by the River Derwent, which at the time I saw it was so very still in its course that I mistook it for an artificial piece of water. The banks of it are too formal.[42] The boundaries of the prospect to the north and south are fine, the first the boldest. The house and gardens are neatly kept though seldom visited by their noble owners. . . .

Thursday 31st July. Before breakfast I walked from the inn to the parish church of Edensor. . . . After breakfast I left Chatsworth . . . at a short distance from the road on the right is a venerable old mansion of the Duke of Rutland, called Haddon Hall. Many projecting and rising turrets render it a picturesque building. There are two irregular courts which lead to different parts of the house. The architecture mainly the different periods at which it has been repaired. The most modern room is said to be the hall, as a painting on the glass bears the date 1589. In this as well as in other rooms there is a great deal of carve work in wood. In a room below are the portraits of King Henry vii and his Queen carved in oak and on the panels. . . . On entering the chapel you see a Roman altar, the inscription of which I could not decypher. On the S. West side are some fine old wyche elms and other trees in character with the building. Many curious and picturesque drawings might be made of this fine old relict of ancient times. . . .

. . . I turned off to the right through some fields just on this side of the turnpike which led me to the entrance to Dovedale. Left my carriage. Picturesque farmhouse. Steep descent to the Vale. A pleasant walk of about a mile and a half on the banks of the River Dove through a valley sometimes so narrow as scarcely to admit the path on the side of the stream, at other times expanding itself into a wider space. The rocks are limestone of a fine grey color, which from the excessive heat have gained many additional warm tints, the mosses and other plants having been burnt up for want of proper nourishment. Their shapes are most fantastic, sometimes formed into curious caverns and arches, at other times rearing their lofty summits into obelisks and columns. . . . In short in this walk all is pretty but nothing very grand and sublime except the view which I have last mentioned. . . .

My carriage met me at the extremity of the Vale from whence crossing a large rabbit warren I soon came in sight of Ilam, the seat of Mr Porte, but now let to a gentlemen. I spent half an hour here much to my satisfaction. The gardener (as is generally the case in show places) extended my walk through a variety of zig-zag paths, much more than he need have done. For the beauty of Ilam in my opinion consists entirely in the fine meadow surrounded by a noble majestic wood. . . . It reminded me of those at Margam and Dynevor Castle in South Wales, but there the trees are not so luxuriant, as they feel the nipping effects of the sea breeze. The extreme flatness of the meadow is a fine relief to the perpendicular wood above which forms nearly an amphitheatre; in some parts the whole circle is surrounded with wood. . . . From Ashbourne to Derby, a heavy stage of thirteen miles through well cultivated and wooded country. Saw the first field of ripe oats. Arrived late in the evening at Derby. George Inn.

Friday 1st August. The town of Derby has nothing very remarkable to boast of in point of buildings, streets or churches. The silk mills are worth visiting; the china manufactory which is brought to greater perfection here than in any other part of England; and the manufactory of Derbyshire Spa by Brown & Co, which is peculiar to this place and has of late years been much advanced towards perfection. The church of All Saints also deserves attention. The tower is a fine piece of Gothic architecture. The interior is modern but contains some fine monuments of the Devonshire family. . . . The situation of Derby is well calculated for manufactures, being built on the banks of the River Derwent. The George Inn is reckoned the best but its situation is dull and not so good as the King's Arms or King's Head in the principal street.

Saturday 2nd August. Left Derby and in my way back to Ashbourne saw Kedleston, the seat of Lord Scarsdale. Enter the park through an irregular grove of fine aged oaks and other trees. Some of the oaks are 100 feet in height and 23 feet in circumference. The house both within and without is magnificent, as to its architecture and ornaments. The architect was Adams[43] who has varied the different shapes of the rooms with much taste and good judgement. The great hall supported by a noble colonnade of Corinthian columns of Derbyshire marble has a very grand and striking appearance. I have seen nothing more so, as indeed so much, in its way. The grates, chairs etc are all done from antique models and correspond with the general taste of the apartment. Music Room: Holy Family Leonardo da Vinci [*Pictures described room by room*]. . . . This house in point of architecture and ornament exceeds any I have yet seen. It bears a foremost rank amongst English country seats, none of which (at least of those I have seen) can boast of so grand and elegant an apartment as the hall and colonnades. . . .

Slept at Macclesfield and found myself again amongst the noise and bustle of [a] manufacturing large town. Built of brick. Cotton and linen trade. The church bears some marks of antiquity and some old monuments without inscriptions.

Sunday 3rd August. From Macclesfield I proceeded through a rich and fertile country. Good level road to Knutsford, and from thence to my friend Sir John Leicester's at Tabley.[44]

Almost exhausted by a long journey in the hottest season ever remembered I enjoyed the thoughts of some days rest of which both my mind and body felt the want. The former was almost palled with the great variety and frequent succession of objects which had attracted its attention and the latter almost died in the pursuit of them. From the 12th of June to this day I had not been at all impeded in my projects by badness of weather and in the whole time had not met two wet days. . . . But the heat was excessive and often incapacitated me from using my pencil as freely as I could have wished.

During my residence at Tabley I descended into the salt mines at Northwich belonging to my friend Sir John Leicester, I cannot say with[out] some degree of apprehension which I have ever felt on descending into subterraneous mines. No such descent however can be attended with less inconvenience or in greater safety. The salt is conveyed up, and the miners down, by means of two large buckets whose motion is directed by a large wheel and horses. Into one of these buckets two of the party placed themselves attended by one of the miners. We seated ourselves on the edge of the bucket and the miner stood on the edge of it holding the rope. We were about the space of two minutes in taking our passage. The motion was steady and all apprehension ceased after the first few seconds.

No words can convey an idea adequate to the surprize and admiration I felt on my first landing in these subterraneous abodes. They had been illuminated with some hundred lights without which all their beauty and grandeur would have been lost. If the hand of the man of taste had been employed in this excavation instead of that of the miner working for his daily bread these caverns could not have under his direction produced more picturesque forms and effects. No attention is paid to regularity; at certain intervals large massive columns are left to support the roof which is worked with a singular and astonishing equality. The substance of the rock salt resembles brown and white sugar candy mixed. Some specimens are found of a fine red color. The blasting of the rock by gunpowder produces a fine effect. The air here is perfectly dry, as well the soil on which you walk. We spent nearly an hour in these curious subterraneous caverns. The passage upward was less steady and more unpleasant. I may class these mines amongst the few grand sights which nature [?art] produces. Few I believe can surpass them.

I left Tabley on Sunday the 24th August, reached Hagley on the 25th and returned to Stourhead on the 30th after a journey of eleven hundred miles in the finest season ever remembered.

VII

Journal of a Tour in 1801

Sunday 12th April. Left Stourhead, dined and slept at Sir William a Court's house at Heytesbury. Weather very raw and cold — a deep snow fall.

Monday 13th April. Weather cold and raw. After breakfast, in company with my friend Coxe, visted the remains of a Roman tessellated pavement discovered at Pit Mead. Part of the pavement had been found some years ago, but another discovery has been lately made by Mr Cunnington,[1] an ingenious inhabitant and tradesman of Heytesbury, in whose company we now viewed it. Rode to Warminster and proceeded in my chaise to Bath.

Tuesday 14th. Dined and spent the evening with the Rev. Mr Leman where I met Dr Bennet, Bishop of Cloyne.[2] These two gentlemen are eminently skilled in the Roman and British antiquities of this island and from their younger days have spent much time in tracing the Roman and British roads.

Wednesday 15th. Dined with my old friend and acquaintance, Mr Morrison. This morning the fortunate news arrived of the death of Paul, the Emperor of Russia.[3]

Thursday 16th. Mounted my horse at seven in the morning and break-fasted at Chippenham. The country on all sides round Bath deserves attention and admiration. About Box, 5 miles from Bath, the scenery is rural and pretty. It soon afterwards becomes dull and uninteresting. Passed by Corsham, the seat of Mr Methuen, containing a very numerous and valuable collection of pictures of the Italian and Dutch schools amongst which is a beautiful landscape by Claude and another by Both.[4] But here as in most collections there is a great mixture of the good and bad, and a judicious selection of the former should be made. The front of the mansion house is in the old English style; the other is now finishing in the rich Gothic style under the direction of Mr Nash, an architect who has shown much taste in the buildings he has erected of that description.

    The country round Corsham is tame and flat. Breakfasted at Chippenham (White Hart Inn, middling). Here I read with that heartfelt satisfaction, which ever animates an Englishman on hearing the naval exploits of his countrymen recorded, the account of the memorable and gallant action performed by Lord Nelson before Copenhagen.[5]

After breakfast proceeded to Malmesbury; the remains of its ancient abbey induced me to take this route. The town is situated on an eminence. Its poor numerous though there are manufactories of lace, hides and spinning machines for cloth. Has three parishes. . . . At the upper end of a long street is the market cross and the abbey. The former is an elegant piece of Gothic architecture, particularly the pinnacle of it, now repairing under the directions of Lord Suffolk. At a short distance is the abbey and near it the steeple of another old parish church. The first part of this venerable building which attracted my attention was the southern doorway which is the richest specimen of Saxon architecture I have ever seen. The arches are ornamented with a great variety of patterns, and numerous *bas reliefs* from Scripture history. . . . The interior of the church affords also some fine specimens of similar architecture. Six Gothic arches supported on massive Saxon columns divide the aisles from the body of the church. The second story above these arches is entirely Saxon, four low and narrow arches supported on columns. The windows in the third story are Gothic. The roof of stone, groined, is also Gothic. In the right of the choir is the figure of K. Athelstan, founder, recumbent on a tomb. . . . There is a tolerable inn near the abbey where the artist and antiquarian may find accomodations during their survey of these monastic remains.

[Agricultural remarks between Bath and Cheltenham.
    Beautiful valley to Box, well wooded and watered, fine pastures near Chippenham. Stone brash, land foul, full of quitch [*couch-grass*]. Harrowing wheat. 3 horses to a plough; wheel is heavy. Oxen at length, in harness.
    Passed Lord Suffolk's seat a little beyond Malmesbury. Cotswold sheep very like the Leicester breed. Thick coarse wool. A small compact sheep. Saw the double-furrow ploughs close to Cirencester in the middle of barley sowing.]

    Dined at Cirencester. Passed the Foss Road. Canal of the Stroud Navigation. Machines erected to try for coal. Fine church at Cirencester, beautiful southern porch of rich Gothic architecture. Ram Inn, old house, civil treatment. Many Roman antiquities have been found at this place which was a celebrated Roman station called *Corinium*. Many Roman roads led here. From hence to Birdlip . . . from Birdlip to Cheltenham.

Friday 17th.   Slight rain. Engaged in looking out for lodgings. Took those at Birch's at 2½ guineas per week and 18s cook and house maid. Quiet, retired house though in the center of the town.

Saturday 18th.   Very fine. Called on Mr Hunt at Charlton. Rode up the hills behind his house to Birdlip and back under the hill through Leckhampton. Rough, bad and wet road.

Sunday 19th.   Very fine. Ascended the hill behind Mr Baghot's. . . .

Monday 20th. Very fine. Rode to Winchbomb, passing by Southam, the ancient seat of the Delabere family. Having ordered my dinner walked to Sudley Castle, the property of Lord Rivers. Finely situated on a gentle eminence, though surrounded and commanded on each side by hills. The effect of the ruins is much injured by the massive buildings annexed and adjoining them, viz the old mansion house and the barn which, if removed, the ruinous group of buildings would have a beautiful effect, being very advantageously placed on an isolated knoll. Their architecture does not bespeak a very early date, being of the broad Gothic. The outside shell of the elegant little chapel remains entire, its effect rendered less picturesque by the fruit trees which are trained up against its walls. . . . The village of Winchcomb in many points of view presents itself as a picturesque object, though the interior of it bears a melancholy appearance. The church is a handsome building. . . .

On my return home I stopt at the summit of the hill to enjoy one of the finest views imaginable. I doubt if England affords a superior. The eye comprehends in one point of view the whole vale from Gloucester to Worcester, in the centre of Tewkesbury backed by the Malvern Hills. The Severn appears and disappears in different parts of this rich landscape. The Sugar Loaf and Blorench Hills near Abergavenny are distinctly seen. Numerous churches and other buildings are dispersed over the plain, and the country so richly cultivated and well wooded that scarcely a barren spot is visible throughout this extensive scenery. The effect was much heightened by the setting sun, partly obscured by clouds and causing some fine partial lights.

Tuesday 21st. Walked out. Fine but cold.

Wednesday 22nd. Very fine. Cold E. wind. Rode to Cleeve 3 miles north of Cheltenham. A handsome and picturesque church. . . . The southern porch is completely Saxon. . . . The western door is still richer. . . .

Thursday 23rd. Walked out.

Friday 24th. Rode to Birdlip Hill. Turned off in a field to the right and rode to the brow of a projecting hill from which I had one of the finest views imaginable.

Saturday 25th. Walked to Charlton Kings. . . .

Sunday 26th. Rode out on the Birdlip Road. . . .

Monday 27th. Rode to Leckhampton, a short distance from Cheltenham, with an intent to visit the church but the clerk and his keys were not to be found. In the churchyard I observed several old tombstones which announce the antiquity of the spot as a place of religious worship. . . .

Tuesday 28th.   Mounted my horse at seven and rode to Tewkesbury, 8 miles. I have always thought this abbey one of the most interesting churches in England, both on account of its beautiful architecture and the fine monuments it contains. The Saxon style prevails. . . . After breakfast I proceeded through Upton, a little town on the banks of the Severn, to Malvern. . . . The distance is 14 miles.

The situation of Great Malvern is truly delightful; the houses and cottages are dispersed in the most picturesque manner on the sides of these noble hills. And the beauty and dignity of the scenery are much increased by the Priory church, which is a large and handsome Gothic building, proudly oerlooking the rich and extensive vale beneath it. I was sorry to find on entering it that no attention had been paid to its internal repairs, and that it still remained in the same damp, mouldering and dilapidated state as when I viewed it last. . . . The architecture of the church is Gothic excepting the six arches which divide the nave from the aisles, which are low and supported by round massive columns. The roof of the transept is of stone, groined, and well preserved. The heavy turret is supported by Gothic arches apparently very light for so great a weight. The roof of the nave and choir are of wood. There are numerous fragments of inscriptions in the painted glass windows.

After dinner I mounted the hills immediately above the house where I took up my quarters, viz the hotel, by a path leading through the garden in the back of it. . . . I mentioned the view from Cleeve Hill as being one of the finest in England, but this I must own as superior . . . when the pear trees are in full bloom and absolutely from their immense numbers whitened the whole surface [of] the plains beneath. The [*County of*] Herefordshire (when the apple trees are in full bloom) possesses the same beauties but as yet they are not come out. The views from the summit are very different. For variety of ground, broken in its forms and fine distant range of mountains the Herefordshire side has the preference. The great beauty of the opposite side consists in the richness and extent of its fertile plains, and the numerous villages, churches etc dispersed over it with the two cities of Gloucester and Worcester and the Abbey of Tewkesbury. . . . But on every account I give the preference to Great Malvern. . . A great alteration has taken place in the face of the country since my last visit to this place by means of a very extensive inclosure. The crops on it appear promising.

Wednesday 29th.   Returned to Tewkesbury to dinner and to Cheltenham in the evening. To vary my route I passed through Little Malvern, a most picturesque and retired situation. . . .

Thursday 30th.   Walked out.

Friday 1 May.   Rode to Dowdeswell, Sandiwell etc. . . .

Saturday 2nd May.   Walked out.

Sunday 3 May.   Rode to Dowdeswell.
My horse having been taken ill I could make no excursions into the neighboring country.
[Agricultural Remarks at Cheltenham.
   Large common fields. Great quantities of beans planted. The wheat also is planted. A very heavy plough with a long beam pointed downwards, no wheel. On the hills the same kind of plough is used but with a wheel. Horses and oxen used indiscriminately. Cotswold sheep in general; I saw no other breed. It is strange that on these dry hills a breed of sheep is not introduced which will bear folding which the Cotswold do not.
   The barbarous custom of trimming up to a point all kinds of trees prevails, but too universally for the beauty of the country and benefit of the cattle.]

Monday 11 May.   Left Cheltenham and breakfasted at Winchcomb. Consists chiefly of one long winding street. Many of the houses by their irregular and mixed architecture denote the antiquity of the place. . . . Having taken views of it I proceeded on my journey to Hayles Abbey on a bad, rough horse road. The ruins remaining are trifling, but from their scattered parts and foundations we may conclude this abbey was very extensive.[6] I was informed that the body of the church stood in the meadow between the present chapel and an old tower which is evidently of a much more modern date than the adjoining ruins of the abbey. . . . Turned off on the right to see Toddington, an old mansion house of the Tracy family, now the property of Mr Hanbury, a family from Pontypool in Monmouthshire. . . . An old-fashioned house presenting a greater abundance of gable roofs than any house I ever saw. Commanding no good qualities in its situation. Improvements both in the grounds and to the house have been making but the work advances slowly. Indeed I cannot fancy any person accustomed to the beauties of Monmouthshire settling himself contentedly at Toddington. [Agricultural Remarks: Between Hayles Abbey and Toddington saw a double plough at work with six horses and the same number to a single one. The man who held the latter told me that the double one was lately come down for an experiment but he did not think it could answer. Land deep and heavy. Large common fields. Beans, peas, tares etc]
   . . .Good approach to Evesham: the three churches situated on an eminence; the River Avon and bridge over it form a pleasing assemblage of objects. Market day. Crown Inn. Having ordered my dinner I walked to the churchyard immediately behind the Crown Inn. The clergyman of the place seeing that I was a stranger and desirous of examining the ruins kindly acted as *Cicerone* to me. The church of All Saints is now appropriated to the religious service of the parish. The church of St Lawrence (in ruins) and a magnificent tower or belfry are all inclosed within the churchyard, and I never recollect to have seen a more picturesque group of Gothic buildings collected in so small a tract of ground and so varied in their forms of

architecture. . . . Every lover of antiquity and national architecture must regret the present deplorable state of the adjoining church of St Lawrence, and particularly of the very elegant Gothic chapel said to have been dedicated to that saint. . . . The belfry said to have been built by one of the abbots as an act of penance is one of the finest and most perfect pieces of masonry I ever beheld. Its character is the broad Gothic. The walls and buttresses are ornamented with blank arches which give it a light appearance. A modern pediment with two figures in armor placed to strike the bells injures the effect of one side of the tower. . . .

After dinner proceeded in a chaise to Worcester; good road, country well cultivated. Stopt at Pershore: a neat town, built of brick, consisting chiefly of one long street. Part of the old church is to be traced in the present one appropiated to divine service. It seems originally to have been of the Saxon order, the tower being supported by Saxon arches. . . . The original nave has been demolished as the present church consists only of the choir and transept. . . .

Tuesday 12th May.   Before breakfast I visited the cathedral. Pure and chaste Gothic prevails here though there are a great variety of different arches. The arches of the choir (as frequently is the case) are richer and more ornamented both in the lower and upper story. Clustered columns with capitals of foliage etc, simple and neat groined roof. The whole has been lately repaired and beautified. A new painted window ornamented with escutcheons of arms is now putting up. This cathedral is rich in sepulchral monuments; contains a great many effigies and some of very ancient date. The most interesting are that of King John whose effigies is very perfect. Prince Arthur's chapel, particularly the back part of it next the south aisle, is a rich, and beautiful specimen of Gothic architecture ornamented with a variety of figures etc etc. . . .

The neighborhood of Worcester teamed in former days with religious establishments attracted by the fertility of the soil, fine water and other natural advantages. They could not have fixed on better situations. . . .

After breakfast proceeded on my journey through Ambersley [*Ombersley*], the seat of the late Lord Sandys (houses generally built of brick though red stone near the suface). . . .

[Agriculture: a fine rain, the first since I left home except a trifling shower or two; country much in want of it]

Kidderminster: built of brick, streets paved with smooth pebbles. Carries on a large carpet trade. The parish church is on an eminence at the upper end of the town. Figures in nitches at the entrance. . . . Left Kidderminster, White Lyon Inn. Saw the first shorn sheep. Long ascent. Boundary stone between Worcestershire and Shropshire. Fine view from the summit of the hill. Northern point of Malvern [*Beacons*] forms a fine abrupt object. The beginning and end of the road sandy. A heavy and tedious stage. Approach to Bridgnorth over a heath. Desolate, a rabbit warren on one side, a gibbet on the other. Long winding ascent up to the town. Picturesque hovels built in the rocks. Fine rich view on the left.

[Agriculture: between Kidderminster and Bridgnorth saw a double plough, and at some distance from the road saw another ploughing up a steep hill by itself, the driver walking on one side with his horse.]

Bridgnorth, built on a rocky eminence above the Severn which is navigable and in some places flows rapidly. Carries on a carpet trade. A foundery for casting iron has been also lately erected. The red soil still continued from Worcester here. The rock also is red. The variety of houses built on the steep declivity and excavated in it have a singular appearance. The whole scenery reminded me of Knaresborough. A large fragment of the old castle remains, consisting of a tower which in falling has been stopt in its course and now leans very much out of the perpendicular. . . . A new church has been lately built here of the Doric order with Gothic sashes.[7] The whole building but ill accords with the antique appearance of the place and adjoining houses and streets; the old church is much more in character. . . .

Wednesday 13th May. After breakfast left Bridgnorth and proceeded on my journey to the Ironbridge at Colebrooke Dale. Road good and not very hilly excepting the steep descent to the inn.

I employed this day in examining the environs of this place where Nature has been very bountiful as to outward appearances and inward productions. Her soil produces iron, coal, limestone, clay for brick etc, etc of which the persevering industry of man has profited. The beauty of these vales is certainly much injured by the great population, extensive ironworks and other manufactories with which the whole face of the country is overspread.[8] Still, however, much remains to admire and the traveller or inhabitant in the beautiful hanging woods and shady well-kept walks of Mr Reynolds will find retirement and solitude interrupted only by the repeated strokes of the hammer in the furnace beneath. These walks are extensive and well laid out. At one extremity a rotunda commands a fine view of the adjacent country; as does, near the other extremity, a Doric building embosomed deep in a fine grove of oaks. In the vale beneath the finest feature is an abrupt and pointed hill, well covered with copse wood and timber trees, at a short distance above the Ironbridge. Below the bridge the sides of the Severn are so thickly beset with forges and other buildings that all beauty of scenery is lost, though the river is oftentimes rapid. The Tontine Inn faces the bridge. The view from it is much injured by a late fall of oak trees etc on the opposite hill. . . .

The Ironbridge is not in itself a picturesque object; it wants solidity. The whole scenery is also (in point of beauty) much diminished by the brick buildings which are general; I have always had the greatest aversion to them and particularly when viewed in a picturesque light. They admit of no variety of tints, no effects of light or shade, and have therefore always a dull and heavy appearance. NB. Painting the windows and doorcases green with the addition of blinds of the same color tends to give them a better effect by relieving the eye from the heavy mass of dull red. Cover them with a wash of soft cream color retaining the green windows etc, and they become at once cheerful and pleasing objects.

The foundation of the Ironbridge has given way and a meeting is now holding to consider about the means of repairing it. Its construction is very simple: five ribs of iron connected by cross bars form the arch which has a gentle ascent.[9] There is a cannon foundry and a procelain manufactory in the neighborhood. The roaring explosion of the former produced a fine effect whilst I was walking in Mr Reynold's woods.

Thursday 14th.   Breakfasted at Much Wenlock, 5 miles from Colebrooke Dale. A poor little inn, the Raven. The ruins of the abbey are both extensive and picturesque. In similar buildings much (in my opinion) depends on the materials of which they have been constructed. In this respect the ruins of Wenlock Abbey have every advantage: the natural color of the stone is good (speaking as a painter) and its effect increased by the variety of plants, wallflowers etc etc, which shoot from the interstices of the broken stones. They present many specimens of architecture, from the early Saxon to a later Gothic. An elegant specimen of the former exists in a chapel or apartment (for I do not know to what use it was appropriated) where the side walls are covered with a double row of blank intersected ribs, and the entrance to it from the west is by three Saxon arches richly ornamented with the zig zag and other patterns.[10] The lancet Gothic windows occur often. A building used as a stable has its roof in two stories, perfect and groined. The cloysters remain and are appropiated to the uses of a farmhouse, neither remarkable for grandeur or execution. Some remains of Saxon architecture are here still visible in an adjoining building.

How many abbeys and monasteries have been converted into farmhouses! Llanthony in Monmouthshire, Llanthony near Gloucester, Valle Crucis, Hayles Abbey and many others. And how few have I seen so fortunately situate near the residence of a man of property as to become an interesting and historical ornament to his place. Of those placed in the latter situation Fountains Abbey in Yorkshire is the only one I at present recollect to have seen. . . .

[Agriculture: Between Colebrooke Dale and Wenlock saw two ploughs at work, one with iron furrow boards which are much used in this country, the other with a double beam and two wheels was in a double plough, both worked with four horses. In light land the New Stanton plough would (I am sure) do the same work with *two* horses.]

Thursday 14th.   After dinner proceeded on my journey to Shrewsbury. Crossed an iron bridge over the Severn about two short miles from Colebrooke Dale to see the ruins of Bildewas [*Buildwas*] Abbey situated near the banks of the river. This bridge is neither so high or wide as the other at Colebrooke Dale and much heavier in its architecture.[11]

The ruins of this abbey in a distant view do not promise much food for the artist and antiquarian, but on turning round a garden wall the eye is suddenly surprized with an extensive and picturesque mass of ruins. They present a great mixture of Saxon and Gothic architecture but I think the former prevails. The shell of the church is nearly entire. The nave consists of seven Gothic arches supported on short round massive columns with Saxon capitals. The upper story is Saxon. The east end terminates with three long narrow Saxon windows. The west end has only two but of the same order and much overspread with ivy. The tower is supported by broad Gothic arches. To the north there is an extensive range of buildings with Saxon doorways now used as stables. . . .

Good road to Shrewsbury; at mile VII see its distant spires. Near M. V to the right is Wroxeter, a famous Roman station, *Uriconium*.[12] Soon after enter the great London Road and which I imagine from its appearance was originally Roman. Lord Berwick's house[13] on the right — too high. Cross the Severn over a handsome bridge. A large inn on the left. Wrekin Hill behind has a good effect. . . .

Friday 15 May. Shrewsbury. I found the Lion Inn much improved since my last visit to this town. Shrewsbury is one of the most irregularly built towns I know, so much so that it is difficult for a stranger to find his way through it. Its suburbs are very pleasant, particularly the walks on the banks of the river. Some of its churches also bear marks of antiquity and deserve notice. The cathedral [*abbey*] near which I passed on entering the town bears many marks of antiquity and of Saxon architecture; in the right aisle the Saxon columns remain which supported the roof. . . . In a garden adjoining the abbey is an elegant and perfect piece of Gothic antiquity (which has been well drawn in Pennant's *Tour*). It is an oratory or pulpit of stone, open on all sides with Gothic arches and figures sculptured in *bas relief*.

From the cathedral I visited St Mary's which also has many marks of early antiquity. On the south is a Saxon porch and doorway, on the north two Saxon doorways. The western entrance is Saxon but unornamented. Several Saxon windows in steeple. . . . From hence I went to St Alkmund's, a church lately rebuilt.[14] Has a fine pointed window, modern (I believe by Eginton) representing a female figure whole length, coloring soft, and well executed. The pulpit is so injudiciously placed as to obstruct the view of the window on entering the church. . . .

There are many other large buildings at Shrewsbury: the goal, Council House (Ionic order), House of Industry so justly celebrated for its good management. The Market House is a venerable old building. In the front are placed the statues taken from the old Welch Bridge, which is taken down and replaced by a modern one.[15]

After dinner I left Shrewsbury and slept at Oswestry, a long stage but level road and good. This town was formerly defended by a castle and walls. A few broken fragments of the former remain on an artificial mound. The gates mentioned by Mr Pennant (vol. 1, page 263) have been pulled down. The church is a large and handsome building but not of a very ancient date. . . .

Saturday 16 May.   Proceeded on my journey to Llangollen and Corwen where I dined, and arrived in the evening at Bala. I found the canal much advanced and the fine aqueduct of ten arches which traverses the vale beneath Chirk nearly finished. When time has given the stone a few mellow tints it will be a most picturesque object. . . . The other fine aqueduct over the Dee and which will be a still grander object than the one before mentioned has not advanced much but the canal is brought up to it and to the lime works above; there are seventeen piers erected to bear the arches.[16] The fine wood on the left of the road between Corwen and Llangollen which I had so often admired is alas cut! . . . Dined at Corwen, slept at Bala.[17]

Monday 2nd [1st.] June.   Tired with the constant succession of bad fishing owing to the east winds, dry weather etc I left Bala on an excursion to the Vale of Clwyd. A tedious, hilly and dreary road over the mountains. . . . The new road from Corwen to Bala through the Vale of the Dee is now rendered passable for carriages and is two miles further, but the difference of distance is sufficiently well compensated by the difference in scenery. Leave Rug, a seat of the Salusbury family on the left. This place is undergoing several material alterations and improvements. . . . A little further on on the left and near the road I observed another artificial mound in a field. All this country was the scene of many bloody battles during the reign of Henry the Second and the rebellion of Owen Glendwr. Whilst my driver was refreshing his horses at Gwyddelwern I visited the churchyard. Here the custom of not burying on the north side is very scrupulously adhered to; on the other sides the graves are crowded. The same custom which prevails in many parts of north and south Wales is adopted here: that of adorning the tombs of the deceased with plants. I observed two infant tombs edged with box and strewed with lime, to prevent perhaps the approach of worms and other insects. . . .

A new road is now making through the vale, by which many steep hills and much dreary country will be avoided. Had I known so much of it had remained undone I should not have attempted it in my chaise, for I found the latter part of it as bad as the beginning of it was good. Continued my route through a well-wooded valley to Ruthin. The principal trees are oak, ash and wych elm. The evening was so far advanced that I could not judge of the country round Ruthin. The features of the mountains, as seen in the dusk, appeared grand, and the vale and sides of the hills appeared well covered with wood.

Tuesday 3rd [2nd] June.   Ruthin. The day was so completely rainy that I had only time to take a view of the church, and a very cursory one of the ruined castle. This church (according to Pennant, vol. 2, p. 55) was originally conventual and belonged to a house of *Bonhommes*, a species of Augustins. . . . The cieling of the church is curious, carved in wood with various devices and

letters, by which Pennant says the names of the workmen were denoted. . . .
The town is built on a hill and its declivities, chiefly of brick. The many
porticos and penthouses give it an ancient and rather a picturesque appearance. . . . The new Town Hall, erected in 1785, is a handsome and
commodious building. A most elegant chandelier, gilt and exquisitely carved
in wood was presented to it by Sir Watkyn Wynne. Part of this building is
occasionally used as an assembly room and the elasticity of the spring floor
is much commended. Though not the county town the assizes are held here.
Though there are considerable remains of the castle the ruins are by no means
picturesque. It was built on a red rock and fortified at intervals with round
towers, several of which still remain. . . .

Wednesday 3rd June. Having made a drawing of the castle I mounted my
horse and made a little detour on my road to Mold to visit the church of
Llanruth, said to be the mother church of Ruthin. . . . The church is a plain
and small building with the simple belfry. This seems to be the original and
oldest kind of parish church we have. I returned to the turnpike leading to
Mold and ascended a long and steep hill commanding a fine view of the Vale
of Clwyd, which has a good effect when seen through the chasm of the
Verres Mountains over which the road leads. . . . I cannot agree with
Pennant (page 417) that the view of the Vale of Mold is so exquisite. It
appeared to me perhaps less striking from having just left that of Clwyd, so
far superior in extent, richness and beauty.

Mold is a neat-looking town, built of brick, and consisting principally of
one long street, near the upper end of which is the church, a handsome
Gothic edifice of the broad style about the time of Henry VII. The steeple
appears of a modern date and has a frieze around it of small animals. . . . At a
short distance from the church the mound and other raised works on which
stood the castle, are visible. The outward form of them will soon be lost by
the plantations lately made on the scite of them. After dinner pursued my
road through Northop and Flint to Holywell. Near Northop the country is
well wooded and chiefly with oaks. I stopped to see the church which
contains some interesting memorials of former days. . . .

Following my road to Flint (which here began to alter for the worse) I had
the first view of the estuary of the Dee and Cheshire coast. Descend to Flint,
a miserable town though the capital of the county. I found however a much
better inn than expected. Visited the castle,[18] situated on the borders of a
marsh. Built of a yellowish stone and on a native rock, which has been in
many places much undermined by wind and water. It is by no means a
picturesque though an historical subject (*vide* Pennant, vol. 1, p. 44). Its
form is nearly square with a round tower at each corner, but the one at the S.
East corner which is larger, is detached from the castle and appears to have
communicated with it by means of a drawbridge. . . . Adjoining the castle
are some lead works. Houses of brick. . . . Drank tea at the Ship and
pursued my route along the coast. Numerous works and manufactories.
Turn to the left, see the ruins of Basingwerk Abbey, St Winifrede's Well and

ascend to Holywell. White Horse Inn.

Thursday 4th. My first visit after breakfast was to Basingwerk Abbey,[19] situated at a short distance from Holywell. It stands on a gentle eminence above and on the borders of the great marsh which extends towards the Cheshire coast, and near the fine spring which runs down from St Winifrede's Well. Its ruins are extensive, the architecture a mixture of Saxon, Lancet and other Gothic. Not elegant in its structure. Pennant vol. 1, page 25 describes the abbey and appropriates the different rooms to their several former uses. Though almost surrounded by the busy clang of manufactories, copper works, cotton mills etc, etc it has not yet quite lost its solitary and sequestered appearance. Its mouldering walls are sheltered by some fine trees. . . . The valley leading from thence to Holywell would be beautiful were the fine spring suffered to continue its natural course unconfined in large pools, and were not the valley crowded thickly with lofty brick houses. St Winifrede's Well, the fine stream, the chapel etc on entering the town form a very picturesque group of buildings.[20] The interior of the well affords a most elegant specimen of Gothic architecture in the arch over it. The chapel above contains nothing very curious. For a more particular account *vide* Pennant vol. 1, page 28.

Having satisfied my curiosity and made the drawings I wished I pursued my route to St Asaph where I dined and slept. . . . After passing over another dreary common the beautiful Vale of Clwyd bursts unexpectedly on the sight, but during my whole tour the mountainous boundaries of the Vale had been so obscured by the thickness of the atmosphere that their more distant beauties had been in great measure lost to me. Cross the River Clwyd, deep banks and narrow. See Rhuddlan Castle on the right. White Lion, a good inn, where for the first time since my journey in Wales I met with the good English round of salt beef. Much cattle is bred in the north parts of Wales but little fattened, the Vale of Clwyd excepted, where many oxen are grazed, some of which have been lately sold as high as seventy guineas p. head.

The inn is situated opposite the cathedral, retired and quiet. The epithet *paupercula* applied by Giraldus to this place in former days may be equally applied at present. The town is small, situated on the declivity of a hill; at the bottom is the parish church, at the top the cathedral whose only merit is its neatness. It contains only one ancient monument. . . . There are some fine ash trees in the enclosure round the cathedral, more spreading than usual. On one side runs the Clwyd, on the other the Elwy which from its wide bed appears at times to be very violent. From the bridge over the Elwy the town, cathedral, parish church etc form a picturesque group of buildings.

Friday 5th June. After breakfast rode to Rhuddlan and returned by Dyserth. The former is a mean village situated on the banks of the Clwyd which is here navigable and a tide river. Near it is the marsh famous for the battle in 795 fought between the Welsh and Saxons, and fatal to the former, and which gave rise to the celebrated Welsh air, *Morfa Rhuddlan*. Very considerable remains of the ancient castle still exist.[21] Its form is irregular; the inner area approaches nearest to an octagon [*sketch*]. The entrances were at NW and SE, the towers round, three of which on the NW side remain tolerably entire. Three sides were furnished with a deep foss, walled on each side. The fourth side, NW, sloping down towards the river was defended by a high wall and square towers, one of which remains and part of the other. . .

. . . After dinner went to Denbigh where I slept. Nothing particularly interesting on the road. Bull Inn: old-fashioned house and as old-fashioned a landlady.

Saturday 6th June.   My morning was employed in taking views of Denbigh Castle and in visiting the neighbouring church at Whitchurch which contains some interesting monuments. This (according to Pennant) is the parish church of Denbigh, vol. 2, p. 731. . . . The town of Denbigh has a very picturesque appearance as seen from the road to St Asaph. Immediately after my arrival I walked out in search of the most advantageous points of view and encircled the castle. I fixed my point at last from the limestone quarries on the road leading to St Asaph. Here the town appears to very great advantage: the ruins of a fine castle at the summit, the modern church and by its side that of one in ruins (or rather begun but never completed),[22] a fine rich country terminated in mountains at a distance with a very good and broken foreground, and the town covering the declivities of a steep hill, well blended with trees. The whole forms a rich picturesque scene, worthy [*of*] the pencil of a Poussin, and similar in many respects to those he chose for his pencil. On the opposite side (I think the SE) the castle has a very different appearance and more that of a strong fortress, being built on a lofty and abrupt rock. But I prefer the former view as the richer. The castle and its outworks are very extensive. The gateway (principal) with a mutilated statue in a Gothic niche over it is a grand and picturesque object. The view from within it over the beautiful and rich Vale of Clwyd is seen to great advantage. The Vale terminates well with the abrupt rock over Dyserth. This entrance faces NE. The town of Denbigh is built partly on the plain and partly on the declivities of the hill. Though the capital of the county it is inferior in appearance (and I believe in population) to Ruthin. . . .

Here ended my excursion through the Vale of Clwyd. This vale is reckoned the finest in the principality; by fineness is meant richness of soil and fertility. With regard to its picturesque beauty I was rather disappointed. Its mountainous boundaries to the east are well-formed and finely broken, but the Vale is in general too wide to furnish good subjects for the pencil. The views however which its different parts present are truly pleasing and the views from its heights are very grand. The hill between Ruthin and Mold and the passage between Holywell and St Asaph afford fine bird's eye prospects. The ground is generally cultivated as high as the sides of the mountains will admit; the country thickly dotted with gentlemen's seats, villages etc, etc and the whole well wooded. Trees of all kinds flourish well.

I never remember to have seen to many of the wyche-elm; the Dutch elm has not yet been introduced. The ride between Denbigh and Ruthin is the richest and most pleasing of any I met with in the Vale.

Sunday 7th June.   Returned by Corwen to Bala on the old road from Ruthin to the former place, hilly and indifferent and longer than the intended new one.

Friday 12th June.   Left Bala, dined and slept at Tan-y-bwlch in the Vale of Festiniog. I have so often travelled this road that no novelty occurred. Nothing had been done towards the improvement of the road. I stopped to fish Llynn Morwynion but the day was unfavorable and I had little sport.

Saturday 13 June.   I went in pursuit of a new lake called Llyn Garmell [*Llynau Gamallt*] passing through Festiniog. Turned off to the left on the road leading to Penmachno. Saw a few of the upright stones mentioned by Pennant. . . . The old road took its course through the valley to the left of the new one, which has been made on the old road (probably Roman) called *Sarn Helen* . . . the lake, or rather the lakes for there are two, separated by a narrow neck of land. . . . The first I came to is the smallest and has the largest fish, which grow to a lage size and at times rise to a fly and, as I was informed, were red. In the larger lake the trout are smaller, white and bad. . . .

Sunday 14 June.   After breakfast I rode to see another lake of which Pennant gives a curious description (vol. 2, p. 129). It is called Cwmallin [*Llyn Cwmorthin*]. . . . I now began to ascend and continued my rough and Alpine track through some oak groves, in some of which the axe has lately been introduced; £900 of timber was cut last year and a considerable fall has been made in the present. It is a lamentable sight for a lover of picturesque scenery; in a few years little wood will be left in Merionethshire. During the few years I have frequented this county the havock has been great; several of my favorite groves which I have so often admired have already fallen, and I hear of more whose speedy doom is impending. But the only evil does not arise from felling the wood but from not properly fencing them out when cut by which the young shoots and prospects of a future copse are totally annihilated. This woodland track intermixed with small pastures, distant mountains etc affords many pleasing points of view and such as I little expected to find before I entered this district. . . .

I was rather disappointed in the appearance of the lake, which from its confined situation amongst the mountains I expected to have found very picturesque. But the mountains slope regularly down without any of those abrupt and perpendicular rocks which render several of these mountain lakes so striking. . . . The vale between it and the mountains admit of two small farms situated at the different extremities of the lake. It is full of trout which rise very freely at a fly and are also caught with a worm; they are white, soft and bad. The approach to this chasm is truly grand. I never saw more grand

25. Harlech Castle; *view from south-east looking towards entry and gatehouse.*

and majestic masses of rock, one in particular on the right of an immense
height, perpendicular and with a square summit, like an enormous tower.
This scenery must be truly sublime after hard rains as the rapid descent from
the lake forms several cascades. The rocks are of the finest masses and most
picturesque forms imaginable. Several rustic bridges thrown over the river
embellish the scenery. . . .

Monday 15 June.   I fished Llyn Morwynion but with no better success
than on the former day.

Tuesday 16 June.   Tired with the bad sport I have experienced with my
fishing rod I sent my Welch guide Evan to try his luck in Mannod Lake, near
Festiniog. Though a disbeliever of the accounts he had heard from his
countrymen of the size of the fish of this pool he returned fully satisfied that
they were of a very large size. . . .
     I employed my morning in visiting a part of the country which I had
before only seen transiently. I began my ride by following the course of the
Tan-y-bwlch river which is navigable within a short distance of the bridge. . . .
The tide coming in prevented my following the river on its sands to the
Traeth Bach, but a horse track over the hill to the right led me down to it.
From the ridge I had a full view of these sands, bounded on the left by
Harlech Castle forming a grand object (though at so great a distance) from
the perpendicular rock on which it is placed. Crossed the neck of land which
divides Traeth Bach from the Traeth Mawr. A few miserable hovels scattered
about a narrow vale of turbary. Descended to the village of Llanfrothen near
to which the present carriage road from Tan-y-bwlch to Carnarvon leads.
The mountains which bound these sands are very majestic and picturesque
in their forms. They are a part of the Snowdonia and are much finer in every
respect than those around the Traeth Bach. There is much pretty scenery
and good subjects for the pencil in this vale adjoining the Traeth Mawr and
which I wish to examine more minutely. Ascend. See a pretty well-wooded
dingle on the left oertopped with rude, barren mountains. Join the great
road, now in a state of improvement and in some parts new making. The
communication to Carnarvon (till lately) was scarcely open for carriages.
Chaise and horse are now kept at Tan-y-bwlch. Much however of the
mountainous tract might have been avoided had the road been led along the
valley by the side of the river.

Wednesday 17 June.   At break of day took my departure from Tan-y-
bwlch which I had never had leisure to examine attentively before. The more
I viewed this beautiful little vale in its different parts the more I had reason
to admire it. It is (as Pennant justly observes) *a gem in a rugged case*,
composed of rich meadows, its sides edged with groves and closed by barren
and precipitous mountains. It is just of the size adapted to the pencil, neither
too narrow or too wide. The forms of the mountains are fine: those on the
western side are beautifully fringed with majestic groves of oak trees, and on

the road leading over the hills to Harlech there is another beautiful hanging wood. The upper part of the vale will soon I fear have cause to lament the loss of its woods, as much has lately been cut down and the axe is still busily employed. The cottages are happily dispersed on the sides of the mountains, some almost immersed in the deep woods and traced by the smoke issuing from their chimnies, and producing a good effect against the dark background. The little village of Maen Twrog adds much to the scenery, nor should I forget the numerous bridges scattered about the vale, the long one of which well bedecked with ivy and nearly in the center of the vale over the principal river has a charming effect. I could dwell much longer on the beauties of this sequestered vale, where the artist and lover of the unadorned beauties of nature will find ample amusement and employment.

Wednesday 17 June. [?]   Beyond Festionig turned off to the left and took the road leading to Penmachno and formed on the scite of the old paved *Sarn Helen. . . .*[23] The situation of this lake [*Llyn Conwy*] is more extraordinary from its high situation than from any beauties of form or features. Situated on a spacious plain surrounded with woodless bogs and commanding on all sides a view of the distant and lofty mountains in Merioneth and Carnarvonshire it is the second in size to Bala amongst the Welsh lakes and full of trout, which are red, firm and good, and in good weather easily caught with fly or corbet. Its shores are much indented. The distance from this pool to Yspythy [*Ysbyty*] is (as near as I can guess) about five miles and the nearest place from which it is accessible. But the accomodations are here so indifferent that no one but a great lover of fly-fishing would put up with them for the chance of a sport so variable and uncertain. In a former tour I had tried them for one night and can therefore speak with experience. . . . Having refreshed myself and horses at Yspytty I returned to Bala in the evening, 12 long miles, heartily tired with my day's journey, through one of the most uninteresting tracts I ever traversed. . . .

On my way met hundreds of Methodists on their return from Bala. An annual meeting is held there by which thousands are attracted, some from devotion, others from curiosity. The man who keeps the turnpike at Bala counted one year above 3,000 who passed his gate and amongst them were 900 horses. Preachers come down from London who relieve each other, so that there is someone officiating almost every hour of the day. The town during this time affords a fine scene of noise, hustle and confusion. Several are now emigrating to America.

Sunday 21st June.   . . .

Monday 22nd June.   In the evening went to Rûg where Captain Salusbury is building a new house near the scite of the old one. It is built of a yellow grit stone, brought from Ruabon, of a good color. The back front has a handsome Ionic portico, large enough to permit a carriage to drive up to the door. The front rooms will command a good view of the Vale of the Dee when the old house and some trees are removed. Much remains to be done: the place must be entirely new modelled. The old house is in part pulled down. I saw nothing curious either in the exterior or interior. Several emblazoned coats of arms handing down to posterity the ancient pedigree of the family. An old ornamented ceiling above stairs. Fine landscapes by Wilson[24] had been removed to an adjoining farmhouse. Near the old house is an ancient tumulus which I understand is not to be removed.

From hence I prolonged my ride on the same side of the river (which together with the vale appears to great advantage from some points of view) to a hill opposite Corwen which I had so often seen from my windows but never visited. On it is a curious British post [*Caer Drewyn*], described by Pennant very minutely and exactly, vol. 2, p. 59. It is conjectured that Owen Gwynedd occupied this post while Henry ll lay encamped on the Berwyn Hills the opposite side of the vale. Owen Glendower is also said to have made use of this fortress. It was encircled by a large stone wall apparently put together without mortar, as I could perceive no signs of any cement, of which its very dilapidated state (no one stone being left upon another) seems to be a proof. . . .

Tuesday 23rd June.   After breakfast left Corwen and proceeded on my journey through Cenioge to Llanrwst. Pass Rug. Leave the Bala road on my left. A pleasing [*country*] cultivated with corn and pastures continues for about six miles. See a curious bridge on the left thrown over a very deep chasm in the rocks through which the river precipitates itself. The dingle is narrow and well-wooded. The descent to the bed of the river appears difficult but after hard rains I should think would amply repay the inquisitive traveller and lover of fine scenery for his trouble. There was so little water in the river that I satisfied myself with a view of it from above. At M.10 pass through Cerrig y Druidion [*Drudion*] (or the Stones of the Druids), see Pennant vol. 2, p. 73. The only antiquity it can boast of is its name. Change horses at Cernioge, a single house. The country which from M Vl from Corwen gradually became more dreary, less wooded and cultivated, is here somewhat enlivened by a few good trees and better pastures. Scarcity of wood is providentially compensated for by a turbary in the neighborhood.

. . . A plan is now in agitation to make a new road by Capel Cerrig to Bangor by which the post road to Ireland will be very considerably shortened. A long steep descent, the sides of the precipice well guarded by a wall. In front an extensive range of the Snowdonia [*Mountains*] present a fine broken outline, and the beautiful Vale of Llanrwst opens itself to great advantage. . . . Amongst the different vales in North Wales this in my opinion bears the superiority. It is neither so expanded as the Vale of Clwyd nor contracted as that of Tan-y-bwlch or Festiniog. I have before observed that the former is too wide to be truly picturesque. The Vale of Llanrwst seems to be of a size between the two, but it has two features in every respect superior to any which the other vales can boast of: the boldly hanging woods above Gwyder and that River Conway meandring beautifully through the center of the Vale. The town of Llanrwst with its elegant bridge, many gentlemen's houses scattered along the well-wooded hills which bound it, good cultivation etc, etc form an assemblage of the most pleasing objects I ever beheld.

In the evening I visited the parish church. The Wynne Chapel contains many curious monuments and brasses belonging to that ancient family. . . . From the church I continued my walk to Gwyder [*Gwydir*], a venerable old house with a picturesque court, situated at the foot of an abrupt mountain covered from its base to its summit with a variety of fine forest trees. I have seen no mass of wood so grand, not even that at Ilam, or at Margam, or at Dynevor, which are the three finest I recollect. In the midst of these sequestered woods stands embosomed a picturesque little chapel in which service is occasionally performed.[25]

Wednesday 24th June.   Pursued my route to Conway. For four or five miles the road is carried at the base of precipitous mountains, from whose rugged sides the waters issuing from numerous lakes on the hills above discharge themselves into the plains, and after hard rains form fine cascades. See the situation of Maenan abbey on the opposite side of the river, for I understand no part of its old walls remain. A large house inhabited by Lord Newborough was built of its materials. See several tents pitched in a field — a very different establishment from its former one.

Hereabouts the cultivation of the Vale ceases and from rich pastures becomes a coarse rushy meadow. Vale widens and becomes less picturesque. Stopped at Caer Hên [*Hûn*] to see if I could find any traces of the ancient Roman station *Canovium* from whose ashes Conway arose. I could gain no intelligence from the natives except that there was formerly part of an old wall adjoining the church, now pulled down. The grass was so high and wet that I had not an opportunity of exploring the fields. I understand that its situation was nearly where the parish church stands, and between that and the river.[26] From an eminence on the road not far from Caer Hên see a fine view of the Vale of Llanrwst, the River Conway forming some grand majestic windings, the vale finely closed by Gwedir Mountain and others more distant. For a short interval the road becomes uninteresting — when Conway's proud towers burst suddenly on the sight. I envy the traveller (if such there be) who not knowing that such a castle existed should be thus unexpectedly and pleasingly surprized.

The outward precinct of the walls remains so entire with the different gates that I fancied myself entering a fortified town.[27] And often in my walks through the interior prts of this noble fortress have I almost expected to see the knights in armor start forth from behind the battlements, so much is the ancient character of the castle still in appearance kept up. Pennant with great truth says: 'A more rugged town is scarcely to be seen within or a more beautiful one without.' To say merely that Conway Castle is a majestic pile of building, boldy situated on a rock and washed by a noble river would be but a faint description of the place. . . .

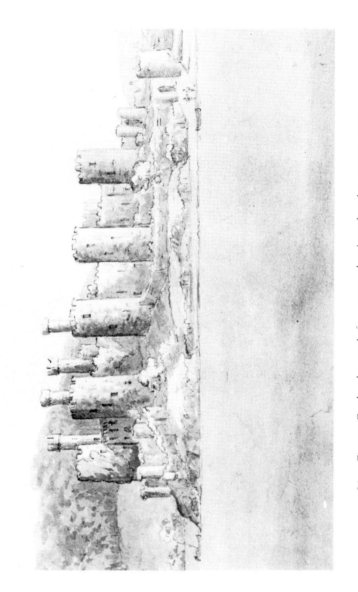

26. Conwy Castle: the north face across the river showing eastern entry.

The castle itself is a most noble structure and of the most picturesque form, and in a much less dilapidated state than most of the baronial and royal castles with which this country abounds. The four smaller towers annexed to the large ones (and which served as their staircases) give a great air of lightness and elegance to the building. The color of the stone with which it is built is at all times soft and mellow and more particularly harmonious when gilded by the rays of the sun. In parts its uniformity is happily broken by ivy which (as in some of the Welch castles and more particularly in South Wales) is not so luxuriant as to hide the material parts of the building. In short the whole is so beautiful in all its parts and so judiciously situated that I could almost suppose the artist, not the engineer, had directed its construction. The present town is built within the precincts of the ancient walls which remains entire with their original gates, fortified at intervals with round towers. On the north side of the castle a noble range of eight of them (sloping down towards the river on the declivity of the hill) may be seen to great advantage. The shape was nearly triangular of the enclosed part of the city, built upon a hard rock. I must not omit mentioning the round tower which has fallen in part, which merits our attention as it conveys an idea of the strength of the materials with which the castle was built. When I look up to this immense tower almost suspended in the air (which I never can without surprize and sometimes even with terror) I no longer wonder that it has withstood the ravages of war and time.

There is a plan in agitation of embanking out the river on the opposite shore and throwing a bridge over from the island to the castle. The convenience will certainly be very great but the artist will have to regret the loss of much fine scenery. The fine expanse of water which now contributes so much to the beauty of the place will be no more, and the course of the river will be confined to a very narrow channel. A bridge also is talked of at Bangor ferry and there it would be rather an ornament than not.

It is impossible not to leave Conway without regret; many more days than I have ever been able to spend here would be necessary to explore all its beauties in their different points. It is a place formed for the artist and man of taste.

Thursday 25th June. Left Conway . . . stopt at Aber. . . . From hence I crossed the Lavan Sands at low water to Beaumaris, distance about 4 miles, flat and sound; went in my carriage to the ferry, which was very narrow. A delightful ride from Conway to Bangor. Was obliged to walk about a mile from the ferry to Beaumaris. Found the town crowded with Methodists and their followers. The first sight was a preacher elevated [*on*] a stage on the green [The same spot was a few hours afterwards supplied with a troop of cricket players] near the sea, preaching *sub die* to two or three thousand people, and ranting away his prose *ex tempore* as readily as an Italian *improvisatore* would his verse. Fortunately I got a bed and a good sitting room at the Bull Inn. I would recommend to every traveller, who consults comfort and quiet during his tour in the Principality, to avoid fairs and

27. Landscape in the Vale beyond Aber (W. of Conwy).

Methodists, particularly the latter, when every private and public bed is engaged.

Beaumaris is a neat town, consisting principally of one handsome street terminated by the castle.[28] Every castle after Conway (which both for architecture and situation is by far the most imposing object I ever saw) must appear to disadvantage. Though an extensive and well-preserved pile of building Beaumaris can boast neither of its architecture or situation, the former heavy, the latter flat [*sketch*]. . . . On entering the southern gates of the castle (the only approach now open) the great hall immediately meets the eye and is a striking object. As far as regards the exterior [*it*] is in good preservation. The windows without are broad Gothic approaching the round; within they are more pointed. A similar room on the opposite side near the southern entrance may be traced from the foundations of the buildings still remaining. The chapel is a dark building with fine narrow lancet windows. In the construction of this building defence and security seem to have been attended to as much as in other parts of the fort. It is the only ornamented part now remaining and has been drawn and engraved by Pennant. . . . I do not recollect having seen any castle of the same extent possessing so few picturesque qualities. This may be attributed both to its uniform architecture and low situation. The towers are low and massive and appear still more so from the situation in which they are placed. The same castle placed on the eminence where stands a modern little fort would hardly be recognised. Were I the proprietor of these ruins and resided so near them as Lord Bulkeley does I should be much tempted to raise some of the large towers and add some smaller ones to them, of which the good effect is so visible at Conway. No difficulty would arise from copying the style of architecture which has been done in the two lodges leading to the castle.

Baron Hill, the seat of Lord Bukleley, though a pleasing object, both on this and more distant shores, certainly receives more beauties than it imparts, from the noble range of Snowdonian mountains which appear to great advantage from its grounds, and I may say constitute the whole beauty of them. It is situated on a gentle eminence and finely backed with wood, which although not individually large as trees, produce a fine mass. The elevation of the house, though the work of the celebrated Wyat,[29] does not please me: nothing to me so hideous as a high house crowded with windows. Such a building gives me always the idea of a cotton or silk manufactory, or an hospital. The front of the house has above forty windows, in a front not far extended, in four ranges, besides an other range of blank windows. Judge then if the effect of this house can be good. It is certainly a striking object being quite white and backed by a fine wood, but I can never allow it to be in character with the place or a pleasing building.

Having amused myself for some time with walking about these grounds and enjoying the unparalleled view from them I ascended the hill behind the house in order, by gaining a more elevated point, to have a more distinct idea of the country. On a rock a little above a modern fort [*p. 267*] built in a wood I found a fit place for my survey. Immediately beneath me were the

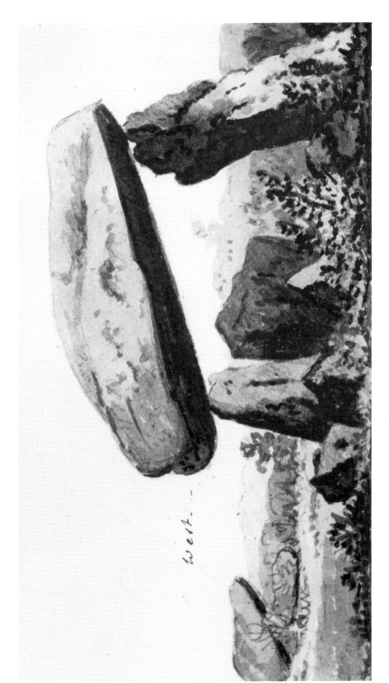

28. Trefor chambered tomb, Anglesey.

town, church and castle of Beaumaris, to the left Baron Hill embosomed in a thick wood, beyond it Llanvaes etc, the coast terminated with the island of Priestholm, opening in the Irish Sea. The promontory of Llandudno appears like another island, the neck of flat land which immediately joins it being scarcely visible. Now begins that noble range of mountains extending on the left. . . . Aber is nearly opposite with its picturesque valley receding behind it between two steep and abrupt mountains. Here commences a fine sheep walk and beneath it a mixture of corn and pasture lands. The background is here rendered very grand by a chasm in the mountains, which assume here the finest and rudest outline of any in the whole range before me. . . . Numerous little white cottages, the habitations of the slate workers, dispersed over the hill on the right side of the valley enliven the view. This range of mountains terminates with the highest (though not the most picturesque) point of Snowdonia under which you pass between Carnarvon ad Bedkelert [*Beddgelert*]. On the near banks of the Menai is Penrhyn, seat of Lord Penrhyn, just appearing amongst the woods and Llandegai church above it. Further to the right is the port of Penrhyn with its shipping, the cheerful and well-inhabited little vale of Bangor, and the entrance of the river towards Bangor Ferry which here becomes very contracted. This whole view is very *riant* and presents a most happy mixture of wood, water, rock and mountain; cultivation and population well blended with the ruder features of nature which they tend to soften and animate. England or Wales can afford few finer or more pleasing prospects.

The situation of Beaumaris is remarkably pleasant and a traveller cannot devote a few days during his tour to a more eligible spot. The walks immediately round the town are good, many of which are conducted through Lord Bulkeley's grounds and open to the public. The views from the green and from the beach before the ferry house are scarcely to be equalled. I know scarcely a finer sea view than that from the latter place where the town of Beaumaris appears to great advantage, as well as the opposite coast. I found good accomodations and civil treatment at the Bull Inn. The church is a handsome Gothic building in the exterior with a turret. The inside has nothing to boast of respecting its architecture but contains some good monuments. . . .

Sunday 28th June.   After dinner I went to Amlwch, a little seaport on the opposite side of the island, 21 M. distant from Beaumaris. A few words will suffice to describe the whole tract of country through which I passed and cannot use more applicable terms than those applied to it by fellow traveller Giraldus: '*Sit autem Mona arida tellus et saxosa, deformis aspectu et inamoena*'. Some of the land is badly cultivated, a great deal not at all. Farmhouses scattered all over the country, now and then a solitary church, and not one village on the whole road, nor a turnpike, which is more singular. Yet the roads are hard and by no means bad; the same horses took me there in four hours without baiting. There are no hills of any consequence, a few steep and short pitches. At Trevawr [*Trefor*] saw a perfect *cromlech* in a

cornfield on the left of the roadside. . . .³⁰ The unusual barren appearance of
the soil announces your approach to the mines. On the side near Amlwch
there is an absolute stop to all vegetation; on the other side a few tufts of
coarse and withered grass show that nature still is alive. Reach Amlwch;
found to my sorrow the best rooms in a small inn already engaged, but by
the landlady's intercession and through an honest Welchman's courtesy I
gained admittance. A good bed and sitting room.

The village of Amlwch owes its present neat appearance, and I might add
existence, to the neighboring copper mines, which has increased the
population very considerably.

Monday 29th. I first visited the large and extensive smelting houses
belonging to Lord Uxbridge and the Revd. Mr Hughes, the two proprietors
of the mines. The ore is brought here, broken into small pieces and put into
the furnace and when boiling is run into places prepared for it. No 1 [*in the
omitted sketch*] is the opening into the furnace. When the metal is ready this
hole is opened, the boilding red-hot metal bursts out of it, fills the first
chamber, No 2, and then runs over into the others. I was told that the real
metal would not fill above one of them (No 2) and that what ran over into
the others was only refuse. It is one of the most beautiful sights I ever saw
and should be seen by everyone who visits these parts. The men employed in
this unhealthy occupation receive only 16d. p. day wages and work 12 hours
exposed to the most pernicious fumes of the copper, a suffocating heat and a
draught of cold air.

I then descended to the port from whence the ore is exported, formed
partly by nature and enlarged by art. Great labor and expence must have
attended this work, and the solid rock has been cut through for a considerable length and breadth, sufficient to admit two vessels abreast, which at low
water lay on sand. This hollow has then a very curious appearance, but what
most strikes the eye is the very singular color of the rocks adjoining the port,
which assume the most beautiful tints from the brightest orange color to the
most delicate pale yellow. This singularity arises from the adjoining copper
mine whereby the springs and soil are strongly impregnated with copper.

Having satisfied my curiosity at Amlwch I proceeded on my way home to
Beaumaris and stopt at the Paris mines. This mountain (according to
Pennant vol. 2, p. 265) gained its present appellation from a Robert Parys,
Chamberlain of North Wales in the reign of Henry IV. He supposes these
mines (the richest in the metal ever known) were not unknown to the
Romans, but from the year 1768 may be dated their modern discovery. Sir
Nicholas Bayley, the proprietor, was induced to try for ore about the year
1762. His undertaking was attended with little success and with so much
more expence than profit that the persons concerned were determined to
abandon the concern. Orders were accordingly given to their agent who,
unwilling to give up the point, divided his men into different parties and
sank shafts in various parts of the mountain. Fortune favored his endeavors
for in less than two days the abundant vein of ore was discovered which has

29.   Caernarfon: East or Exchequer Gate in its earlier form. Note pantiles (?) on roof.

been worked ever since to so much advantage. The lucky day was March 2nd, 1768; the anniversary has ever since been kept by the miners, and I was informed that till lately the miner who hit upon the vein was on that day carried in triumph by his comrades. He is now dead. The two proprietors are Lord Uxbridge and the Revd. Mr Hughes, the former in by far the largest proportion.

As all description would fall short of the singularly romantic and picturesque forms of this mountain I shall not even attempt it. The grotesque shapes of the rocks, caverns, arches etc, the dreadful perpendicular height of the mountain, the rich and beautiful and varied tints occasioned by the metal, added to the various instruments employed in working these mines, the constant explosions by blasting the rock etc etc render this one of the most sublime and interesting scenes I ever beheld, superior to the rocky scenery at Maum [*Malham*] Tarn which (till I had seen the Parys Mountain) stood the first in my opinion of any I had ever beheld. The copper is procured by various processes. The rough metal [*ore*] is taken from the native rock, broken into small pieces and carried to the smelting house where it is melted down (No 2). But I believe the most valuable ore is procured by another process which is very curious and well worth notice. An extensive range of oblong pits are made and filled with old iron articles of every species. The spring of water flowing immediately from the mountain is then introduced into them. The effect is so great that the iron [?] is in time dissolved and changed into copper.[31] It is turned continually and at times the copper is scraped off. . . . The naturalist may see a particular account of this ore, processes etc, etc in Mr Pennant's account of the mines as above (vol. 2, p. 265).

I returned to dine at my old quarters at Beaumaris and on

Tuesday 30th June   proceeded on my tour. I hired a good sailing vessel intending to go to Carnarvon by water but tired by the continual tacking occasioned by adverse winds I landed at Bangor Ferry and pursued my road by land. Occasional views of the Menai are the only interesting objects in this tract of country. Approach Carnarvon by a straight and handsome road terminated by the proud towers of Edward's strong castle. Employed in the evening in visiting the ruins of the ancient *Segontium* etc, etc. On the left hand of the road leading to Pwllheli, at a short distance from the castle, see the remains of an ancient Roman wall of some height.[32] This fort according to Pennant was designed to secure a landing place from the River Seiont at time of high water. Above and more to the left are still more considerable remains divided by the great road leading from Carnarvon to Bettws and Bedgelert. The whole area of a square encampment, a little elevated above the surface of the adjoining grounds, may be with certainty traced [The walls consist of rough masonry; I could observe no facing left in many parts overgrown with ivy and bushes]. . . . From thence I walked to the neighboring church of Llanbublic [*Llanbeblig*], the parish church to the town of Carnarvon, which may be seen by the very numerous and crowded gravestones in its churchyard. In some I observed the new made graves encircled with basket work of straw in addition to the flowers etc strewed and planted on them. . . .

July

Wednesday 1 July. Having employed my morning in re-visiting the castle and in making some drawings of it I proceeded on my journey after dinner to Pwllheli on the opposite coast 20 miles distant from Carnarvon. . . . Observe a fort on an eminence near the shore to the right arising out of an extensive marsh which I imagine is Dinas Dinlle [NB. Visited this encampment in 1804 H.] described by Pennant. . . . Leave Glynlyffon [*Glynllifon*] on the left, seat of Lord Newborough. Some new plantations lately made, the older ones (as usual in every part of England) choaking up each other for want of thinning. . . . Approach nearer the sea coast and reach Clynnog Fawr, a retired little village surrounded with a grove of fine trees. The church surpasses I think in size and grandeur either of the cathedral churches of Bangor or St Asaph. Two handsome Gothic arches divide the choir from the transept. The arch on entering the nave from the west is taller but not so wide. The east window is large. . . . Adjoining the church is a detached building called the chapel of St Beuno. His tomb mentioned by Pennant no longer exists. I saw an old mutilated statue said to have been the effigy of the saint, also an old wooden box, said to have belonged to him also, to which is annexed some fabulous history. A fine old bell in the chapel on the ground, date 1622. . . .

. . . The horses being baited I pursued my journey to Pwllheli. Approach the sea on the right and mountains on the left. . . . Dreary country destitute of wood. At M.5 from Pwllheli a view of Cardigan Bay I found a comfortable inn lately built at Pwllheli, a little town on the coast without a church, the one appropriated to it at Denyo [*Denio*] being at some distance, as is often the case in Wales, for instance Carnarvon, Bala etc, etc. This little town seems in a flourishing condition. I saw a large Guineaman on the stocks fitted for 600 slaves.

Thursday 2nd July. Pursued my route on horseback through Abereirch, Llanystymdwy, a picturesque little village on the banks of a rapid river with a rocky bottom, to the miserable and desolate borough town of Criccieth, situated immediately on the coast Its castle[33] of which the principal remains consist in the two entrance towers of a round form is boldly situated on a high and steep rock projecting into the sea, and from the sea shore beneath forms a good subject for a drawing. . . .

Friday 3d July. Proceeded on my road to Bedgelert across the Traeth Mawr sands. Since my last visit to this part of the country very great alteration and improvement has taken place on the face of it owing to the spirited and expensive exertions of Mr Madocks who has made a large purchase in the narrow plain leading from the sands up to Penmorfa, and, by means of a considerable embankment, hopes to recover the whole tract from the ravages of the sea. And as the water flows over a level and even bed of sand and in a great measure are sheltered from very violent storms his undertaking will probably be attended with the success it deserves.[34] The approach over the sands to the entrance of the River Glaslynn presents in front the grandest range of mountains I have yet seen in Wales. The highest point of Snowdon called the *Wyddfa* rises in the center and by its oertopping height shows its ascendancy, though another mountain adjoining nearly rivals him in height. The foreground of this landscape is singular, being the most even and smooth bed of sand imaginable. Its effect however is good, perhaps owing to the contrast formed between the mellow color of the sand with the fine purple tints of the mountains, which by wood and rock are finely varied. On a nearer approach to the termination of the vale no visible means appear of getting out of it, except by traversing one of the rude mountains before you. Much less does there appear room for the descent of a rapid river. The road however unexpectedly winds round a steep rock and leads you into some pleasant meadows through which the river winds its serpentine course and soon afterwards comes the great road leading to Carnarvon.

I again took up my abode at my old quarters at Bedgelert and after dinner re-visited Llyn Dinas and afterwards ascended the mountain of Dinas Emris, celebrated in ancient British history. Here Vortigern is said to have built a fortress. There are remains of buildings, particularly of a square fort on the highest summit[35]. . . . It was formerly entirely cloathed with fine wood much of which has suffered from the axe.

Saturday 4 July.   I made an excursion to the vale and lakes described by Pennant, vol. 2, p. 180. . . turned off amongst the mountains through a pass called Drws y Coed or the 'Door of the Wood'. Lofty mountains on each side. Copper works which had been neglected for some years are now again working. A very rough and steep descent safe only for a horse well accustomed to Alpine paths. . . . Walked round the upper lake in search of views and trout. Was more successful with the former than the latter. From the upper lake the pass of Drws y Coed appears to great advantage: on each side of the pass the mountains are abrupt and precipitous, and Y Wyddfa, the highest point of Snowdon, fills up (to great advantage and effect) the chasm between them. . . .

Sunday 5 July.   Returned to dine at Tan-y-bwlch Inn. Much still remains to be done to the new carriage road; though much has been done, and well done, it is still very hilly and steep in parts. Observe one immense mass of fine rock which overhangs the road and from its slaty and crumbling quality carries with it some degree of terror.

Monday 6th July. Returned to Bala in hard rain. Here ends my Welsh expedition which has been attended generally with good weather. . . . Two such favorable seasons for tourists as the present and the last were hardly ever known.

Thursday 9 July. Left Bala, slept at Corwen.

Friday 10 July. Dined and slept at Chester and remained there till

Sunday 12 July, when I proceeded to Sir John Leicester's at Tabley.

Monday 20 July. Went to Liverpool. Found Bate's Hotel noisy and hot. A new inn under the name of the Liverpool Arms Hotel just fitted up in Castle Street, the best situation in town. Dale's house is also very good.

Wednesday 22nd July. Returned to Tabley.

Sunday 26th July. Left Tabley, dined and slept at Tarporley. . . . In the evening visited Beeston Castle, four miles distant.[36] The high perpendicular rock on which it is placed attracts the general attention of every traveller, and appears the more conspicuous from the flat country with which it is surrounded. The approach to it (which I think is on the southern side) is so easy that I rode up to the entrance of the castle and a chaise may come to the foot of the hill. This side was defended by a strong wall and round and square towers at intervals. Many of the former and one of the latter still remain entire. The western and northern sides [not having my compass with me I may perhaps not be quite correct in my account of different aspects of the castle] are naturally fortified by an abrupt and precipitous rock. . . . Thus the keep was insulated and approachable only by a drawbridge. A round tower on each side of the entrance (which was narrow and irregularly cut in the rock to the south) still remain. From the highest summit the eye commands a most extensive and magnificent view of the distant country. The estuaries of the Dee and Mersey are plainly seen with the town and shipping at Liverpool, the steeple of Wrexham church etc, etc. [I was credibly informed by the landlord of Tarporley of this; the haziness of the weather prevented my ascertaining the fact. I saw plainly the Mersey]. The rich well-wooded plains of Cheshire have also a fine effect. Having made a drawing of the entrance I descended and rode round the base of the hill, hoping to find some striking point of view but was disappointed. . . .

Monday 27th July. I visited the church at Tarporley. . . . After breakfast parted with my friend Sir John Leicester and proceeded on my way to Nantwich etc. Returned half way to Beeston Castle to take a view of it which (as I before observed) has a more picturesque appearance at a distance. . . . the village of Bunbury. The parish church is a handsome large stone building with pinnacles and picturesque projections. The whole is

Gothic but of different aera, one very early. An inscription on a tablet in the church informs us that it was a collegiate church founded 11 Richard II. . . . I met my carriage at the third milestone on the Nantwich road and continued my road to Acton where I stopt to view the church and its monuments, both of which are well worthy of notice. The former is particularly neat both withinside and outside. . . . A short distance from Acton is Nantwich, an old-fashioned dirty town, with saltworks etc, etc. The church is a handsome and picturesque building and would be much more so were it not built of a red stone which assumes a dirty and dismal hue. It contains some monuments worth notice . . . near the altar are four Gothic niches or seats. The choir is handsome with a rich stone groined roof, stalls very richly and well carved in wood. . . . On the front of the singing gallery are the arms of the Earl of Chester in several escutcheons. The architecture of the church is rich Gothic of the middle aera. Close to the church is a curious old school house built with plaister and wood carved, ornamented with escutcheons and other devices. On it is the following inscription [*omitted*] on two tablets which I think worth preserving as I understand the building will shortly be pulled down. . . .

From Nantwich I continued my road to Whitchurch and a road so bad, so heavy, and so sandy I never before travelled. It reminded [*me*] of some of the heavy stages in Westphalia. From Tarporley to Nantwich the road is paved and very good, and though no friend to paved roads I often regretted that this stage was not paved. I sent my saddle horses on meaning to ride through Combermere Park, the seat of Sir Robert Cotton but a violent storm of thunder and ligtning prevented me. There is one of the finest pieces of water there of any in England. Whitchurch . . . is built of brick. At the upper end of the pricipal street on rising ground stands the church, a handsome modern building, lofty and circular. A tablet informs us that the old church fell 31 July 1711, foundation of the new laid 27 March 1712, consecrated 8th October 1713. . . . After dinner proceeded to Hawkstone Inn. The road in many parts heavy but far superior to that from Nantwich.

Hawkstone

Tuesday 28 July. After traversing so many miles of flat, uninteresting country, dirty towns and bad roads and noisy inns the eye rests with pleasure on the well-wooded hills and neat retired inn at Hawkstone. In point of appearance and situation it resembles more the private mansion of a country gentleman than a public hotel for the reception of company. To the worthy and hospitable owner of Hawkstone, Sir Richard Hill, the traveller is indebted for these comforts. Though the natural beauties of this spot have sufficient attractions no one will regret that the conveniences of a good inn have been added. The description of any place where all is pretty and no one particular feature predominates is very difficult, none more so than that of grounds where art has been called into the assistance of nature. My friend

Coxe often complained that Piercefield[37] gave him more trouble than any other part of his *Tour in Monmouthshire*. I find the same difficulty with respect to Hawkstone. I shall therefore endevor only to trace the leading features of the place, adding a few remarks on some of its buildings etc. etc.

Every person who visits these grounds must be sensible that their principal beauty arises from the happy combination of wood, rock and hill, all of which appear the more striking and, I may add, more grand in their proportions as they are placed in flat country without any other similar features in their neighborhood. These hills, which are three, are all varied both in shape and character. The first (the nearest to the inn) is well wooded to its very summit, on which are the ruins of an old castle called Red Castle, which at a distance are seen occasionally peeping through the trees, which begin to encroach rather too much upon it. Its position is wonderfully strong, accessible only on one side and by a steep ascent. The well which has been cleared out presents a most dreadful chasm to the person who looks down into it. In one part the rock has been cut down perpendicularly to an immense height, so as to form a side passage, but there appears to have been no communication by means of it with the castle, unless one should be found under the rubbish which the gardener intends clearing away. The present archway at the upper end of the ascent leading to the summit of the hill is modern.

The next hill is insulated and the grandest object in the grounds. The masses of rock are fine, strongly tinged with verdegrease and in a variety of points of view shew themselves amongst the wood to very great advantage. In this hill is the grotto into which you enter through a long and dark passage, but the first approach to it is through a long and winding chasm in the rocks, which have been very evidently disjointed by some convulsion of nature. At the end of the grotto some yellow painted glass has a good effect on your first emerging out of darkness. In my opinion the effect of this cavern would be much better and more harmonious were the colors of the class confined to yellow only; as the blue, purple and green are discordant and unnatural, whereas the yellow gives the most natural effect of bright sunshine. In another part of this cavern the trick of introducing a figure dressed up as a Druid has not a bad effect. This grotto (like many others) is most unnaturally adorned with shellwork, spar etc. The view from the precipice on the western side of the grotto is very rich and finely varied with views of the distant country, the foreground bold and well-wooded.

The third hill extends considerably in length; its sides are well wooded and slope down in an irregular form to a pretty vale beneath. On this hill is the *terras* and at the highest point is a handsome obelisk erected in 1795, dedicated to the memory of one of his ancestors, Sir Rowland Hill, whose figure is represented at the summit in his Lord Mayor's gown, which office he filled in the year 1549-50. On it is a brass plate commemorated [-*ing*] his good character etc. The obelisk is of a columnar shape with a base built of stone; its summit (which you ascend by numerous but easy steps) commands a most extensive view [Castle Dinas near Llangollen appears very visible through the opening between the mountains. . . .] I have often heard it remarked that from no one spot the eye could see a clear horizon of seven miles; but from this summit you certainly can for the nearest ground is the Wrekin which is above that distance. But *this* is the only place from which I have ever seen it, though from every high ground I have visited I have ever had the above remark in my eye. Near the extremity of this *terras* is another building commanding a fine view but by no means appropiate to the place as an object. There is a very picturesque little glen on this hill with some fine rock scenery in which is an urn with an inscription to the memory of Rowland Hill. In this hill also is a building wherein is the figure of a hermit who moves and speaks. The face is natural enough, the figure stiff and not well managed. The effect would be infinitely better if the door of the building were placed at the angle of the walk and not opposite you. The passenger would then come upon St Francis by surprize, whereas the ringing the bell and door opening into a building quite dark within renders the effect less natural.

As I said before the principal beauty of Hawkstone is derived from these three hills. The rock is in general of a light colored grey and of a good tint, that on Castle Hill excepted which is red. And I have often expressed my dislike to that color being totally void of harmony. Though the buildings are numerous and a motley crew they are not so placed as to offend the eye, except the white tower or rather summer house at the end of the *terras*. The woods are fine, the different sorts of trees well varied, some of the oaks very old and of large dimensions. Underwood and fern. In a walk under the grotto there is a very happy mixture of wood and rock. Here the latter appears very grand on looking up and seeing them frown over your head. From two points the grounds appear to great advantage where you see them in their simple and unadorned state and uninterrupted by any buildings except the old castle: one point is from the head of the water going from the inn to Hawkstone House, the other from the opposite extremity of the valley towards the citadel. I prefer the latter; the center hill and its fine rocks and wood appear to very great advantage as you walk along the vale, as does the fine hanging wood on your right.

The house is old fashioned, of brick and stone, not in any way pictur-esque. The lawn before it is extensive. The water though very repectable in point of size (for it is near two miles in length) bears too many marks of the surveyor's hand.[38] It was planned by Eames, and like most of *his*, indeed all professor's works in that line, deviates widely from the great original they ought to endevor to copy-Nature. As it was said of some avenues at Farnal Place 'Grove nods at grove, each alley has its brother'[39] so you may say truly of Hawkstone 'Bank nods at bank, each winding has its brother', for the convexities of one side correspond regularly with the concavities on the other. And the water is in general so nearly of the same breadth that it has more the appearance of a large canal than a lake. Its effect might be assisted by making plantations in the round, projecting parts and thereby breaking the formality and regularity of the banks.

The walk is long and fatiguing owing to the many ascents. These are rendered more easy by steps cut into the rock. They have too formal an appearance but are absolutely necessary in order to make the walks practicable. The Castle Hill being unconnected with the other two hills may be reserved for the evening's walk. So may the walk along the valley which the gardener does not point out; perhaps because it is simple nature unadorned with buildings. There are a variety of seats of different architecture and shapes. The Otaheite [*Tahitian*] Cottage is one of the prettiest. The spot fixed on for the menagerie is also well chosen.

Wednesday 29 July.   Left Hawkstone and proceeded through Newport to Trotsey Bank. By the following the advice of my landlord and taking a nearer road to Newport I experienced much delay. Passed through Hodnet. [A great deal of buckwheat is sown and ploughed over in the neighborhood; it has a good effect in loosening the soil of stiff lands.]. . . In the evening rode to Boscobel about 1½ miles from the inn to see the royal oak[40] which stands in the middle of the field [in the same field three beasts were killed by lightning on Monday last during the same storm which prevented my visiting Combermere] encompassed with a high wall on which there is a brass plate with this inscription:

> *Quercus Amico Jovi*
> *Felicissimam hanc arborem quam in*
> *Asylum potentissimi Regis Caroli*
> *Deus optimus maximus per quem*
> *Reges regnant hic crescere voluit. . . .*

From hence continued my road for some distance and then turned off to the right to Tong, a retired little village with handsome mansion belonging to Mr Durant, and picturesque little church. [Tong was formerly the property of the Duke of Kingston who sold it to Mr Durant. He took down the old mansion and rebuilt it, though in its domes and turrets its appearance is by no means modern] It is well built of grey stone, battlements and pinnacles. The steeple is an octagon rising from a square base out of which issues a stone spire. On the west side of the church are some trifling remains of an old building said to have been an hospital. Other remains of a nunnery adjoining the church had been taken down by the late proprietor. The architecture is Gothic of the middle aera. I have met with few parish churches so picturesque without and none so interesting to the antiquarian within. . . .

Thursday 30th July.   Proceeded to Lichfield, a long stage of 19 miles, the greater part of it on the scite of the old Roman road, of course in a very direct line. In general flat and good. The evening was devoted to a more minute examination of the cathedral than that I made during my last year's tour.

The character of this cathedral is Gothic, of which it presents many elegant examples, particular[ly] in its west front and in the north and south doorways. The western front is the most striking part of this building; a wide open area before it enables you to view its several parts to advantage. It is ornamented with many statues, blank arches etc. The doorway is singularly elegant, particularly the inner one. The arches of both are supported on figures in the form of caretides [*caryatids*] (I do not recollect at present having met with a similar example) and richly decorated with other light Gothic devices: foliage, figures etc. etc. The north door is very rich with five retiring circles. . . . The south door is in the same style but less rich than the northern. . . . The interior has a very neat and clean appearance and has undergone both alterations and repairs under the direction of the modern Gothic architect and innovator, Mr Wyatt *(Note on the Present Mode of Altering the old Gothic Cathedrals and Churches).* The lower row of arches which separate the nave and side aisles are narrow Gothic supported on columns with capitals of foliage. . . . The windows in the transepts are of a different aera, some broad Gothic, others more modern. The skreen which divides the choir from the nave is a patchwork of old and modern Gothic, some of it very rich and beautiful removed from the Lady's chapel. . . . The choir which in its original state was rather narrow has been rendered still more disproportionate by removing the skreen which separated the Lady's chapel and the choir. At the end is the whole length figure of Christ by Egginton (in painted glass) similar in effect and design to that at Salisbury. One evident and very striking error here occurs in the stalls which are of Graecian architecture. . . . The chapter house is an elegant building. Its approach through a winding passage is similar to that at York. The columns are detached from the wall so as to form a narrow arcade between them and the wall. Handsome entrance door, *bas relief* between the lancet doors. The sides of the chapter house are ornamented with blank Gothic arches pointed at top, trefoils within. The roof (as usual in similar buildings) is supported by a clustered column with a capital of foliage. The doorway leading out of the left side aisle has the Saxon zig-zag ornament.

Friday 31st July.   Dined and slept at Birmingham.

Saturday 1st August.   Went to Hagley.

VIII

Journal of a Tour in 1802.

On *Sunday 25th April* I left Stourhead, slept at Bath and remained there till

Wednesday 28th, when, in company with my friend Mr Coxe we pursued our route first to Devizes and then to Beckhampton where we dined and slept. The church nearest the old castle at Devizes (I think St Mary's) is remarkable for a very fine tower of Saxon architecture in good preservation. Within. . . . Our object in going to Beckhampton was to examine the Druidical remains at Abury [*Avebury*] and other interesting pieces of antiquity.[1] We found but indifferent accomodations at the inn.

Before dinner we ascended Silbury Hill which may be called the King of Barrows, as it is far superior in size to any existing in our island. Its original destination is rather uncertain. Some antiquarians have supposed it to have been a tumulus erected to the memory of some great prince and Stukeley mentions human bones having been found within it. Others think that it may have been an altar, a consecrated mount or a place of religious worship connected with the Druidical temple at Abury. Whatever its purport may have been it is certainly a very singular object as well as a wonderful effort of human art.

In the evening we walked to Abury distant about a mile from our inn. This temple may boast a much earlier existence as well as a much larger extent than Stonehenge. In the latter the stones were evidently shapen into a regular form by the tool, as the signs of the chisel are very apparent in the stones of the great trilithon which fell a few years ago.[2] In the former the stones are erected in their natural state, rude and unshapen, as they came from their native quarry. Had not the original plan of this immense building been fortunately preserved by Stukeley[3] modern antiquarians, I fear, would have found it impossible to have traced it, particularly the most singular part of it, viz the majestic avenues, the Snake's head etc, etc reduced at present to a few scattered stones. Neither is the interior part of the temple in a much better condition, and a few years probably will annihilate all traces of this wonderful structure except the high circular mound of earth that surrounds it. The country being destitute of natural quarries these stones have been beaten to pieces to supply the want of others, every wall bearing witness to the destruction of the adjacent temples.

The parish church deserves some attention. On the southern side of it is a very perfect Saxon doorway decorated with the zig-zag orament. Within are four Saxon arches . . . a most curious and ancient Saxon font. . . . Over the entrance to the chancel is a beautiful Gothic roof loft painted and gilt. This fine fragment of antiquity till lately had been covered over with lath and plaister. . . .

Thursday 29th.   The greater part of the morning was employed in tracing the Roman road which led from Bath to Silchester of which these were the stations: 1) *Verlucio* XV; 2) *Cunetio* XX; 3) *Spinis* XV, Sheene or Sheenham-land; 4) *Caliva.* Only one of these stations has been completely ascertained. . . .[4] About half a mile from Beckhampton the present turnpike traverses the old Roman road which took a straight direction to Silbury Hill. From the above spot we followed it in the line leading towards Bath. It ascends the down in a direct line and the holes from whence materials were drawn to raise the causeway are still visible on its sides . . . its line is not quite straight but makes a gentle curve [Our friend Mr Leman,[5] so well skilled in the antiquities and formation of the Roman roads, observes that that nation never varied from the straight line without some apparent reason, but here certainly none exists as the ground would have admitted of a straight line equally with a curve]. Leaving Oldborough Castle on the right it ascends another hill. Here you will see a hedge planted on its ridge. It continues its track on the northern edge of Roundway Hill, vulgarly called Morgan's Hill from the name of a person hanged on its summit. . . . At Calston limekilns we lost it for a moment but were soon convinced that it took another bend to the right. Following the steep edge of the hill it joined the deep foss called Wansdyke. . . .

Wansdyke is supposed to have been a boundary between some of the ancient nations who inhabited Britain. It is an immense ditch with high banks on each side. Its course is as irregular and curved as that of the Roman roads is in general direct and straight, by which we may fairly conclude that whenever the Wansdyke assumes a straight line (as mentioned above) it has made use of the Roman road and follows its track; and therefore that Wansdyke was a work subsequent to the time of the Romans.

After dinner we continued our researches after the Roman road which is supposed to have passed near Marlborough. I before mentioned that we saw evident traces of it pointing directly towards Silbury Hill. Stukeley and antiquarians agree that it passed on the south close to the above hill. It then probably continued nearly the same track as the present turnpike road. A little beyond the village of Kennett we again saw evident remains of it on a piece of maiden down, to the left of the turnpike on which are several barrows. . . .

Friday 30th April.   Marlborough. The church of St Mary's has a rich Saxon doorway to the west, the only part of the building not consumed by a fire which destroyed the rest of the church. . . . After breakfast continued my journey to Swindon. . . . Leave the downy country, pass Birdlip Park on the right, country more enclosed. Swindon: a neat little town. Church pleasantly situated on an eminence; I could discover no traces of antiquity except in two busts from which the arch of the chancel sprung. . . . Through

Cricklade to Cirencester, 16 miles. Enter the Foss Road between Swindon and Cricklade, a little way before you reach a public house called Cold Harbour on the right of the road (In many of the Roman roads places still retain the name of Cold Harbour. .). . . I continued on the Foss Road [*Way*] as far as Birdlip Hill where I left it for Cheltenham. In no place have I seen the Roman roads so perfect as about Cirencester. Dined at Cirencester and reached Cheltenham in the evening. Lodged at Mrs Hales, Somerset Place, a single house and excellent lodgings, 3-13-6 p. week.

During my stay of three weeks there I made occasional excursions to Tewkesbury and Gloucester. The former was described in my tour of last year [*p. 164*]; of the latter I shall now give a brief description. This cathedral presents a mixture of Saxon and Gothic architecture. All the arches in the nave are Saxon except the two first at the western entrance. . . . Our Lady's Chapel, and the other smaller chapels, and most particularly the cloysters afford beautiful specimens of rich Gothic architecture in their fretted roofs and cielings. I have seen no cloysters so beautiful and in so fine a state of preservation. Those in Westminster Abbey would perhaps vie with these in elegance were not they shamefully converted into repositories for wood, coal and every kind of rubbish. This cathedral contains many curious and well-preserved monuments some of which boast of high antiquity. The shrine and tomb with the effigy of King Edward the Second is of superior excellence and elegance. . . . Like many other of our fine Gothic buildings this is sadly disfigured by a skreen and two altars, a barbarous mixture of Italian and Gothic architecture. . . .

Till within a few days of my departure from Cheltenham the weather had been unusually cold. We had continual frosts and falls of hail and even snow. All the French beans, potatoes and young shoots of ash and oak trees were cut off, and the apples and pears much injured.

I left Cheltenham on

Saturday 22nd May. Proceeded through Tewkesbury to Upton on the Severn, 17 miles (road flat). From thence to the village of Little Malvern . . . descended to Ledbury, an old-fashioned looking town in Herefordshire. Feathers Inn — middling. XI miles. The parish church is a large and spacious building. The belfry with a lofty stone steeple is detached from the church. [lofty stone steeples prevail much in this county] The churchyard is well-shaded by some lofty elms and lime trees. The western front has a picturesque appearance. The doorway is Saxon. . . . Adjoining the northern transept is St Catharine's Chapel with richly ornamented Gothic windows. . . . After dinner we proceeded to Hereford, 17 miles, road good and flat, country finely wooded, corn and pastures. Some hop grounds and numerous orchards, many of which were cultivated with corn. New Inn (Green), good.

Sunday 23rd May. After breakfast accompanied by Mr Watten, an inhabitant of the city and well versed in the history and antiquities of the county, we made an excursion on horseback. The gate leading out of the town from the same street in which I lodged had been pulled down since my last visit to Hereford. A little way without it on the right is Coningesbye Hospital and adjoining are the ruins of the Grey Friars, the most interesting part of which is a pretty little Gothic oratory atanding in the middle of a farmyard. At first we followed the turnpike road leading from Hereford to Leominster . . . to the Roman station at Kenchester. This is supposed to have been the *Magna*[6] mentioned in the *Itineraries*. . . . Within there are several foundations of buildings and one small arch of stone and brick intermixed which from its structure evidently proves it to be Roman. . . . I was much disappointed in not seeing a Roman altar at Hereford which had been found at Kenchester but lately destroyed. . . . We deviated a little on the left from our direct track to Hereford in order to see the farm and stock of Mr S. Tulley, famous for having the finest breed of cattle in Herefordshire. Like the North Devon breed these cattle possess the good quality of keeping themselves always in good condition and of fattening quickly. Of course they are not capital milksters. They are generally bright red with white heads. Westcar, the celebrated grazier in the Vale of Aylesbury, has for some years past gained the annual prizes at Smithfield with oxen of Tulley's breed. . . .

Monday 24th May.   Before breakfast we examined the cathedral. The most picturesque parts of it in point of architecture are an elegant Gothic porch, which serves as the northern entrance to the church, the east end with the Audley chapel projecting. . . . The tower is square and massive with rich Gothic [*ornament*]. Wants pinnacle to lighten it. The west end is beneath criticism, the work of the modern Goth, Wyatt, who in his endevors to restore and improve has destroyed the beauty of many of our most interesting Gothic buildings.
     Interior of Hereford Cathedral. Seven Saxon arches support the roof but on one side (viz the south) the arch nearest the choir is Gothic, and the two first arches on each side of the western entrance are modern Saxon. Four of the Saxon capitals on each side are uniform, the others very richly ornamented. . . . There is a beautiful specimen of this Saxon architecture on each side of the altar. . . . The Saxon architecture in the southern aisle appears of very ancient date. . . . The Ladies Chapel: early and rich Gothic with elegant clustered columns, now used as a library by which the general beauty and effect of the building is much injured. . . . On the opposite side is the Audley Chapel, a precious morsel of Gothic antiquity with a richly fretted roof, painted and gilt. . . . The northern transept which is of rich old Gothic architecture is converted into a parish church. It contains the ancient and curious shrine of Bishop Cantelupe enriched with *bas reliefs* etc. On the southern side of the church are some picturesque remains of a rich Gothic cloyster. . . .

Monday 24 May.   After breakfast left Hereford and proceeded towards Kington. Turned off to the right to pay a visit to Mr Price[7] at Foxley, who accompanied me round a large part of his grounds, which are highly gratifying to the lover of picturesque scenery. The house is of brick, old and indifferent in every respect. The form of the grounds resembles a horseshoe, the outside lines being a ridge or terrace commanding a most rich and extensive view of the distant country [*sketch*]. The highest eminence bears the name of Lady's Liff and exceeds all the others in point of prospect. The declivities on each side are cloathed with very fine wood through which the distant prospect often introduces itself with a very happy effect. In the center of the horseshoe is a valley, partly cultivated, and on one side of it stands the house, the approach to which is through an extensive and irregular lawn. The chief beauty of Foxley consists in the irregularity of its hills and woods, the variety in which the different sorts of trees are grouped and the extensive views it commands from the high grounds.

The road to Kington is good and in general flat. We found a remarkably clean inn at the King's Head. In the evening walked to the church. . . .

Tuesday 25th May. The object of this Summer's tour is to follow the interesting and highly curious *Itinerary* of Giraldus Cambrensis through North and South Wales in the year 1188 and to make a collection of drawings to illustrate it.[8] The first place he mentions is Radnor, most probably Old Radnor. This morning I rode first to New Radnor about six miles distant from Kington on the road to Rhaiader. Passed through a pretty valley; country begins to assume a mountainous appearance; hills rocky in parts and well-wooded. . . . New Radnor is situated at the foot of a hill. It was formerly surrounded on three sides by walls and guarded on the fourth, viz the north, by a castle built in a strong situation on an eminence. The line of the walls is still visible and from their regular and square form bear much the appearance of Roman art, but I have never heard of a Roman station in this part of the country, nor are there any signs of bricks in the walls or buildings. . . .

Leaving New Radnor I turned off to the right and ascended to Old Radnor whose church stands on the rocky summit of a high hill with a few shabby houses near it. I was informed that the parish was however very extensive. It has probably seen better days for the church is large and very well built of stone, and I make no doubt was the place visited by the archbishop and Giraldus. . . . There is some very beautiful carved wood-work of foliage, grapes etc, painted, with Gothic canopies, rich frieze etc which extends entirely across the church, viz the nave and side aisles, and a curious carved pulpit or singing desk. . . . Leaving Old Radnor I descended by some limekilns to the pretty little retired village of Gladestry, situated in a bottom surrounded by hills. I then turned off to the left to the small village of Huntingdon where there are trifling remains of an old castle . . . I am inclined to think . . . it was the *Crukeri Castrum* mentioned by Giraldus. . . . After dinner continued our journey to Hay, 14 miles (Swan Inn). . . . Hay appears to very great advantage as you approach it, situated on the side of a hill with distant mountains above it. Inn good.

Wednesday 26 May.   Remained at Hay, an irregular, ill-paved town with narrow streets built on uneven ground. On the summit stood a castle some remains of which are extant, particularly the Gothic gateway with its portcullis and part of its ancient walls to which an old-fashioned house is annexed. Between the church and Swan Inn there is a high tumulus where probably there stood a castle of more ancient date than the one before-mentioned. The church stands in a beautiful situation and is surrounded with a variety of Scotch fir, beech, ash etc. which add to its retired and picturesque appearance. . . . A long wooden bridge with no piers and arches of stone separates the counties of Radnor and Brecknock. The church contains no monuments worthy of notice. . . . A great part of the old walls still is visible on the northern side of the town. In the evening I rode to Clifford Castle about two miles distant from Hay and situated on an abrupt precipice hanging over the Wye. . . .

Thursday 27 May.   After breakfast continued our route to Bualt [*Builth Wells*] (20 miles). Followed the Brecknock Road for upwards of four miles and then turned off to the right. . . . On approaching Buallt cultivation increases and the vale widens. Inn at Buallt — King's Head, indifferent. Bualt is an irregular built town on the declivities of a hill. Houses in general old, some better in the suburbs. The scite of its ancient castle remains and a few foundations of the walls. A handsome stone bridge of six arches over the Wye. Church a simple structure, nothing antique about it.

Friday 28 May.   After breakfast we mounted our horses and proceeded first for a few miles on the Llandovery road to a place called Keven y bedd [*Cefn y bedd*], a little farmhouse on the right and adjoining the road near which place is a dingle called Cwm Llewellyn [These places become interesting to the traveller by being intimately connected with the history of Wales: 'Prince Llewelyn tired with continual action with a few men privately separated himself from his army in Cardigan . . . he was killed by Adam Francton who, not till he had returned to plunder his dead, knew that Llewelyn had fallen his victim. His head was cut off and sent to King Edward at Conway who ordered it to be placed on the highest pinnacle of the Tower of London. Thus fell in the year 1282 the last Prince of British blood']. . . . We continued over a rough and stony road for eight miles along the Vale of the Wye, the river being constantly in sight on the left hand. It still retains a broad channel and flows in a rocky bed. On approaching Rhayader there are some fine woods on the opposite banks of the river and some pretty scenery. A new road is making, a very necessary accomodation for those who may wish to see this tract of country in a carriage. We found very decent accomodation at the Red Lion Inn and very civil treatment. The landlord, Richard Evans, is an intelligent man.

   Rhaiader. A small market town in Radnorshire on the banks of the Wye which here begins to contract its channel, and a little below the bridge (which consists of one bold arch) forms a cataract from which circumstance the place derives its name. . . . The scite of an old castle belonging to Prince Rhys still remains on a strong position a little above the bridge, where a deep fosse as been made to strengthen its position by cutting through the rock. Several barrows are also extant in the neighborhood of the castle. . . .⁹

Saturday 29th May. After breakfast I followed my author Giraldus to St Harmons, a little village in a dreary plain, surrounded by mountains, about three or four miles from Rhaiader on the direct road to Llanidloes. This church was formerly dedicated to St Germanus. After an early dinner we mounted our horses and accompanied by our landlord varied our route home by Llandrindod Wells which are situated about halfway between Rhayader and Bualt. . . . A large house was open for the accomodation of company on the plan of Harrogate, Matlock etc, but not answering the expectations of the owner and the place being of late little frequented it has been converted into a farmhouse. The rain which commenced yesterday afternoon now poured down upon us in torrents and prevented our visiting the principal object of my curiosity and which induced me to take this track home to Bualt: a Roman camp or station on the River Ithon [*Castell Collen*] wich lies on an estate belonging to Mr Williams and not far distant from the Wells. . . .

Sunday 30th May. Proceeded to Brecknock, long and steep ascent, road good. . . .

Monday 31 May. A heavy rain having fallen in the night the whole of this day was devoted to view the different churches and other antiquities of Brecknock. The priory which stands on high ground at the upper extremity of the town was originally founded by Bernard de Neumarch, the Norman who about the year 1090 gained the lordship of Brecknock and nearly at the sametime [*as*] Robert Fitzhamon obtained the Lordship of Glamorgan. It bears many marks of antiquity, but its architecture (which is entirely Gothic) from the different reparations it has undergone is of course much varied. The choir, however, is uniform: of the early Gothic with lancet windows . . . adjoining to the south aisle were the cloysters, taken down fifteen years ago. . . . In the body of the church on the left side are some seats, belonging formerly to some companies in the town. Over each seat the tools and implements characteristic of their employment are carved in *bas relief*. This venerable old church is in a very dilapidated state and the pavement sadly disfigured by the horrid custom of burying corpses and digging graves within it. The Priory walls also are much more neglected than they were in former years.

At the opposite extremity of the town and on the other side of the River Uske is an ancient building, first a convent of Dominican or Black Friars, and afterwards in the time of Henry VIII converted into a college. The choir of the original church remains and entire parts of some of the detached buildings, the outside walls of the nave etc, etc. Occasional service is per-

30. Brecon Priory from the north-east, not then of cathedral status.

formed in it. . . . There are still some remains of the old castle, a part of which bears the name of Ely Tower, from Dr Marten, Bishop of Ely, confined there by order of Richard III. . . . The other church in the center of the town is a large building with a lofty tower, but contains no marks of antiquity but a few heavy Saxon columns with rude capitals.

The situation of Brecknock is admirably calculated to produce a picturesque effect in landscape, abounding with remains of ancient buildings and having the advantage of two rivers on which are many bridges and mills etc. The distant scenery of the mountains is also truly grand; I know of none which produce a finer outline than the Brecknock Van or Beacon to the south of the town. The views on the little Honddy [*Honddu*] surpass those on the Uske: the course is winding and on approaching the town by its rapid descents forms a variety of waterfalls. Between the Priory and its confluence with the Uske it has no less than three bridges over it, all of which are highly picturesque, particularly the high one leading to the castle, and the other near the mill at the confluence of the two rivers. In short Brecknock is a place made for the artist and landscape painter where he will find a wonderful variety of fine and rich subjects for his pencil.

The accomodations of even the reputed best inn (and the only one where post-horses are kept), the Golden Lion, are very indifferent, the beds excepted which are good. During a residence of five days here I made several excursions. In tracing the footsteps of my leader, Giraldus, I visited the church of Llhanhamlach situated near the Uske, exactly three miles from Brecknock. . . . I found it in a very picturesque state for the pencil and a modern ruin, the roof of the nave and side aisles having been stript for the purpose of rebuilding. . . . I made another excursion to Trecastle Xl miles from Brecon on the great road leading into Carmarthenshire in order to visit the church of Luel [*Llywel*] mentioned by Giraldus. . . . At Trecastle the tumulus and scite remain of an ancient castle, and the Black Mountains of Carmarthenshire form a bold outline. Dined at Trecastle and returned in a heavy rain to Brecon. I visited also the little church of Landu [*Llanddew*] mentioned by my author. Followed the Hay road to the first turnpike and then turned off to the left. There are the remains of a large castle contiguous to the church. . . .

Friday 4th June.   After breakfast we left Brecknock and proceeded on our route to Abergavenny. I stopt at Crickhowel to see its church and dined with a fine old veteran tar, Admiral Gell,[10] who has lately built a pretty villa on the banks of the Uske. The Vale of the Uske through which we passed stands unrivalled for its beautiful and happy mixture of wild and cultivated nature, which it presents to the admiring and astonished eyes for the distance of about thirty miles, viz from Trecastle to Abergavenny. The woods and mountains are finely intermixed with the cultivated grounds, and the numerous cottages and churches, scattered over the whole face of the country (and which in general are whitened) add much to the general gayety of the scenery. I am inclined to think the Roman road followed nearly the same track as the present turnpike to Abergavenny, the *Gobannium* of the ancients. In many places the road is evidently much raised . . . the old stone with the inscription of *Victorini* on it, as mentioned by Camden, still maintains its position in a wall by the right hand side of the road between miles IV and V from Brecon. . . .[11]

Few villages are more delightfully situated than Crickhowel. I reviewed with pleasure the spot where in the year 1793 I had spent so many pleasant days. My ardor for monumental antiquities had not then begun, nor had I ever seen the inside of the parish church which contains food for the artist and antiquarian. The church contains a magnificent marble monument to the memory of Sir John Herbert, Knight, and his lady, 1666. . . . In the evening I rode to Abergavenny. . . .

Saturday 5th June.   There are three objects at Abergavenny which deserve the attention of the traveller who visits it: its fine situation, the castle and church. Few places are more pleasantly situated near the banks of a fine river and surrounded by three magnificent mountains, grand and diversified in their shapes: the Sugar Loaf, Skyrid and Blorenche, of which my friend Coxe has given a very just and animated description in his *Historical Tour of Monmouthshire*. [One of the old city gates remains and is called Tudor Gate] The castle is more deserving of notice on account of the fine view which its terrace commands than for its ruins which are not particularly striking. . . . The church, a handsome Gothic edifice, is very rich in monumental stone. Indeed few parish churches can surpass it either for the number or richness of its sepulchral effigies. Those of the Herbert family are very costly in their decorations, and good execution, in alabaster. These have been minutely described by my friend Coxe. The church has lately undergone considerable repairs and unfortunately in the general whitewash some of the old effigies have not excaped the brush. In the evening I adjourned to my brother's[12] at LlanStfrede [*Llansanffraed*].

Monday 7th June.   Rode to Ragland [*Raglan*] to see the ruins of its ancient castle, which for its grand entrance between two fine machicolated towers may vie with any in the principality. I cannot but regret whenever I view this grand relict of baronial magnificence that it has been so long neglected and uninhabited. And every lover of fine architecture must also regret that one of the noble entrance towers is so completely covered with ivy as to leave no trace whatever of its architecture. However picturesque ivy may be in its general appearance it is here overloaded.

Wednesday 9th June.   Left Llansanfrede and proceeded through Uske and Caerleon to Newport where we found the new bridge, and inn, completed, both of which in my last tour through Monmouthshire were in an unfinished state. I fancied that I could discover traces of a Roman road between Uske and Caerleon; a great part of the present turnpike runs upon a high causeway. . . . [I have been since informed by Mr Evans at Newport that the

31. Cardiff Castle, the south west corner, after some restoration by first Marquess of Bute but before massive reconstruction by the third Marquess and Burges.

Roman road ran on the other side of the Uske — through the valley].
Newport: a dirty, ill-paved town with the remains of a large castle immediately on the banks of the river, but by no means picturesque. Ascend
through an irregular street to the parish church of St Wollos where there are
some curious examples of Saxon architecture, fully described by Mr Coxe in
his *Tour*. Drank tea with Mr Evans.[13]

Thursday 10th June.   From Newport to Cardiff 12 miles. A fine view of the
Severn with the embouchure of the Uske, the Somersetshire coast (nearly
opposite Bridgwater), the Steep and Flat Holms etc, rich plain on the left.
Cross the River Rumney and enter Glamorganshire. Three miles from
Newport the turnpike road intersects Tredegar Park, the seat of Sir Charles
Morgan. Cardiff Arms — good inn.

Friday 11th June.   Rode to Llandaff, between two and three miles distant
from Cardiff, and on the other side of the River Taff. A poor village though
the seat of a bishop. The greater part of its ancient cathedral is in ruins and
presents a picturesque appearance. In this building the early Gothic architecture prevails. The western front is decorated with lancet windows of
various height[s] and dimensions. Over the entrance door is the figure of a
bishop holding up one hand in the act of benediction and in the other his
pastoral staff. Higher up and near the top of the facade is another figure
sitting, holding up one hand and in the other a book. On the north and
south sides are two Saxon doorways, the former very rich and well executed.
On entering by the western door the nave and two side aisles appear in
ruins. Three Gothic arches on each side. By a fragment now left we see that
the upper story was formed of one wide lancet between two narrower
windows. The columns are taper[ed] and clustered with their capitals
diversified and very neatly carved; some of them resemble the foliage of the
Corynthian and Composite orders. Many of the small heads with which the
ribs of the arches etc terminate are full of expression. Indeed I have seldom
seen neater and sharper workmanship than in many parts of the building.
Thus far the ruin is uniform in its character. The remainder of the building
which composes the modern cathedral now in use is beneath criticism. An
Italian building rears itself within the walls of the Gothic shell: nothing can
be more discordant or ridiculous. . . .
    Cardiff or the city on the Taff, large and neat, and rendered more
interesting to the inquisitive traveller by the remains of British antiquity
which it contains. The city was reserved by Robert Fitzhamon, the
Norman, as his own portion, after his conquest of the county of Glamorgan
in 1091. There he resided and held his several courts of justice. At that time
it was also strongly fortified to guard it against the attacks of the neighboring
lords. A large extent of the ancient walls still remains, and the southern gate.
Of the castle buildings the keep, elevated on a high mound, and the Black
Tower (in which according to vulgar tradition the unfortunate Robert, Duke
of Normandy, ended his days after twenty-six years imprisonment) still

retain marks of antiquity, but the main body of the castle has been so modernised and thickly beset with sash windows that little of its ancient character can be perceived. The grand octagon tower on the western side may still give some idea of this ancient structure. The modern reparations were made by Lord Mountstewart[14] who intended it as a residence but premature death prevented him accomplishing his designs; it remains in an unfinished state. Three rooms contain some family portraits [*20 portraits described*]. . . The area of the castle yard is formed into a shrubbery and pleasant gravel walks. The keep is a low polygon building from which another higher and of the same form projects. On the N. East of the town are the ruins of the convent of Grey Friars, of no great antiquity in point of architecture, the windows being similar to those used in the time of Queen Elizabeth.

Saturday 12th June. Left Cardiff; passed through Cowbridge, a town consisting of one long street; and stopt at Pyle. A magnificent inn built some years ago by Mr Talbot of Margam. Nothing particularly interesting in this tract of road except some occasional fine views of the Severn and Somersetshire coast. . . . Numerous villages and houses whitewashed [The cheapness of lime enables the meanest cottager to wash the face of his habitation continually, if not annually] dispersed over the whole face of the country greatly enliven the landscape, which is in general in want of trees. . . .

I quitted my chaise at Ewenny bridge, 6 miles from Pile, to visit the remains of Ewenny Priory,[15] distant about half a mile from the little inn at the foot of the bridge. According to Leland it was founded for Benedictine monks and dedicated to St Michael by John de Londres, Lord of Ogmore, but here I think the antiquarian is wrong as in Powel's pedigree of the Londres family I do not see the name of John, and I was fortunate enough to ascertain the real founder. . . . The different gateways, turrets, embattled walls which surround the church nearly on three sides give it the appearance rather of a fortress than a place designed for religious purposes. It is situated on a marshy plain near the banks of the little River Ewenny which abounds with trout and whose waters never fail. Its outside is massive and adapted to the style of architecture which the interior presents. This is wholly Saxon and one of the most ancient, complete and interesting specimens of that order which I ever beheld. The only Gothic work I could see was the wooden skreen separating the choir from the transepts.

To me this building had double charms, as I could fancy it had existed nearly in its present state at the time when Giraldus travelled through Wales and had not undergone any architectural innovation. Few such specimens of ancient art now remain; the love of innovation and the bad taste, or perhaps I might better say ignorance of the most intelligent of our architects have robbed many of our churches and cathedrals of their original beauties. During my various excursions it has been my misfortune to witness the many absurdities which have been committed in the modern repairs of our cathedrals and which is now called *beautifying*. It is singular that architects having the finest example of pure Saxon and Gothic architecture dispersed throughout the kingdom from which they might improve, or rather form their taste, should put all rules at defiance and produce such a motley, unmeaning farrago of architecture as I have seen frequently collected in the modern productions of their art.

If I may judge from the present state of this church I should think it had remained *talis qualis* since the days of its foundation. I before said that its foundation had been attributed by Leland to John de Londres but the monument of the real founder still extists in the choir. Mr Wyndham has noticed it in his *Tour* as being erected to the memory of Maurice de Londres but he failed in decyphering it completely. . . . The choir deserves particular attention from its Saxon roof of stone, groined and ribbed. . . . A large old mansion house (which has seen better days) adjoins the church and is still in a more ruinous condition than the Norman sanctuary. Two gateways to the east and west remain perfect, besides a high embattled wall which, as I said before, nearly surrounds the church which is open only to the north.

Sunday 13th June. The morning was fully employed in riding to Bridgend, Coity and in revisiting Ewenny Priory . . . we directed our course northerly in order to see Coity, a small village situated about 2½ miles NE of Bridgend. The Lordship of Coity was granted by Robert Fitzhamon to Sir Paine Turbeville whose family or name exists still in the possession of Ewenny Priory etc, etc. The remains of the castle are still very considerable though their forms are not at all picturesque. A gatehouse towards the east remains entire. The walls on this side were defended by a deep fosse. The castle was placed on rising, though not high, ground, and its present remains bespeak its ancient strength and grandeur. . . . My second visit to the Priory was attended with success for I then decyphered the two old inscriptions which I believe till now have never been clearly understood. Returned to dinner at Pyle. . . .

After dinner we walked to the little village of Kynfeg [*Kenfig*] [*a little*] above a mile distant from Pyle. The church is on an eminence overlooking a large stagnant lake and beyond it the sea coast. Between these two and near the church I saw the remains of an encampment. Robert Fitzhamon reserved the castle of Cardiff and Kenfigg for himself when he had conquered the County of Glamorgan. A small fragment of a stone wall in which is one arch, seated on an artificial mound to the west of the church in the midst of numerous hillocks of barren sand and a rabbit warren are now the sorry remains of this ancient castle. . . .[16]

The landlord at Pyle is an intelligent farmer and first introduced the culture of turnips into this country. He has tried a variety of instruments and finds the Rotheram plough, made strong, answers best.

Monday 14th June. In my way to Neath I visited Margam, three miles from Pyle. Near the roadside on the right is an old cross with an inscription on it but illegible. It serves as a sort [*of*] bridge over a little rivulet [*sketch*].

In the village street is the top and pedestal of another cross in a better state of preservation and richly decorated with fretwork etc.[17] The parish church is in exterior as curious a specimen of Norman architecture as that of Ewenny is in the interior. I allude particularly to the western front which appears to me the most perfect Norman façade I have yet seen.[18] The arches in the nave are lofty, circular and supported on pilasters. The windows in the left aisle are small and circular. On the south side of the choir is a chapel rich in sepulchral memorials of the Mansell family but so crowded together that their good effect is somewhat diminished. The features in general are well preserved and the execution good. . . .

Quitting the church I repaired to the ruins of the abbey but the mortification I was destined to feel on viewing this once celebrated monastery had been anticipated by a friend, who had informed me of the sad change it had undergone since I had last seen it. That *chef d'oeuvre* of elegant Gothic architecture is now, alas, no more, and every passing traveller will weep over its sad relicts, especially those who have had the good fortune to have seen it in its days of perfection. Its memory however will survive in the description, and accurate view of it by Grimm, given by Mr Wyndham in his *Tour through Wales*. Some years afterwards I also witnessed its perfect beauties; in the year 1793 its dissolution had commenced, but even then, with a little care and trifling expence it might have been saved from the ruin which daily impended over it [*p. 55*]. Two of the arches had only then fallen; the central column which supported the roof still stood firm, and the remaining groins and arches would have been a sure and easy guide to any workman who might have undertaken its reparation. But that happy moment passed by; the central column gave way and with it the whole roof fell in, so that nothing but the shell or skeleton of this unique *morceau* now remains. How often has the possession of this beautiful ruin been envied? And how little care would have preserved it for many more centuries in its original state of perfection? Hundreds and perhaps thousands have been spent in the same ground in conservatories and greenhouses and this interesting relict has been suffered to perish.

This Cistercian abbey is said to have been founded by Robert, Earl of Gloucester A.D 1147. It was granted 32 Henry 8 to Sir Rice Mansell and is now the property of Mansel Talbot Esq of Penrice. From the superior elegance of this Gothic architecture it well deserved the epithet of *nobile monasterium* given to it by Giraldus. The outside shell of the chapter house overhung with ivy and other plants (to which I fear its present roofless state may in great measure be attributed) still presents a very picturesque subject to the artist. Its situation is beautiful, at the foot almost of the finest hanging, precipitous wood imaginable. [The hanging wood beneath Dynevor Castle, Carmarthenshire and one at Ilam in Derbyshire are the only woods which can vye with this at Margam (at least of those I have seen in my travels).] Several gravestones have been lately discovered when removing rubbish from the chapter house; they were ornamented with very simple crosses and bore no inscriptions. The church certainly is of a much more early aera than the abbey, and was built probably by one of the Norman knights who settled in Glamorganshire after the conquest by Fitzhamon, but I see no notice taken of it in Powell's *History of Wales*.

In addition to the noble greenhouse of 327 feet in length, including a room at each end, in which are several busts, statues, vases etc, etc, a fine picture by P. Veronese, still left unarranged, a noble conservatory has been lately built, where the orange and lemon trees are trained against the wall on a *treillage* and their fruit thereby very much forwarded.[19] These trees have been sadly diminished in size and beauty since I first saw them. . . .

Continued my journey to Neath. . . . The appearance of the country mends towards Breton [*Briton*] Ferry, whose scenery has often been mentioned and admired by travellers. The only desideratum is a permanent, in lieu of a tide, river. Descending towards Neath this town appears to great advantage, seated in an extensive vale and surrounded by well-wooded hills and mountains, whose shapes are well broken. . . . Neath is a populous and commercial town, surrounded with iron, copper, tin and coal works, and having the advantage of a canal and navigable river.

Tuesday 15th June.   The morning was employed in examining and making drawings of the abbey at Neath, situated about a mile westward of the town on the road leading to Swansey and Carmarthen. [The remains of the castle, consisting of a gateway between two round towers, stand nearly in the center of the town and afford no good subject for the pencil]. . . . The ruins cover a large tract of ground and the ichonography of the church may be easily made out.[20] Adjoining is the shell, nearly entire, of a very spacious building, probably the abbot's house, the upper part in ruins. The ground floor is converted into habitations for colliers, miners etc, and surely a set of more miserable dwellings or more dirty inhabitants were never seen. The dingey and sombre appearance of these ruins (caused by the neighboring copper and iron works) at first sight prejudiced me much against them, but on closer inspection I found a good subject for my pencil in each separate front. In a field near the roadside called Court Herbert is an upright stone placed at the head of an old effigy, removed from the adjoining abbey. It represents the figure of an abbot holding the model of a church in his hands, designed perhaps to represent the person who built or repaired the abbey. Two angels supported a canopy or cushion at his head. The sculpture is good for the time it was executed. . . .

Wednesday 16th June.   From Neath to Swansey 9 miles. . . . 4 miles from Swansey is Morris Town, created by a gentleman of that name. Continual works, furnaces etc in the vale till you reach Swansey. We found a good inn at the Ivy Bush and a charming dining room, large and lofty, looking out to sea. Swansey: a populous busy town. Some good houses, particularly in the suburbs, and streets wider than in the generality of Welsh towns. The bathing however is not good, being only practicable at high water or ebb, the shore being muddy and the sea retiring a very considerable distance from it. There is a public lodging house with bathing machines half a mile from the town, and one nearer. Swansey however can never be looked upon as a good place for sea bathing, both on account of the muddy shore and want of other conveniences. A handsome pier is now building projecting far into the sea, and at high water the number of vessels going in and out of the river produce a very lively scene. The old castle (made use of as a prison) stands so pent up in the middle of the town that a stranger might visit Swansey and not even see it. It cannot therefore be considered as a picturesque object. Its parapets resemble those at Saint Davids and Lantphey Court.[21] The parish church is a mixture of modern and ancient architecture; the nave is of the former description, the chancel of the latter. It contains some interesting monuments. . . .

Friday 18 June. Left Swansea, rode to the village of Llugher [*Loughor*], 7 miles, where I crossed the river of the same name at low water, and leaving Glamorganshire entered Carmarthenshire. This place is upposed to have been a Roman station under the name of [*Leucarum*], and the straight road from Swansea hither in many places resembles a Roman causeway, particularly where it traverses a common about halfway between the two places. It is a small village on an eminence above the river, with the remains of a square tower on a mound. From hence I rode three or four miles to Llanelly and visited the church. . . . From hence to Kidwelly eight miles. . . . My carriage was obliged to go round by Pontardulas, the ford at Llugher not being safe.

Kidwelly is situated between two tide rivers called Gwendrath [*Gwendraeth*] Vawr and Gwendrath Fach, the former of which I crossed over [*by*] a long bridge[22] in my way to Kidwelly. The latter runs through the town. It lies about a mile distant from the channel and the river is navigable to the town. Kidwelly has a large and picturesque castle seated on a rocky eminence above the river.[23] It had two entrances, both accessible only by drawbridges; they were nearly opposite to each other; that to the south west between two large rounded towers was the principal. The walls on the SE side are nearly straight except where the projection of the round towers and octagon building break the line. Here the castle was strongly fortified by nature, the grond sloping abruptly down to the river [*sketch*]. On the opposite side, NW, the line is nearly semi-circular and the walls defended by round towers at certain intervals. On this side also is a deep fosse. Four large towers form the angles of the inner court. . . . The architecture of this building is simple and grand, calculated for defence, not show; the windows are small and narrow, the towers loft and massive. On walking under the S. East side of it, by the banks of the river, the castle appears to great advantage, and the parish church with its lofty spire forms a pleasing addition to the landscape.

Sunday 20 June. Pursued our journey to Carmarthen, road good but hilly, nothing interesting on it. Carmarthen appears well at some distance from the town: seated in a rich vale, watered by the Towy, country around it cultivated but barren of wood.

Carmarthen is the best Welch town I have yet seen during my tour. Situated on rising ground above the River Towy which runs on the south side of it, where some fragments of the old walls and towers are seen intermixed with the houses. It is a tide river and navigable up to the town, and over it is a long and narrow stone bridge of seven arches.[24] It is supposed to have been a Roman station and the *Moridunum* mentioned in the *Itineraries* but no relicts of that remote aera are now left to testify the supposition.[25] Giraldus says: '*Haec urbs antiqua coctibilibus muris partim adhuc extentibus egregie clausa*'. But I could perceive no bricks in the old walls, and should imagine it probable that he mistook the red stone of which they are built for brick. The few remains of the castle have been converted into a goal. . . . The parish church with regard to its antiquity has little to recommend it (broad Gothic arches on octagon pillars and one aisle only to the south), but it contains the interesting monument of Sir Thomas ap Rhys, a celebrated character in our history who assisted Henry vii on his landing at Milford. . . . We have to lament the loss of three other fine alabaster effigies in memory of personages of the same illustrious house which were absolutely beaten to pieces by masons and converted into plaister for the mouldings of the cornice of the church then repairing about 12 years ago. There are a few other badly executed busts and effigies of a more modern date. Here also rest the bones of Sir Richad Steele[26] but not even a tablet to perpetuate his memory. . . . We found a very good inn at the King's Arms, much better than the original Ivy Bush.

Monday 21st June.   This morning's ride was delightful and interesting: to Llanstephan 8 miles, to Llaugharne 3 miles, to St Clear 3 miles. Between Carmarthen and Llanstephan I had occasional views of the River Towy. . . . I descended to the banks of the Towy which (the tide being up) here presented itself as a wide noble river [not fordable but a ferry]; and continued my ride along the sands till I came under the castle. . . . This castle[27] is prettily situated on a bold and verdant promontory, the declivities of which are well covered with wood. The shell is nearly entire, its entrance to the north; a broad Gothic arch between two semi-circular towers is now stopt up, but on one side is an arch (though not so wide) by which you enter the castle court. . . . This castle guarded the western entrance of the Towy and was often taken and retaken and destroyed and rebuilt during the frequent wars in which the princes of Wales were engaged. . . .

A short ride conducted me from hence to Llaugharne [Some of the cliffs near Laugharne are very beautifully overhung with the most luxuriant elm trees growing from the interstices of the rocks] where I forded the River Tave [*Taf*]. The castle at this place is in point of situation very different from that I had just visited. Its walls are washed by the tide and one front only (viz the South) affords a good subject for the pencil.[28] Lanstephan in situation far exceeds it. I had not time to visit either of the churches. . . . This line of coast in Camarthenshire and the adjacent one in Glamorganshire is wonderfully intersected by tide rivers: the Tave at Laugharne, the Towy at

Lanstephan, the two Gwendraths at Kidwelly, the Lwghor, the Tawy [*Tawe*] at Swansey and the Nedd at Neath. Laugharne is a large village consisting of a long street with a decent-looking inn; the church stands at the upper end of it. . . .

I found a tolerable inn at St Clear (the Blue Boar, a single house where post-horses are kept). A long straggling village at the junction of the River Kathgenny [*Cynin*] with the Tave. Immediately above the banks of the former and not far from its junction with the other stood the castle but not one stone is left; the tumulus on which stood the citadel, and other broken ground, mark its ancient scite.

Tuesday 22nd June.   Continued our journey through Narbeth to Tenby: a most interesting country, very hilly, roads rough and bad, country void of wood though in general cultivated, numerous coal pits and limeworks. The teams in general use are light carts with two oxen (small) in the shafts, or rather a stout pole between them, and two light horses before.

Having a few hours to spare I mounted my horse at Narbeth and rode to Llawhaden, about four miles, where there are considerable ruins of a strong well-built castle of whose history I have been able to gain no information.[29] It belongs (I believe) to the Bishop of St Davids. Its situation is very picturesque, particularly when first seen from the same road I went: where it first meets the eye proudly seated on a lofty eminence covered with fine wood down to the banks of the rapid river which flows beneath it. A handsome stone bridge, the parish church, a mill etc unite in adding to the general pleasing effect of this landscape. The ascent it very steep but worth the trouble of ascending. A handsome circular archway between two semi-circular towers forms the SW entrance. A long range of wall still remains on the S. side with two fine octagon towers.

I returned to dinner at Narbeth, a poor place with the ruins of a castle; and proceeded to Tenbigh [*Tenby*] where I took up my quarters at the White Lyon Inn, commanding a most beautiful view of the bay etc, etc. The approach to Tenby is particularly striking and unexpected, and perhaps appears to as great advantage from this road as from any other point of view. The eye comprehending nearly the whole town forms a good idea of its plan. It is built on the semi-circular ridge of a high cliff sloping abruptly down to the seashore. The extreme point is a verdant round knoll covered with a few remains of an old castle, between which and the town is a little harbour, completely sheltered from the wind. On the south-west side of the town a long range of the ancient walls and towers remain [*sketch plan*]. The former are very high and embattled, the latter chiefly round though there are two of a square form. These fortifications apparently extended all along the coast on the south-east side till they joined the castle. The walls terminated on the opposite side nearly in a line parallel with the White Lion Inn. In short it appears to have been fortified on three sides by art, and on the other by nature, the cliffs being nearly perpendicular on the NE side.

The interior of the town still bears a very antique appearance; numerous old walls and buildings covered with ivy, Gothic windows etc meet the eye in every street. Tenby seems made purposely for the artist and antiquarian, but especially for the former, as I have seen few places so abounding in fine studies, and where he may pursue them with so much ease, quiet and economy. But when I speak of studies from nature I do not mean to imply subjects for landscape in general; I allude more particularly to sea views and rock scenery. The latter are indeed superiorly fine, both as to form and coloring. I have never seen it richer or more harmonious. The ivy seems to take particular affection to the rocks and old walls in this place, for the cliffs are covered from their base to their summits with (I might almost say) copses of that plant. The rock scenery along the sands towards the north is as fine and grand as imagination can fancy, or the pencil of a Salvator Rosa can figure. . . .[30] But in praising the rock scenery the town must not be omitted, which in every point of view, when seen from the heights or from the sands beneath it, preserves its singularly picturesque form. And the cliffs beneath it are so completely covered with plants that the town seems rising from a wood. The number of ruined houses etc, many covered with ivy, intermixed with the more modern habitations, soften by their mellow tints the glaring white color of the modern habitations.

The parish church is a venerable old structure and both within and without bears marks of antiquity. The arch of the western door is of a curious form resembling the Saracenic. On this as well as on several doorways near the church are Latin mottos in old characters repeated *'Benedictus Dominus in donis tuis'*. . . . Its roof is curiously decorated with various devices. Amongst them in the nave is the figure of a priest holding a crucifix, and of two officiating priests with him. The ribs of the roof in the chancel are supported by figures in religious habits holding escutcheons of arms and these, having their hair curled round and not shaven prove that the church was collegiate. . . .

Tenbigh as a sea-bathing place stands unparalleled: its bay is so sheltered by the projecting promontory of the castle that the SW winds cannot affect it; the shore also is so even and gradual that bathing may be had at any hour of the day. It is well supplied with machines. The White Lion in point of situation certainly bears the preference to any other house, being situated on nearly the very highest ridge of the cliff and immediately over the sea. The *Hotel* is more resorted to as a boarding house. The town affords many lodgings and the charges in general are reasonable. Fish of great variety and abundance: soles, pipers and gurnets predominate. A dory[31] was caught a few days ago of the extraordinary weight of 7 lb.

During my stay at Tenbigh I made two excursions to Manorbwr Castle, distant about five miles to the westward. This place being the *natale solum* of my author, Giraldus, was particularly interesting to me. His description [*is*] also very accurate but rather inclined to partiality (a very natural one, I confess) when he adds: *'Restat igitur ut Cambriae totius locus hic sit amoenissimus'*. Healthy indeed it may be but by no [*means*] delightful as a residence; the country being in general stoney and destitute of wood has a dreary appearance. [*The*] castle is situated on an eminence between two other hills, facing the sea. Its entrance is towards the east, [*a*] fosse on each side of the gateway. Inner court inclines to the oval or oblong and becomes narrower towards the west. Has the remains of many apartments within, one modernised. Without all is simple and calculated for defence: high plain walls no windows; and from the uniform style does not appear to have been rebuilt or suffered much during the civil wars in this country. I know nothing of its history as I do not recollect its being once mentioned by Powell in his history. The lake, fishponds etc as described by Giraldus are easily to be traced; a mill is still supplied by the never-failing stream which issues from a hill a little distance from the castle (the miller informed me that water was never wanting, even in the driest seasons). The parish church is seated on a hill south of the castle; [*it*] is a plain stone building with a lofty square tower. Its arches are of the simplest and rudest Gothic, no bases or capitals, exactly as if a Gothic aperture had been cut out of an even line of wall. There are the debris of a rich carved Gothic canopy skreen which divided the choir from the nave. This, as well as the pulpit, was painted and gilt. . . .

Sunday 27th June.   Rode to Llaugharne, distance about sixteen miles. A pleasant ride and tolerable horse road but rough and stoney, the usual qualities of a Pembrokeshire road. Descended occasionally to the sea coast. . Passed by a ruinous old mansion house on the left and near it the trifling remains of Roch [*Roche*] Castle. The range of hills on my left, after having descended into the marsh, are well wooded having many gentlemen's houses at their base. One of these places is called Westmead near which in a limestone quarry a skeleton was found with several coins, two of which the landlord at St Clear showed me, both of Carausius. . . . At Spring tides a road is practicable on the sands the whole way to Tenbigh. I dined at a decent little inn at Llaugharne. . . . I supped and slept at my old quarters at St Clear and on

Monday 28 June.   Pursued my journey on horseback. About five miles on the road to the right, and having just passed the residence of the clegyman of St Clears, I turned off to visit the remains of the celebrated abbey called Whiteland [*Whitland*] or Alba Domus, where Howel Dha[32] summoned the princes and nobles of Wales and formed a new code of laws in the year [*c.945*]. A few fragments of rude walls and some foundations alone exist to testify the former existence of this celebrated Cistercian abbey, but the beauty of its sequestered situation still remains. It was built in a little valley sheltered from the E. and North winds by a long and magnificent range of hanging wood extending along the declivities of the hill for more than a mile which still remains in high beauty. It was formerly called Ty Gwyn ar Taf [*Daf*], the White House upon the Taf, though that river runs to the westward of his valley. 'Qui color albus erat, sed hunc contrarius albo'; for two smoking iron forges with their noisy and busy attendants occupy this

32. Haverfordwest Priory, north-west view in 1793.

33. Pembroke Castle: the interior with keep in 1802.

spot once dedicated to retirement and religion. . . .

At Narbeth I met my son and chaise who came from Tenby. Proceeded to Haverfordwest, a large and populous town, built on the steep sides and summit of a hill, watered by a navigable river; its ancient castle, built (according to report) by Gilbert Earl of Clare in the reign of King Stephen is situated on an eminence and made use of as the County Goal. In the southern suburbs of the town and immediately on the banks of the River Cleddau are considerable remains of a Priory[33] of Black Monks [*Canons*]. The north and south transepts remain in part, the former the most perfect in which there is a large arch leading into it from the nave. Considerable foundations to [*the*] south also testify the extent of this building. The Early Gothic architecture and lancet windows prevail. The town has three churches, neither of which contain any monuments worthy of notice. The Gothic architecture of Saint Mary's, the principal and most central church is light and elegant and uniform in the nave and east and west windows. It has only one aisle, viz northern, in which, as well as in the nave, is a handsome carved roof. . . . Saint Martin's church is on a hill near the castle; has no particular marks of antiquity except three old stalls and a niche for holy water on the south side of the altar. The third church, St Thomas stands on an eminence above the priory. The best inn at Haverfordwest is the Castle, though by no means capital. The town is very badly situated for both pedestrian or equestrian exercises, the streets being very steep and roughly paved.

Tuesday 29th June.   After breakfast in pursuit of my author's track I rode to St Ismaels, a small village about ten miles SW of Haverfordwest and a few miles to the right of the turnpike road to Hubberstone, and also at no great distance from the shores of Milford Haven. The village is straggling. I think I observed a tumulus covered with furze and low wood. The church is of a picturesque form and situated in a sequestered valley remote from the village. The only thing I observed here worthy of notice was a piece of pottery [*sketch of amphora*] which appeared to me Roman. My female *Cicerone* told me that it had lain there many years and that it belonged to the Romans.

From hence we directed our course to Hubberstone, where we had a most satisfactory view of Milford Haven with numerous ships riding at anchor and so completely landlocked as to bear more the appearance of an extensive lake than a branch of the ocean. Towards its embouchure are some bold projecting rocks but its shores are in general tame and want wood. Opposite to Hubberstone is the newly-created town of Milford,[34] more pleasing in its appearance to the eye of the merchant or trader than to that of the artist, for at present the houses are unconnected and like so many spots. Sir William Hamilton and his nephew, Mr Greville, have created this new colony. Thus have art and industry begun to make use of those advantages which Nature has here pointed out to the merchant and adventurer. We now see a dockyard established and ships riding in the finest bay perhaps in the known world. People however have their doubts about the success of these new establishments, and all lament that so much public money has been lavished on useless fortifications in the defence of the harbour.

Wednesday 30th June.   We went in a chaise to Pembroke Ferry and from thence walked up to the town, a distance of about two miles. On many accounts I should have preferred going up to it by water, the approach to the castle and town being so much more picturesque, but the tide did not suit, and my time and impatience did not allow me to wait. . . . Pembroke is one of the most interesting places which will occur to the tourist during his rambles in South Wales, and the ruins of its ancient castle, priory etc will afford many good subjects for the pencil of the artist. This castle is situated at the west end of the town on a rocky height which at high water is peninsulated. Its entrance is nearly south-west and remains entire towards the inner court. Its original foundation is attributed to Arnulph de Mont-gomery, *temp*. Henry I, about the year 1105. . . . It still preserves much of its Norman character. The round tower in particular is a most grand and conspicuous object rearing its majestic summit high above every other part of the building. It had three stories besides the ground floor and a fine stone roof in the form of a dome, which remains entire. It is beautifully mantled with ivy. The whole area is still surrounded with walls and many remains of towers and other buildings. A lofty building to the north faces the river and was perhaps used as a chapel. . . . On this same side facing the river is a curious natural cavern, called the Wogan, which penetrates a considerable way into the rock. . . . It resembles much many of the natural caverns I have seen in Italy . . . used as places of amusement; they were called *nymphaea.*

There are evident traces of three of the gates which formed a communi-cation through the walls to the interior of the town. The north gate leading to the ferry remains entire; the west and east gates are down; on the southern side there stands a tower and a road into the town close to it. . . . From the north to the east the line of the walls run parallel with the river or rather a large mill pool, at which latter angle a very perfect round tower still remains, called Barnard's Tower. On the southern side also the lines of the walls, which at intervals were fortified with round towers, may be easily followed. The ground on this side was low and marshy. . . . Pembroke has two churches within its walls and another adjoining them on the western side. St Mary's in the middle of the town [*has*] a great chasm in the walls of the tower said to have been occasioned by the bombardment of Cromwell . . . Saint Michael stands on the western side of the town and in its architecture bears some marks of antiquity. . . . At Monkton adjoining the western suburbs of Pembroke are the remains of a priory of Benedictines. It is dedicated to St Nicholas. . . . The two doors on the southern side are Saxon but not rich. The ruins to the east of the present church and annexed to it show that it formerly extended much more that way. . . . Numerous old buildings are dispersed about the environs of this church and farmhouse adjoining, where a great part of the enclosure wall of the Priory still exists.

34. Roch Castle, Dyfed, west view of the ruined tower in 1793.

In every point of view Pembroke may be considered as a rich treat to the artist and antiquarian. The ruins are grand and truly picturesque. The best point of view for the castle is the opposite side of the river where the town and bridge and massive steeple groupe well with the castle and river, and form a very rich and picturesque mass of building and landscape. There are two tolerable inns here but no post-horses.

1 July. We returned to Haverfordwest; crossed the ferry in a very rough sea, and not finding our chaise ready on the opposite shore, pursued our journey on foot; and did not meet our conveyance till we had got halfway back to H'West. . . .

2 July. I pursued my route to St Davids on horseback through the little village of Camros mentioned by Giraldus. . . . From thence to Newgal Sands, mentioned by Giraldus, where a horse race was on the point of commencing. Leaving Roch Castle built on a land rock on the right I continued my road to St Davids, through a most dreary and rugged country. The description given of it by my friend Giraldus is true to this day: '*Hic autem angulus est supra Hibernicum mare remotissimus, terra saxosa, sterilis et infecunda; nec silvis vestita, nec fluminibus distincta, nec pratis ornata: ventis solum et procellis semper exposita.*' [If I objected to anything in this description it would be the epithet *infecunda*, for the land when properly tilled is very productive; its barley is particularly celebrated. Sea sand [? *weed*] is frequently here used as a manure].

However unfavourable and accurate this description may be yet on many accounts Saint Davids merits the attention of the traveller. Its ancient fame and character will render it interesting to the historian; its ruins and monuments will attract the notice of the artist and antiquarian. Its environs abound in old incampments and Druidical remains. Its origin is of a very early aera: British history reports that at the first planting of Christianity in this island there were established several episcopal sees and that three of them were archbishoprics. That of Wales is generally agreed to have been fixed at Caerleon-on-Usk in Monmouthshire. . . .[35] Certain however it is that he [*St David*] removed the see from Caerleon to *Menevia* which afterwards took his name.

The cathedral church dedicated to St Andrew and St David, having suffered much by the continual incursions of the Danes and other pyrates, was pulled down by Peter de Leia about the year 1180 and re-edifyed. Thus we can ascertain the aera at which the oldest part of the present cathedral was built. In the time of Iorwerth, 53rd bishop, 1220, it is recorded that the new tower of the church fell down, and that in 1248 under the presidency of Anselmus, his successor, a great part of the church was thrown down by an earthquake. To Bishop Martyn who died AD 1327, the 58th bishop, we owe the building of St Mary's Chapel in which he is buried. But to his successor, Henry of Gower, 59th bishop, the antiquarian is most indebted for the beautiful remains of a magnificent palace in which the bishops resided. He

died AD 1347 and was buried in a chapel he had built and dedicated to St
John under the rood loft. To Adam Houghton, 63rd bishop of the See, is
attributed the building of St Mary's College, an elegant Gothic structure
adjoining the cathedral on the northern side. . . . To the aforesaid bishops
we owe the different structures at St Davids forming so noble and grand a
groupe of architectural skill and elegance.

The fame of this celebrated sanctuary was so great that princes came
barefoot to its shrine: in the year 1085 William the Conqueror. . ., in the
year 1171 Henry the Second. . . ., AD 1284 Edward the First with his
Queen Eleanor came on a pilgrimage to the shrine of this saint. The offerings
were so great and its riches so abundant that it is said the monks divided
them equally. In short once it was the British Loretto; now, alas! the
Palmyra of Saxon and Gothic antiquity![36]

Three distinct but adjoining buildings form this massive groupe of varied
architecture: the cathedral, the college and the Bishop's palace (the two
latter of which are in ruin) and offer the most picturesque subjects for the
pencil. On entering the close through a fine octagon gateway they unexpectedly burst upon the sight and the *coup d'oeuil* cannot fail to strike
with surprize and admiration even the most indifferent spectator. But how
much more impressive would the view appear, if the modern chapter house
were removed, or had never been erected.[37] For it unfortunately interupts
the most essential part of the view, the bishop's palace. The exterior of this
cathedral (except a rich Saxon doorway to the north side) presents no fine
specimens of architecture and is entirely Gothic with the above exception.
The old west front was much admired for its Saxon workmanship but the
modern one, like the adjoining chapter house, is beneath criticism; such an
heterogeneous mixture of Saxon, Gothic and castellated architecture I never
before beheld. [The architect was Mr Nash, then a young man, now much
improved in his art as an architect]

[*Detailed description of cathedral and tombs omitted.*]

I shall now take my leave of the cathedral (having mentioned everything
which has occurred to me worthy of notice) and take a short survey of the
adjoining ruins which, as I before said, are more fertile in picturesque
subjects than the building just described. The College is situated on the
northern side of the cathedral and very contiguous to it . . . its architecture
was Gothic and the shell of the chapel bespeaks its ancient magnificence. To
the south-west of this college stood the bishop's palace, erected by Henry
Gower. . . .[38] The original form of it was a quadrangle two sides only of
which now remain. The bisops occupied the eastern apartments. The
kitchen with its curious chimnies was perfect till very lately but they are now
fallen. . . . The southern side was said to have been the royal apartments. . . .
The hall is a magnificent apartment 88 feet by 30, and the circular last
window has been often and very justly admired. It still remains in good
preservation. The entrance to this hall is formed by a singular arch [*sketch*]

over which were the statues of the royal personages, now nearly annihilated. This building derives the greatest beauty from an open parapet which surrounds it. This open parapet has a very light appearance and answered a double purpose: for shooting the rain off from the roof, and, as a walk, in which second light it might answer the defensive purpose of a battlement. . . .

There are two small public houses, for they do not deserve the appellation of inns, where the curious and not overnice traveller may procure a frugal meal and a decent bed (no wine or post-horses). I had again occasion to experience the hospitality of the resident archdeacon, Mr Williams, who kindly offered us board and lodging. But the independence of an inn, however homely, has to me charms which the stately mansion often fails affording. . . .

Sunday 4th July.   Rode to Fishguard over a most dull and dreary tract of country. The situation of this port is picturesque and has a very good effect on going down to it one way from the town above, where the bason, quite land-locked, with houses around it, and enclosed by high hills, make[s] a good subject for the pencil. There is some pretty scenery in a little retired valley watered by the River Gwain [*Gwaun*] where my friend Mr Fenton has built a neat house in a romantic situation under some cragged rocks. A decent inn (Captain Langharne's — no sign) afforded me a good bed and dinner but no wine.

A late event has rendered this place more conspicuous in history than it was when I last passed through it. I allude to the landing of the French in its neighborhood on 22 February, 1797, under General Tate to the number of between twelve and fourteen hundred. Their place of landing was a point of land called Cerrig Gwastad to the west of Aberfelin Bay. This was on the 22nd inst. and they surrendured their arms on Goodick [*Goodwick*] Sands near Fishguard on the 24th to an English force far inferior in number. [The object of this French expedition hitherto remains a mystery.[39] My friend, Mr Fenton, told me a circumstance in which providence seems to have almost miraculously interfered to save the neighboring country from their depredations. For a short time only before their landing a ship laden with wine was wrecked on that coast. Every cottager profited of the spoils attending the wreck; so that the French on plundering in their turn the cottages drank so freely of the wine that they were in a complete state of intoxication and were heard explaining: '*Vive le Roy d'Angleterre*' etc. etc. and such loyal expressions.]

Monday 5th July.   From Fishguard to Cardigan. Nothing interesting occurred till I came to Newport where there are the remains of an old castle, built by the Lords of Kemaes (the name given to this district). Near this place some fine woods belonging to Mr Bowen give animation and interest to the surrounding scenery. I here deviated from the direct road to Cardigan by turning off to the left to the village of Nevern where there is a picturesque church and one of the most perfect crosses I have yet seen, ornamented with frets, knots and other devices in compartments, and, according to Camden who has described it[40] an undecypherable inscription. On an eminence to the west of the church and adjoining it is the scite of a large castle, and this, I conclude, was the one alluded to by Giraldus and not that at Newport, as his annotator supposed. This neighborhood abounds in curious Druidical and British remains. At Pentre Evan, not far from Newport, is a well-preserved cromlech, the finest I have yet seen, and the highest after Stonehenge. This I visited in 1793 [*p. 42*]. There is another very fine one between Nevern and the sea and but little out of the way from that place to Cardigan, but the wet weather prevented my taking it en route. It is called Lech y Drybed [*Llech y Drybedd*]. From Nevern I did not return to the turnpike road but rejoined it before I reached Cardigan.

In the evening we walked to the abbey of St Dogmael[41] [a monastery of the Order of Tiron, begun by Martin of Tours. . .], adjoining to which stands the parish church. The ruins are trifling. Part of the northern transept (as it appeared to me) remains. . . . This village which is populous is inhabited principally by a hardy race of fishermen. The houses are dispersed and intermixed with trees forming a pleasing *tout ensemble*.

Monday 5th. [*Tuesday 6th*] *July*   This morning was delightfully spent in viewing the natural beauties of the Rivery Tivy [*Teifi*]. The tide serving we hired a boat to take us to Killgeran [*Cilgerran*] Castle [seven shillings and sixpence boat, 2/6 to the men], which by land is only two miles distant from Cardigan but more by water. After passing alongside an extensive and flat marsh a sudden bend of the river, contracting its channel, conducts you into a narrow pass, surrounded on each side with a perpendicular wall of rock and wood [chiefly slate quarries which are rather too numerous]. Banks steep and precipitate feathered down to the water's edge with oaks and copse wood. The first view of the castle just peeping at a distance between a perspective range of well-wooded hills is very striking, and what on a nearer approach it may lose in picturesque beauty it certainly gains in grandeur. The proud remains of a large castle appear in full front. The hill on which it stands is void of wood but boldly broken with projecting rocks, and perhaps this contrast to the woody scenery around may add to the general effect of the scenery. I have never seen ruins more happily combined with rocks, wood and water, a more captivating scene, or more pleasing composition. Numerous coracles at the proper times of the tide are seen busy in taking salmon; they add much to the animation of the views.

I quitted with reluctance the beautiful scenery below and ascended to the castle.[42] Its foundation has been assigned to various people and its remains bespeak a very early antiquity, although the Welsh historians inform us that it was very frequently attacked, destroyed and rebuilt. The most conspicuous part of the ruins is two round towers of large and massive proportions, one of which from the uniformity of its round arches seems to have differed but little in its external [? *aspect*]; indeed I only recollect having seen one Gothic arch in the whole building. A staircase is still practicable up to the summit of

one of the towers. The whole is built of the dark slaty stone of the country. . . .
I returned to Cardigan by land, but how different is the appearance of the
castle on the land side! It might almost be passed by unnoticed; whereas by
water it forms the grandest and most pleasing ruin in South Wales, and
cannot fail to leave a lasting impression on the recollection of every traveller
who visits it.

We took an evening's walk along the banks of the River Tivy and nearly
opposite to St Dogmael's . . . observed an old entrenchment of an oblong
form with an outwork. . . .[43] We afterwards bent our steps homewards and
visited the goal, a new and handsome edifice in the suburbs of the town on
the Aberystwyth Road, and the Priory, now the parish church. . . . A few
old walls and towers mantled with ivy and built with the dingey, slatey stone
of the country, on the banks of the River Tivy, mark the ancient site of the
castle. In vain I looked for the chapel said to have been built at the head of
the bridge by Giraldus on the spot where he preached the Crusade.

Wednesday 7th July. From Cardigan I pursued my journey to Newcastle
in Emlyn, passing along the Vale of the Tivy and through the picturesque
little village of Kenarth [*Cenarth*] where there is the salmon leap recorded by
Giraldus. NB. This is not the direct or shortest road to Newcastle but by far
the most eligible, the road being good and leading through much beautiful
scenery. At a short distance from the village of Newcastle are the remains of
a castle, which from the marks of the foundations etc appears to have been a
considerable building. It was built in a strong situation on high ground and
almost insulated by a singular bend which the river makes. The present ruins
are not of very ancient date, the arches being of the later kind of Gothic, viz.
broad. The entrance to the west forms the most conspicuous part of them. . .
I found a good inn at Lampeter (the Black Lion) but no chaises or post-
horses are kept. This little village is situated nearly a quarter of a mile from
the River Tivy over which there is a bridge. This place is called *Pons
Stephani* by Giraldus and in the maps of the county it is also named Pont
Stephan. To the south is a rich vale, inclosed and cultivated to the summits
of the hills. The parish church is on an eminence at a short distance from the
town. Its font is ancient. . . . A large old mansion house near the town
belonging lately to the Lloyd family but now roofless and dilapidated.

Thursday 8 July. Continued my journey towards Aberystwyth. The first
object which attracted my attention was the large old church at Llandewi
Brevi, eight miles from Lampeter. The condition of this ancient church is so
miserable that it bears more the appearance of a ruin than of a building still
appropriated to the service of God. Four lofty Gothic arches supporting a
massive square steeple bespeak its ancient grandeur. The south aisle only
remains, divided from the nave by three arches supported on octagon pillars.
In this aisle also is a fine broad Gothic arch. The appearance of this once-
celebrated sanctuary is really melancholy: no pavement but the plain earth,
no ceiling but the rafters and beams as in a barn, which it certainly resembles

35. Strata Florida Abbey, Dyfed, western doorway of the church.

more than a church. The stone bearing the following inscription *(Hic iacet Idnert, filius Iacobi . . . Sancti David)*, mentioned by Camden,[44] still serves as a headstone to a little window adjoining the pulpit. The characters are rude and badly cut. There are two other stones with inscriptions. . . [Llandewi Brevi was a college founded by Thomas Beck, Bishop of St Davids, AD 1187, in honor of St David who preached at the Council held here AD 519 and thereby put an end to the Pelagian heresy]. The church is situated on rising ground backed by high mountains and surrounded by a miserable collection of thatched cottages. In short the whole place bears a most miserable aspect. The parson was my *Cicerone* to the antiquities of the place, and on my enquiry about a place in the neighborhood called Llanieo [*Llanio*] asked if it had anything to do with Io whom he had heard mentioned by Ovid!

The Roman station at *Laventium* is supposed to have been not far distant and Camden mentions some inscriptions existing at Llanieo I [*he*] saw, about a mile from Llandewi Brevi on the other side of the river.[45] The bad weather preventing my making personal enquiries on the spot I pushed on to Tregaron, a small village on the River Tivy, famous for good trout fishing, and affording tolerable accomodations for a fisherman (but no wine). Red Lion public house.

Having refreshed myself and horses I pursued my road to Strata Florida, 6 miles from Tregaron and a mile out of the main road to the right. The situation admirably adapted to the severe and recluse order of Cistercians: surrounded on three sides by mountains many of which still retain their sylvan cloathing, open only to the west. The relicts of this once-celebrated abbey are very trifling, but time has, fortunately for the lovers of antiquity, spared a most beautiful specimen of its early architecture: a very rich Saxon doorway differing in its patterns from any I have ever met with. It is in the most perfect preservation, but being shut up within a garden is seen to great disadvantage. As it faces nearly west it may have been the western entrance to the church.[46] A high fragment of wall is standing towards the east, and these alone mark the existence of Strata Florida.

I continued my ride over a most dreary tract of hills through Rhosefair [*Ffair Rhos*] to Spitty [*Ysbyty Ystwyth*]. On the descending from this place the rich groves of Havod begin to make some compensation for the many tedious miles I had this day crept along over rough and dirty roads. The scenery is now very grand and truly Alpine: well-wooded hills, waterfalls, picturesque bridges etc. Leaving Havod I had another sad interval of barren moors before I reached my quarters at Devil's Bridge, distant between three and four miles from Havod, tired and fatigued after the long and dreary journey my guide, Giraldus, had this day led me.

Friday 9th July. I reviewed the romantic scenery of this place with pleasure and, I may add, wonder. The waterfalls owing to the late rains were in high beauty, but I could not reach the lower one which in my last visit to this place I remember to have preferred to the large one [*p. 63*]. I found the

Havod Arms improved in one respect: that of keeping chaises and post-horses. This little inn in point of situation I believe stands unrivalled with any, perhaps I may say, in Europe. It is built on the edge of a rocky precipice covered from top to bottom with wood, and its windows command a most sublime view of wood, mountain and water, the lower cataract being exactly in front and the roaring of the upper one distinctly heard. In the immediate environs of this place the scenery is perhaps grander than at Havod: abrupt mountains, fine wood, numerous roaring cataracts; in short all the necessary ingredients for a grand romantic composition. We are naturally inclined to think that wood is absolutely necessary to constitute the picturesque, and the country here is proof of it. For in the neighborhood there are many other abrupt, bold and rugged mountains and precipices which, undecked with wood, pass by unnoticed by the traveller, whereas the well-cloathed scenery of Havod and the Devil's Bridge cannot fail to attract the notice and admiration of every passing traveller.

In going from hence to Aberystwyth the River Rydol [*Rheidol*] winding its serpentine course through the vale beneath relieves the insipidity of the cultivated hedgeless country around. The end of the vale towards the sea is closed by the town of Aberystwith filling up the whole space between the hills. Aberystwyth is situated near the confluence of the Rivers Ystwith and Rydol, but nearer the latter. They both unite their streams on the seashore and flow into the ocean. The scite of the ancient castle on a bold rock exposed to the main ocean has been converted to the amusement of the public by having been formed into public walks. The ruins are insignificant and appear the more so from being scattered about in different fragments over the hill. On [*the*] confluence between the two rivers is an encampment, rendered interesting to the historian by the account transmitted to us of its formation when Gruffydd ap Rhys encamped there previous to his attack on the Normans in Aberystwith Castle (Powell, p. 147). . . .

Aberystwith, though certainly an indifferent place for bathing, is much frequented. A new bridge over the Rydol and several houses have been built since I last visited it, and [*the*] town paved. The chalybeate spring also in the marsh has been covered over and secured from the weather, [*omission by author*] though well built and roofed. The town has rather a melancholy appearance from the dark-coloured stone of which it is built. The beach is pebbly and irksome to walk upon. On the coast to the N. West are some singular slaty rocks with dark gloomy recesses etc. How different do they appear in the painter's eye to the richly tinted cliffs of Tenby. The two places cannot in any respect bear a comparison either for beauty, convenience of bathing or the luxuries of the table. Fish is scarce, and the surface of the waters is seldom animated by the appearance of vessels. The accomodations both at inns and lodgings is good.

The foundation of the church of Llanbadarn Vawr is attributed to a very early aera as in the year 1,111 it was given to St Peter's, Gloucester. . . . It has also been called the church of Saint Paternus. Its architecture is uniform of early lancet Gothic, the church large and very resembling that of

Llandewi Brevi in its massive square tower and lofty Gothic arches which support it. . . . On the south side of the churchyard is an old cross decorated with fretwork, knots, heads etc, similar to those at Nevern etc. . . .[47]

Sunday 11th. In the evening I quitted Aberystwith and slept at Machunleth [*Machynlleth*]. The former appears well from the hill on looking back towards it, as it did on approaching it from Havod. In vain searched for a near view of the town and castle, but could find none well-adapted to the pencil. Passed by Gogarthau where some large plantations of firs by their flourishing growth show that the want of wood in this country is not owing to any deficiency or bad quality in the soil. . . . Cross the River Lysnant [*Llyfnant*] and enter North Wales. A pretty waterfall, mill, bridge etc. The country now assumes a more mountainous appearance; lofty and cragged mountains prettily intermixed with woods, pastures and cornfields. The navigable Dovy takes a very meandering course. Machynlleth in Montgomeryshire where the elections are held for the county is situated in a plain surrounded on all sites by mountains and watered by the clear streams of the Dovy.

Monday 12th July. Quitted Machuneleth and sending my chaise round to Dolgelly pursued my road to Touyn [*Towyn*], Merioneth. In my way passed through Penalt [*Pennal*] a little village four miles from Machunlleth, mentioned by Camden and other later authors as possessing some Roman antiquities; in the search of which a kind of fatality seems to attend me for at each of the Roman stations (viz Llandrindod, Llanieo and Penalt) I have been stopt in my researches by bad weather and nearly wet through. The only marks of antiquity I saw were a tumulus planted with firs. . . . Towyn, Merioneth: a small town with a good inn. Built in a bad and unhealthy situation flanked on one side by a turbary and marsh, and distant about a mile from the sea where there is an extent of the finest hard and level sands I ever saw. A nasty sulphureous pool (never cleared out) is flocked to (like the pool of Bethesda) by all the neighborhood. In high tides it is in some degree purified. . . .

On leaving Towyn pass a seat of Mr Corbet's on the left and crossing the River Desunny [*Dysynni*] see a tumulus to the left a little below the bridge [*Domen Ddreiniog*] Ascend a dreary tract from which the eye is somewhat relieved by a magnificent range of mountains, closed by Cader Idris on the right. . . . The road is now formed on a steep precipice more tremendous than that of Penmaenmawr, having no parapet against it. Towering rocks above on the right and numerous sea gulls and cormorants etc uttering their wild notes in the air accord well with the scenery around. A ride of two miles on hard sands brought me to the ferry over the River Maw [*Mawddach*] and landed me at Barmouth. I found good accomodations and very reasonable at the Cors y Gedol Arms (Mr Lewis). This place is most singular in its situation being built so immediately under a steep rock that the windows of one house look into the chimneys of its neighbor beneath. The dingey color of the stone so like the natural rock of which the houses are built hurt the general effect of the town, which if of a lighter color would produce a much more interesting *coup d'oeuil*.

Tuesday 13.   Enjoyed a most romantic ride on the banks of the river Maw to Dolgelly which is navigable nearly up to that town. Dolgelly contains so many grand and natural beauties in its neighborhood that they merit a minute examination and as accurate a description as the united efforts of the pen and pencil can produce. I look forward with pleasure to the time when I may have leisure and opportunity to survey them well and with the attention they merit.

Wednesday 14th.   In the evening we reached Bala.

IX

Journal of a Tour through North and South Wales in the Year 1803.

I left Cheltenham on *Saturday 14th May* and in order to vary my route proceeded through Michel Dean [*Mitcheldean*] to Monmouth. Turned out of the Ross road near the village of Huntley to the left. Michel Dean is a pretty little village in a retired situation, the country around well varied with wood, hill and dale, and abundance of orchards now in full bloom. This road was formerly much frequented but now neglected and deserted. One or two pairs of post-horses still kept. Ascend from Michel Dean and enter the Forest of Dean. Coal mines and wooded scenery. Trees much mangled by the axe. . . . Pass through Colford, a small village and afterwards close to High Meadow, a large and heavy building, the seat of Lord Gage, commanding a fine view towards the Wye to which the road soon leads, and conducts you to Monmouth.

Sunday 15th.   Weather fine. Ascended the Kimen [*Kymin*], a high hill above Monmouth commanding an extensive view, where a naval temple (in very bad taste) has been erected to the memory of our naval heroes. Retired and shady walks affording some good views of the adjacent country have been cut in the woods adjoining. Parties of pleasure resort much to this spot in summer where a house is opened to supply them with refreshments.

Monday 16th.   Fine weather. Proceeded on my road to Abergavenny.

Tuesday 17th.   Weather fine. Visited once more and probably for the last time the ruins of Llanthony Abbey, which are now, alas, approaching rapidly to dissolution. I was informed that last year a part of one of the fine Gothic windows in the western front had given way, and now I had the sad mortification to find that all these three elegant windows (by far the most elegant part of the whole window) had in the preceding winter fallen to the ground. The Saxon tower, I fear, from the present unconnected state of the stones which compose its masonry will soon follow the same fate. It is a melancholy sight to the traveller who frequently revisits the same ground and object of antiquity to witness the progressive ruin of these fine specimens of ancient architecture; the chapter house at Margam is now no more and Llathony will soon no longer excite nor deserve the attention of the traveller.[1]

Dined and slept at Admiral Gell's house near Crickhowel [*p. 205*].

Wednesday 17th [18].[2] Weather fine. I spent this morning in a most satisfactory manner with Mr Payne, a clergyman resident at Lhampeter [*Llanbedr*], distant two miles from Crickhowel. A most beautiful and picturesque situation, well worth visiting. From Mr Payne I gained much information towards the illustration of Giraldus's *Itinerary*.

Thursday 18th [19th]. I left the Admiral's and proceeded through Abergavenny and Uske to Newport. Fair day (fine).

Friday 19th [20th]. (fine weather). Rode to Cardiff with Mr Evans, vicar of S. Wollo's. Passed by Machen. . . . From thence to Caerphilly through a pleasing well wooded valley. Visit the ruins of this immense castle whose history is very imperfectly known. . . .[3] I found the buildings and population of this place much encreased. The castle belongs to Lord Bute.

Saturday 20th [21st]. The whole morning was spent at Llandaff in examining the cathedral and in taking views of it, and in comparing the present cathedral with the plan drawn by Browne Willis. . . .[4]

Sunday 21st [22nd]. After breakfast Mr Evans and I took a chaise and visited Barry Island, ten miles distant from Cardiff. Leave the great road about 4 miles from Cardiff, and turn off to the left. Pass by Wenvoe, a modern castle, seat of Mr Jenner: a handsome and large stone building, grounds well disposed and covered with wood. Road from thence to Barry rough, narrow and bad. See to the right some trifling remains of Barry Castle. The parish church seated on an eminence commanding a fine view of the Channel, and opposite coast of Watchet and Bridgwater. Being low water the chaise crossed the sands and beach, very rough.

This island consists of 300 acres, chiefly pasture land and mountains. A few sheep and cows. A large warren. It has only one house which in the Summer season is frequented as a lodging house and can accomodate about twelve persons.[5] Its annual rent is £80 p. annum which without the additional profit of the boarding house would with difficulty be made. The island has mines of lead and calamine but not worked. I saw several barrow ducks [*sheldrakes*] in this island. These beautiful birds lay their eggs in the rabbit holes, and as soon as their young are sufficiently strong their parents lead them off to the sea. Mr Evans told me that one of his neighbors had reared a brood and domesticated them. On the west side of the island, nearly opposite to Barry church, a few straggling stones testify the former existence of a chapel. And further on towards the same point I was told that at low water the ruins of another chapel are visible. One of these was probably that mentioned by Giraldus. On the south point (called Nell's Point) is a fine well to which numbers of women resort on Holy Thursday and after having washed their eyes with it each drop a pin in the well. The landlord of the house told me that on cleaning out it lately he took out above a pintfull of pins.

Monday 22nd [*23rd*]. Very fine. Quitted Cardiff. In a few miles enter a narrow defile guarded by Castle Coch, a small fort on the steep declivity of a rocky mountain to the right, well-covered with wood which from its sloping position could never have been very large.[6] [*Quere*: this fort being in the hundred of Senghennith may it not have been the one mentioned by Powel in his *History*, and not Caerphilly as is generally supposed?] Cross the Merthyr Canal and continue the road between the canal and the River Taf. Cross the former again near New Bridge. A neat little inn, Bridgwater Arms, 12 miles. This tract affords much pleasing and picturesque scenery. . . . Continue my ride on horseback to Merthyr Tydvael [*Tydfil*] 13 miles, the Taf flowing on the left of the road the whole way and the canal following nearly the same line. A glorious specimen of the successful efforts of art and industry in conducting a canal through apparently so impracticable a country [*p. 89*]. I had heard such exaggerated accounts of the romantic beauties of this vale that on being an eye witness of them I confess myself somewhat disappointed. This ride however affords many fine points of view and certainly deserves the attention of every traveller.

At a considerable distance you see Merthyr seated in a rich luxuriant vale, backed by a magnificent range of finely-formed mountains. At the further end of the town I found a better inn than I expected (Plymouth Arms), and four good post horses which conducted me in the evening to Brecon. All manufacturing towns and especially those in the iron trade have a dirty and dreary appearance, however beautiful their local situation may be, for instance Colebrook Dale etc etc [*p. 167*]. Iron is the chief manufacture of the place and in one of the works belonging to Mr Crawshae [This gentleman without any capital when he first came into this country has by industry amassed a most immense fortune]. A little way out of the road leading to Brecon, is the largest overshot wheel in England, made of cast iron. The ore is here melted, then cast into thick bars, and afterwards into long ones; the process is rapid and curious to see. The cultivation and population of this thriving place has taken place within the last 30 years.

To Brecon 18 miles. Road excellent through the hills, affording some wild mountain scenery. Followed the River Taff nearly to its source. The whole of the road from Cardiff very good and the tract of country through which it passes highly interesting.

Tuesday 23rd [*24th*]. Weather fine. Spent the morning at home. In the evening walked with the Fortescues to the Gaer three miles distant [*p. 37*]. . . . I was much struck, as well as my companions, with the delightful situation of this station. This was probably the summer station of the *Legio secunda Augusta* whose headquarters were at Caerleon; some of the bricks are to be seen at a farmhouse on the opposite side of the River Uske. We descended from the Gaer to the banks of the Uske and pursued a meandering path by the water's edge through the noble wood which feathers down to the water's edge, and more beautiful and natural scenery of wood and water can no where be seen. The fine bend of the river adds great variety to the landscape.

It reminded me of the scenery at Mr Knight's at Downton Castle [*p. 108*]. These woods happily belong to an English peer (Lord Camden) for had they been the property of any Welshman the axe would probably have been very active amongst them. This circuit (though well worth the additional fatigue) extended our walk to at least seven miles before we reached our quarters at Brecon.

Wednesday 24th [*25th*].   The rain so much wanted at last began to fall. I dined and spent the evening with Theophilus Jones[7] and met Mr Payne, and from each got some useful hints for my Giraldus.

Thursday 25th [*26th*].   Fine morning, wet evening. Left Brecon; dined at Llandovery, Castle Inn, newly fitted up, very good; and slept at Llandilo, Bear Inn, old house, middling. Continue through the Vale of Uske by Pen y Pant. Rich and pleasing scenery. . . . Llandovery, small remains of an old castle. Forded the River Towy three times and proceeded to Llandilo. Road more hilly but good. See the rich Vale of Towy, too expanded and cultivated to be very picturesque. . . .

Friday 26th [*27th*].   Rainy morning. Left Llandilo. Fate seems to have decreed that I never see the beauties of the Vale of Towy in perfection. The thick fog on the hills obscured the sight of this upper part of the Vale. On approaching towards Carmarthen it cleared away and exposed to my view the fine vale with the town of Carmarthen at some miles distance between the hills, which are very finely broken in their forms and beautifully varied with wood and pastures. The whole of this vale presents a rich scene of luxuriant cultivation, the fields well inclosed with hedges and the hills cultivated to their very summits. The beauties of this vale should be viewed in detail and on horseback. And Grongar Hill celebrated by our poet Dyer, and the bold insulated eminence on which are seated the remains of Dryslwyn Castle, merit attention from their beautiful situation in the center of the vale. . . .

   Dined at Carmarthen (King's Arms, Edward Morris, good inn) and in the evening pursued my journey to Lampeter, a most dreary track of twenty-four long miles over a most rough, jolting and stoney road. What a contrast does this tract of country form to the neighboring Vale of Towy! Not one interesting object occurs, till the eye is somewhat relieved for the last five miles on entering the Vale of Tivy [*Teifi*], which I crossed at Llanybydder [*Llanybyther*], the road on the north side of the river being better than that on the south side. About one mile to the left of the turnpike road and about a mile and a half from the New Inn (a miserable little ale house, the only place of refreshment for man and horse) is Pencader, a village consisting of a few houses (no church, or rather a meeting house supplies its place). A verdant artificial mount marks the scite of an ancient castle. Here Prince Rhys paid homage to King Henry the Second, as is recorded in Powel's *History of Wales* and also in Giraldus. . . . After crossing the Tivy at

Llanybydder pass an artificial tumulus on the right adjoining the road. Found much civility and tolerable good quarters at the Black Lion, Lampeter — Lewis, landlord, who contrary to the modern custom of most Welsh landlords made his appearance before his hosts [*guests*] at meal time.

Saturday 27th [28th]. Wet morning. River too muddy for a fly. The morning however was neither unprofitably nor umpleasantly spent in drawing out the Life of Giraldus from Warton's *Anglia Sacra*.[8] He was indeed a fine, spirited and independent fellow!

Sunday 28th [29th]. Showery weather but not bad. Mounted my horse and rode to the little hamlet of Llanio. . . . Whether Llanio occupies the place of *Laventium* mentioned by Pliny as being situated in the country of the Dimetae [*Demetae*] or not I cannot ascertain but certainly a very large Roman station was here placed.[9] Every field for a considerable circuit around the present little farmhouse (the property of Mr Johns of Havod) contains fragments of bricks. Its situation (like all others chosen by the Romans) was on a gentle eminence. . . . I saw several fragments of Roman masonry consisting of small pieces of brick mixed up with lime, so hard that by repeated blows agaist other stones I could not break them. To the SE the inequality of ground shows evident marks of ancient buildings having existed on that spot. I was informed that there were several traces of Roman roads in this neighborhood. . . .

Monday: stormy.

Tuesday evening (Rainy morning) *31st May*. The dread of a Welch fair with all its accompaniments of noise and riot drove me from hence sooner than I intended. Slept at Llandovery. . . . The road continues winding through the hills, chiefly on the ascent for a considerable distance till you descend towards Llandovery and cross the River Towy. The distance is not certainly as much as is charged for post horses. The road in some parts rather rough but on the whole tolerable and infinitely better than that from Carmarthen to Lampeter. Horses must be sent for from Llandovery as none are kept at Lampeter.

Wednesday 1st June. Stormy weather. Returned through Trecastle to Brecon.

Thursday 2nd June. Rainy morning.

Friday 3rd June. Rainy morning.

Saturday 4th June. Rainy morning. Rode to the Gaer. . . .[10] Saw two Roman bricks with the impression *LEG*. II *AUG*. at the farmhouse of Mrs Price, the impression stamped transversely. . . .

Sunday 5th June.   Very wet morning. Went on a visit to Mr Payne at Llanbedr.

Monday 6th June.   Fine morning, very stormy afternoon. Rode to the Coed Gron mentioned by Giraldus. In our way home visited the little church of Patricio in which is a most singularly elegant Gothic skreen or roodloft carved in Irish oak, representing foliage of holly leaves and berries etc, etc. An ancient font with a Latin inscription. How so elegant a piece of sculpture came into so sequestered a situation we are at a loss to know.

Tuesday 7th June.   Fine day. This whole day was devoted to antiquarian researches. At Crickhowell visited the old gateway called the Porth Mawr. . . . Between M.IX and X from Brecon and opposite a little public house called the Beaufort Arms on the left of the roadside, turn down a narrow lane to a farmhouse called the Gaer. Here is certainly a large Roman station or more probably a town, for besides the usual oblong enclosure there are traces and foundations of many surrounding buildings. . . .[11] It is very singular that so large a Roman station should have hitherto remained unnoticed and particularly by Mr Strange who investigated most of the Roman antiquities in this county. Immense quantities of fine Roman brick lay scattered over all the adjoining fields, and I picked up one small fragment of very fine red-glazed pottery. The farmer who lives on the spot says that in a field behind the house, north I think, a great many urns and vases of this red pottery have been found, and that the poor people had begged them of him to keep their milk in. In this field was also an arched way with a walk composed of gravel and pebbles. On this side I imagine was the cemetery. Coins also were frequently found here some years ago. . . . It is rather singular that we should find a large station so near the other two, ie at the Gaer the other side of Brecon and *Gobannium* (Abergavenny). I conceive this to have been considerably larger than the other Gaer. . . . This therefore I take to have been a town. . . . A few fields to the NE of this farmhouse is an inscription in bad Latin characters (being read *Catacus hic jacet Filius Testerhacus*).[12] Leaving this place we visited the old Bwlch road which bears strong marks of having been the old Roman road which connected the three stations; the straightness of the pitching and upright stones left at intervals reminded me much of some of the fragments of Roman roads in Italy.

In our way to Brecon we visited an old cromlech about half a mile NE of Llanhamlach church, situated on top of a hill, marked by an old yew tree. It still retains the name of Ty Iltyd [*Illtud*] or house of St. Iltud who is mentioned by Giraldus as having lived here a hermit's life.[13] I think there was probably a small cell or chapel on this summit. The crosses and other figures cut in the stones in the inside of the cromlech are certainly only the playful handiwork of those who have visited the hermit's cell. Camden mentions this cromlech. . . . Visited the church at Llanhamelach now modernised and repaired since my last visit to it [*p. 205*]. Found the effigy I mentioned in my last tour had changed her situation from a recumbent to an upright posture. . . .

Wednesday 8 June. Fine weather.

Thursday 9 June. Very stormy. Paid another visit in company with Mr Jones to Llandew but found nothing very interesting there. The round tower, a Gothic doorway and some of the outside walls mark the scite of the ancient residences of the bishops of St Davids, which like the others belonging to the same see at Llawhaden and Lantphey Court were castellated. For in turbulent times which prevailed for so long a series of years in this country not even the mansions of the clergy were safe from plunder; their buildings were therefore constructed with a view to defence. The remains of the chapel are the most prominent part of these ruins. Would that I could have ascertained the scite of my friend Giraldus's abode, *in cellula*, as he calls it. . . .

Friday 10th June. Stormy weather. Left Brecon. Tedious ascent for three miles. . . . Pass through Glasbury IV miles from Hay and enter the Vale of the Wye. Distance from Brecon XV M. Inn — Swan.

Saturday 11th June. Stormy weather. Leave Hay. From thence to Hereford XX miles, chiefly level road. Cross the Wye about V miles from Hay. On approaching Hereford good cultivation, fine cattle, hills more richly wooded.
   NB. This tour, owing to ill-health, ended very abruptly. R. Hoare.

1804

[*No record in the quarto volumes of journey this year but some of the leaves in volumes 2 and 3 of the folios may belong to a lost journal. Mr Woodbridge has worked out from the place diary at Trowbridge that he took the New Passage across the Severn on 29 April and after an extensive period of travel first in south and then in north Wales returned to Chester in August. Fenton refers to Hoare in his company in this year in Wales.*]

1805

[*No record in quarto volumes but on folio 128, vol. 3 of the folio volumes Hoare wrote:* '. . . year 1805 was memorable . . . in private as well as public accounts. My only son came of age . . . and I served the office of High Sheriff for the County of Wiltshire. Yet I breathed a little Cambrian air between the assizes but was suddenly summoned from my shady retreat at Vachdeiliog by a requisition to a County Meeting. . . .']

Itinerary through Wales etc June 1806.

Tuesday 17 June. Weather fine. Left Bala. turned off at M VI on the Corwen Road and by a narrow road joined the great Irish turnpike. . . . Cernioge, a single post house. People (like the country) rude and uncivilised: roads infested by herds of beggars and children trained to begging by incessantly following the carriage for great distances . . . the Vale of Conwy leading to Llanrwst breaks upon the sight like enchantment; nothing can be richer in woods and cultivation. . . .

Wednesday 18 June. Fine weather. The approach to Conwy is singularly striking and lost nothing in my eyes upon a renewal of long acquantance with it. During my former visits to it I never could quit its precincts so much pleasing employment did they afford for my pencil. . . . This morning was devoted to a part of that promontory extending in a NW direction from Conwy and terminating with the point called Great Orme's Head. . . . From hence we continued our walk to a seat of the Mostyn family called Bodscallan [*Bodysgallen*] a truly sequestered spot surrounded by fine groves of oak, sycamore and other forest trees. . . . We proceeded about a mile further across the fields to Gloddaeth. . . . The steward showed us some of the antiquities that had been discovered in different parts of Wales, amongst which was the curious golden torque found at Harlech. . . .[14] In the evening we rowed down the river to the embouchure of the Conwy (a dangerous bar for vessels to pass). Landed to examine the hill on which the ancient fortress of Deganwy was situated. . . .

Thursday 19th June. Weather fine. This morning was devoted to the same promontory . . . quitted the path leading to the church of Llandudno and turned off to the left close to some copper mines and from thence to the signal post, established by the Navy Office. There we found Lieutenant Wright who pointed out to us by means of glasses the different signal posts on the coast. I plainly distinguished (without their aid) the Isle of Man. . . .

Friday 20th June. Fine weather . . . having hired a boat, took advantage of the tide and went up the River Conwy as far as Caer Hen [*Hun*], five miles. Saw many of that beautiful species of wild fowl called burrow ducks [*sheldrakes*] with large broods of young [*p. 234*] . . . landed at Caer Hen. . . .[14] We saw the marks of excavations that had been made by the late Mr Griffith who died in the prime of his life, and who had just acquired a taste for the investigation of his national antiquities. These excavations were made not within the area of the camp but in a field beneath [*between*] it and the river. .

Saturday 21st June. Fine weather. Employed the morning in taking views at Conwy. . . .

Sunday 22nd June. Mist and rain, cleared up before noon. . . . Crossed the Menai at Bangor ferry. . . . To Holyhead two stages of M.Xll each; change at Gwyndy, a large single house apparently a good and quiet inn. For the space of twenty-five miles I never saw so tedious an uniformity of uninteresting country. . . . Jackson's Hotel, Holyhead; noisy and inattentive, as is the case in most bustling towns from whence there is a passage. . . . Parish church built within a square enclosure . . . perhaps not so old as the time of the Romans; they [*the walls*] are built herring-bone fashion. . . .[15]

Monday 23rd June. Fine weather. Set sail in the evening at 8 o'clock in the Union Packet, Captain Skinner. Rough swelling sea. . . .

[Expence per packet

Berths for Self and Son	£2.	2.		
Berths for two servants	£1.	1.		
Chaise 2.2., Shipping 10/6	£2.	12.	6	
Custom house fees Holyhead		6.	6	
	£6.	2.	6	[£6-2-0]
Gave the Steward		17.	6	
	£7.	0.	0]	[£6-19-6]

[*Hoare's Journal in Ireland was published by himself in 1807 and so is omitted here.*]

1807

[*Hoare did not travel this year and so no journal exists*]

1808

[*No journal in the quarto volumes but there is a journal in folio volume 3, ff. 46-77, and Fenton refers to Hoare in his company in Wales in this year. The following brief extracts are from the damaged folio leaves*]

. . . *South and North Wales . . . in the year 1808*

Tuesday 7th June. Sailed for Cambria with a wind directly contrary. Mounted my horse and proceeded *via maritima* to Newport. . . . Looked down on the *Urbs Legionum* (Caerleon) and observed a new stone bridge substituted for the old one of wood. . . . But with what different sensations do I now view this tract of road? When I last traced it in company with the historian of Monmouthshire, and my friend, Mr Coxe, the spirit of curiosity and investigation animated our pursuits and enlivened our rides. Novelty is one of the most essential ingredients in the traveller's recipe, and I never experienced the want of it so much as on the present occasion. . . . Railroads begin to be preferred to canals, being less expensive in their original formation, less expensive as to repairs and less subject to risk and damage.

Wednesday 8 June.   Saw the ruins of Ogmore Castle to the left and another large house is building nearer to the road. The trowel seems not to want employment in this district.

Thursday 9 June.   . . . Passed by Margam for I had not the resolution to see what further dilapidations had been made upon its elegant and once perfect chapter house, nor inclination to witness the modern improvements lately made (as I was now informed) to its interesting Norman church. Aberavon — smoking with furnaces. . . . See the ruins of Neth Abbey in a bottom on the left, a shapeless and dirty mass, as viewed from this distance. . . .

Friday 10 June.   . . . Aberdulas. Turned off a few paces on the right to see a mill and another waterfall. A delightful scene and perfect composition for the pencil. The masses of fallen rock are particularly grand and the whole scene appeared to me to merit attention. . . .[16]

Tuesday 14 June.   From Narbeth to Tenby 11 miles, shocking and shaking road torn up by the continual carriage of lime and stone. I hailed with joy the first sign of the chearful town of Tenby, which on all sides and in every point of view merits the epithet of picturesque. My stay at Tenbigh was extended. . . .

Monday 20th June.   This day was employed in viewing Pembroke where there is much to attract the pen of the antiquary and employ the pen[cil] of the artist. Pembroke with its stately castle is to South Wales what Conway is to North Wales, but the round tower of the former has certainly no rival. Each are built upon a rock and each is washed by salt water. A commodious walk to the natural cavern called the Wogan has been nearly completed. . . .

Friday 24 June.   . . . continued our ride through Hubberstone to the battery where we enjoyed an advantageous view of this fine harbour. . . . When we both view and consider the sudden formation of the town of Milford (the work of one individual, Mr Greville) it cannot be viewed without interest.[17] A new church is lately completed; I like its interior better than its exterior. . . .

Tuesday 28 June.   From Haverfordwest went to St Davids. Roch Castle on the road singular from being built on one of those land rocks so peculiar to

Pembrokeshire. It is so commanding an object that it is seen on all sides for many miles round the country. . . .

Wednesday 13 July. From Llampeter to the Devil's Bridge. Took shelter during a storm at *Laventium*. . . . The stately mansion at Hafod with a portion of its valuable library has been burned since my last excursion to this place but phoenix-like is again rising most rapidly, and with renovated splendor. . . .

Thursday 14th July. . . . Crossed the Dovey again near Mallwyd over a picturesque bridge and the only one in the long inter-space between this place and Machynlleth.[18]

Thursday 4 August. After a fortnight's rest at my delightful villa at Vachdeiliog I again mounted my horse and directed my course towards Dolgelley. . . . I found the town of Dolgelley much improved since my last visit: many new buildings, and a goal placed in a healthy and elevated situation at a short distance out of town, a new inn. . . .

. . . [5] *August.* Ascended . . . Cadair Idris . . ., these bird's eye views defy the descriptive powers either of the pen or the pencil. . . . We also rode up to Nannau, the residence and park of Sir Robert Vaughan who has lately built a large and solid mansion house, not in the most appropriate style of architecture.

Sunday 7 August. Rode from Dolgelley to Barmouth, one of the finest rides in North Wales *when the tide is up*.

Tuesday 16 August. Returned to Vachdeiliog where we remained till the 25th.

Friday 26 August. Once more I sallied forth in search of the Roman station of *Mediolanum*,[19] so frequently mentioned in the *itineraries* and so often looked for in vain. I had heard of coins and earthworks. . . .

Sunday 4 September. . . . Not far from our present abode is Kinmel,[20] a handsome new house lately built by the Rev'd Mr Hughes, the fortunate proprietor of a part of the Parys Mountain [*p. 188*].

Wednesday 7 September. To St Asaph, Holywell and Chester.

Here end my rambles in Cambria. The interval betwen their termination and my return to Stourhead was filled up by visits to my friend Sir John Leycester at Tabley in Cheshire and Mr Parker at Browsholme near Clithero in Lancashire in the environs of which there are many objects deserving the notice of artist and antiquary

R.C.H.

1809

[Hoare did not travel this year so no journal exists]

X

[The following table occurs on pp. 111-2 of volume 6 of the quarto volumes following the journal but has been here transferred to the front. It does not correspond exactly to the route of the tour but seems to represent draft headings for a proposed 'historical tour' of this area.]

Tour in Caernarvonshire

Iter 1. From Bala to Ysbytty, follow the Conwy to Llanrwst-Gwydir.
Iter 2. Follow the River Conwy to Caer Hen and Conwy. Conwy and environs. Roman road.
Iter 3. From Conwy to Aber and Penrhyn. Penmaenmawr. Slate quarries. Llandegai etc.
Iter 4. Bangor etc to Caernarvon.
Iter 5. From Caernarvon to Clynnog. Nevin. Madryn. Tre'r Caeri. Vortigern's Vale.
Iter 6. Bardsey Isle. Pwlheli. Mr Ellis's.
Iter 7. Criccieth. Tremadoc. Bedgelert. Snowdon and back to Bedgelert.
Iter 8. From Bedgelert by Llyn Dinas and Gwyned to C. Cerrig.
Iter 9. From Capel Cerrig down the Vale of Lugwy up the Vale of Lleder to Dolwyddelan Castle. Penmachno.
Iter 10. Vale of Llanberris and Dolbadarn Castle.
Iter 11. The Irish Road by Llyn Ogwen to Bangor Ferry and Anglesea.
Iter 12. The whole extent of the banks of the Menai.
Iter 12. [*sic*] From Beaumaris. Plas Gwyn.
Iter 13. Paris Mines etc.
Iter 14. From Amlwch to Holyhead etc.
Iter 15. From Holyhead through the interior to the Menai.
Iter 16. From the Menai by Aberfrau etc and western coast.

A Tour through Caernarvonshire. Anno 1810.

A complete and comprehensive tour of the County of Caernarvon being the object of this excursion we made the best of our way from Vachdeilliog on the *2nd of July* to Yspytty Evan [*Ysbyty Ifan*], the first village on the banks of the Rivery Conwy or great water from [*blank*]. . . . Its principal source is derived from a large lake in the County of Caernarvon called Llyn Conwy, situated in a most barren and dreary waste, the sound of whose waters are interrupted only by the discordant shrieks of a large species of sea gull which frequents the lakes, and the wild notes of the grouse. It abounds with trout which are excellent and ranks second in size to Pimble Mere or Bala Pool. . . .

A dreary ride brought us to the little village of Yspytty Evan, distant about 12 miles from Bala. . . . A small neat village situated in Denbighshire on the banks of the Conwy which flows over a singular bed of rock. Pennant (p. 131) says there was formerly an hospital of the Order of St John of Jerusalem here which was succeeded by another charity.[1] The church is a neat building, well paved and neatly kept, not often the case in Wales. But these matters have been better attended to since the establishment of the office of rural deans whose business it is to overlook and order the repairs necessary to ecclesiastical buildings. In this church are preserved the mutilated remains of three alabaster effigies whose names have been recorded by Pennant. The mutilation of these monuments may be attributed to the wanton tricks of schoolboys who, according to the Welsh custom, resorted to the church as a schoolroom. . . . Leaving Yspytty turn off to the left on a common and descend gradually till we enter the Vale of Conwy near a fine bridge of one lofty arch and large span. . . . Here the new road from Shrewsbury to Capel Cerrig [*Curig*] and Holyhead joins the river and continues its track along the west and Denbighshire side. The country now encreases in interest and arrests the attention by the boldness and richness of its features. The Conwy flows in a very confined channel over a very uneven bed of rocks forming occasional cataracts which only after heavy rains deserve notice, but is so hidden in its deep bed and by the wood on its sides that only occasional views of it are caught. On reaching a second fine bridge and the spot where the road leaving Denbighshire crosses it into Caernarvonshire on its course to Capel Cerrig my pencil was drawn forth from its case to catch an idea of the surrounding scenery, so peculiarly adapted for that purpose. We continued our route to Llanrwst on the Denbighshire side of the river. . . .

Llanrwst, ie the church of Saint Rystyd or Restitutus (see Pennant, vol, 2, p. 143), Archbishop of London in 361, is situated on the east or Denbighshire (side) of the River Conwy. Its church is one of the most interesting in N. Wales, containing many curious sepulchral and architectural memorials. It consists of one aisle or a simple nave with a chapel belonging to the house of Gwydir attached to it on the south. It has a very simple roof of wood, not ceiled. The choir is separated by a very rich skreen of oak. . . . A circular arch with a rich carved border in wood separates the Gwydir chapel from the church. It is also decorated with other carvings in wood and contains many sepulchral memorials of various ages and in various styles; the recumbent effigy of Howel Coetmor (probably derived from Coed Mawr), formerly owner of the Gwydir estate claims the preference in point of sculpture and the coffin of Llewellyn the Great in point of antiquity. . . .

Gwydir (so spelt by the modern Lord of the Estate). Part of the ancient building attracts the attention as you pass the modern habitation: an arch or gatehouse date 1555, and a pleasure house 1592. A neat little chapel in the wood above, date SRWB 1673, marks the site where another mansion formerly stood, called Gwedir, far superior in point of situation — see

Pennant 2, p. 140.[2]

Wednesday 4 July. The heavy rains of yesterday recompensed us for a day spent within doors by the fireside; for the rocky bed of the Conwy was now full and the cataracts in high beauty. For a considerable way our road led us under the majestic and towering woods of Gwedir which are well fenced and attended to. I could not but regret the injudicious and sombre mixture of the Scottish fir with the brilliant forest trees of different species. . . . We now come to a bridge over the Llugwy near its confluence with the Conwy which has been celebrated for its picturesque form and surrounding scenery. There is a good representation of it in aquatinta by the veteran Paul Sandby.[3] The river falls above it very precipitously over a bed of rock. At a little distance is Bettwys [*y Coed*], a small village through which the *Sarn Helen*,[4] a Roman road passed on its course from the station of *Eryri Mons*, now Tommen y Mur, to *Canovium* or Caer Hên. We could not find the clerk nor the key of the church so we were obliged to leave the monument of the Knight of Bettws unseen [*p. 249*]. . . . The river continues to fall rapidly and forms numerous fine cataracts, the most celebrated of which falls through a very deep ravine surmounted by a lofty rock and fine wood of oak and birches and is called Rhaiader y Wenol, or the Waterfall of the Swallow (Pennant, vol 2, p. 135). . . .

   Capel Cerrig [*Curig*], ie the chapel of St Cyric. We fixed on this central spot for our different excusions in the Snowdonian district. When I last visited these parts some years ago there was no accommodation even for the fisherman or even a pedestrian-tourist, but the public zeal of the late Lord Penrhyn has remedied all these inconveniences by establishing a large and commodious inn at Capel Cerrig and by rendering the rough places plain. The whole country is now become practicable in every direction, and a chaise rolls on with ease and safety where a timid equestrian would not have ventured. The inn and its appendages occupy a large space of ground and its different sides afford a singular contrast. On one side you will see numerous carriages hastening to or from the *dear country* and all the posting bustle of Hounslow or Salthill; on the other side all is retirement and wild solitude. . . . In front of the house is a rugged mountain covered with partial rock and wood of birch trees. The remaining scenery is wild, rugged and mountainous. I cannot commend either the architecture or materials of the house, particularly those of the principal front which is entirely lined with slate, giving it a most funereal appearance when viewed from the lake and other places. Had it been built with the stone of the country, and not faced, it would have proved a good and enlivening object from many points of view in the neighbourhood. The architecture is a medley of square and pointed windows etc, and irregular in its plan. The bedrooms are in general small but the whole is commodious, and so good a refuge in so desolate a country could hardly be expected.

Tuesday 10th July. Having been confined to our fireside for the two last days by storm and tempest we gladly mounted our horses. The heavy rains induced me to shew my friend [*Fenton*] the savage beauties of Llyn Ogwen and its neighborhood. A day succeding rain should always be selected for seeing a country abounding in rivers and waterfalls, especially in Wales, where from the sudden rise and fall of the mountain brooks the fine natural scenery is either increased or totally derived.

The road from Capel Cerrig to Bangor owes its origin and existence to the spirited efforts of the late Lord Penrhyn. . . . A dreary and narrow vale bounded by barren mountains unenlivened by the chearful verdure of wild foliage, leads us for some few miles to the embouchure of the valley of Ogwen. The fissures made by water testify the former abundance of trees in this valley as the peaty soil is full of their roots. On the left is a mountain of a curious form called Trifan. . . . The road towards Ogwen Lake increases in interest and expectation is kept on the watch to see where the road will lead the traveller for all seems embosomed in impracticable mountains. The scene at length discloses a fine lake, along whose banks the great road leads for a mile or upwards. Wildness prevails all around: barren rock boasting of no herbage but fern and heath, not a tree to be seen, rills and cataracts rolling down from the lakes above amongst the huge fragments disjointed from their native bed by some great effort of nature. All around you, I repeat, is wild but in character; no cottage, no pasture, no plot of corn or potatoes interrupt the savage scenery. . . . On this same spot I fancied I could discover a cromlech overturned; in this land of stones it may probably be only fancy. . . . The trout in Llyn Ogwen rank amongst the best in Wales and of the many I have tasted are only exceeded by those of Llyn Morwynion and perhaps Llyn Conwy. They rise freely at a fly and would afford excellent sport to the fisherman if nets were not made use of to entrap them. . . .

Wednesday 11 July.   Followed the Vale of the Llugwy . . . we gained some information from an intelligent farmer concerning the Roman road called *Sarn Helen*. He told us it passed on our left through the meadow on its course towards the Vale of Conwy. A steep descent led us to the Vale of Dolwyddelan, a little village in a most retired situation accessible only by a mountainous tract and bad roads. . . . The *Sarn Helen* is well known all over the district. It passed immediately through the Vale of Penmaen on its course to the Roman station at Tommen y Mur '[ERYRI MONS] and must have crossed the fine meadow in the vales, and ascended the hill a little to the south of the present road from the mountains into the village, close to a spring still reserving a memorial of it in the name of Ffynnon Helen. On reaching the valley we eagerly looked for the chief object of our journey, *viz* the Castle,[5] but none was to be seen. It is distant near a mile from the village in a most retired and vital situation well fitted for the residence of a man disgusted with the world. Such was its quondam possessor and inhabitant Iorwerth Drwndwn, the unfortunate son of Llewellyn the Great (Pennant vol. 2, p. 136). . . .

The clouds began to collect round the mountain tops and the bad account of the mountain road to Penmachno deterred us from putting that part of our intended plan into execution. We therefore took a more circuitous road homewards following the course of the Lleder from Dolwyddelan to the spot where it mixes its stream with the Conwy. I am rather surprized that more has not been said about this little, secluded and beautiful valley; but tourists are too apt to follow the unvaried path of their predecessors and in these mountainous regions seem to be afraid of losing their way in search of novelty. . . . We were highly delighted with this valley of the Lleder; some of the scenery is on the grander scale and all is beautiful. A picturesque bridge of the native architecture attracts the attention and a bold Alpine road above it. [The native bridges consist of stone piers, and wooden rails between them, built of the rough unhewn stone of the country and produce a very picturesque and appropriate effect.] The stream flows over a very rough and rocky red, and is always lively and animating. . . .

Saturday 14 July. Our progress had been impeded for the last two days by bad weather. We this morning returned to Llanrwst and in our way endevored to fill up some gaps which had been left in our former *iters*. From this road the mountain Moel Siabod appears in a more picturesque point of view. . . . On the left of the road where the River Llugwy flows close to it and where the vale is rather broader than usual are the decided remains of a Roman settlement, ascertained by the bricks, tiles, columns and peculiar mortar made use of by that nation.[6] A part also of the square or oblong enclosure with its rounded corners is very distinguishable. The situation was (as usual) on a slight eminence. In a neighboring wall of a little inclosure are six or seven of the rude stone pillars that divided the upper and lower stories of the hypocaust or sudatory, a building and luxury attached to every villa of the Romans. We were led to this discovery by some notes made by my companion, Mr Fenton, in the Bodleian Library at Oxford, from MSS of the celebrated Cambrian, Edward Llwyd,[7] to whom Bishop Gibson was so much indebted in the publication of his improved edition of Camden's *Brittania*. He merely mentions bricks having been found on the spot; and this is not the first instance where from such slight evidence or hints we have made similar Roman discoveries, for instance the stations at Tommen y Mur, Tre Coch near Llandovery etc etc. . . .

A litle beyond this spot is the Cascade of the Swallow, mentioned before, page [247], but slightly. Our curiosity tempted us to descend to it by a very steep and slippery tract and highly were we repaid for our risk and labor. . . . An easy descent might be made at a trifling expence and would be highly acceptable to the numerous passengers who at present pass by it unheeded.

Proceeded to Bettws where we at length obtained the key of the parish church and paid our homage to its gallant knight, Gruffydd ap Dafydd Goch, whose well sculptured and well preserved effigy still remains within its walls. The church is rude and is only distant six feet from the perpendicular bank of the River Conwy which is of a shivering and crumbling soil, and in the corner of the walls near the river there is a settlement which forebodes a future ruin.[8] The view on each side is delightful and the cemetery abounds in fine yew and forest trees, and is nicely kept by the close-biting sheep. From Bettws we deviated to the south to fill up a gap occasioned by the weather of last Wednesday and to see the falls of the River Machno. . . .

Sunday 15 July.   After visiting Mr Burrell at Gwydir we proceeded on our route to Conwy. Many parts of this respectable old mansion will attract the antiquary's attention: the entrance gateway, the general view of the quadrangle, a most singular mixture of ancient architecture, and a very curious figured chimney piece in a room above the gateway. The scenery for some distance along the vale is fine: boldly aspiring mountains cloathed with old and modern wood, cascades falling precipitously from the lakes in the mountains above etc, etc. The Conwy is navigable for vessels to the village of Trefriew. Further on the right is Caer Hen [*Hun*], the site of the ancient Roman city of *Canovium*, just below the seat of the Griffiths family where numerous relicts dug up there are carefully preserved. Near this spot crossed the Roman road. . . . Cultivation improves and agriculture has converted the rocky waste into chearful corn fields, and in this sad year of failure and apprehension no one can view the excellent crops in this district without satisfaction. From the heights above Caer Hên on the right of the road there is a pleasing retrospective view of the rich vale of Llanrwst, and soon afterwards the astonished eye greets the proud towers and embattled walls of the modern Canovium. This, I think, is the fourth time of my appearance [*experience*] of this stage of wonder and delight, nor is my ardor abated or attention diminished; such scenes of novelty and magnificence can never tire.

Monday 16 July.   Returned to Caer Hen. At two miles from Conwy the river being at high water appeared to great advantage and the eye now dwelt with rapture on it where yesterday its muddy bed was passed over almost unnoticed. . . . Called on Mrs Griffiths to see the antique Roman fragments found at *Canovium*. Amongst these was a most curious circular shield lined with strong leather, with a projecting umbo of iron in the centre and ornamented with circles of iron, embossed with brass knobs [*drawing, 13 in diameter*]. NB. A particular account of Caer Hen and its discoveries was published in the *Archaeologia* of last year by Lysons.[9]
    From Caer Hen we ascended by a long, rough and steep ascent of about two miles to an ancient British camp situated on a high hill and called Pen Caer [*Pen y Gaer*]. Mr Pennant, vol 2, p. 336, has slightly mentioned this fortress. . . . Passed through Lanpeder *(Llanbedr-y-cennin)* . . . in the churchyard is a stone bearing the marks of considerable antiquity [*sketch*]. It is of hard blue stone and has a projection at top resembling the mortis [*tenon*] on our stones at Stonehenge. . . .[10] Our path led us to the very entrance to the fortress which took a slanting direction through two aggers of stone into the area of the camp which occupied the whole apex of the hill

which naturally sloped towards the uppermost *vallum*. This as well as the others was raised by loose stones without cement. Following the circle of the encampment from the entrance at the west, near to which are two small *tumuli* of stone, towards the south are found three *aggers*, which towards the east terminate in one. Here the hill becomes stronger by nature and did not require the assistance of art. Towards the N. West the number of *aggers* is again increased to two which are continued to the aforesaid entrance. But the greatest singularity of this work is a strong barrier made below the lower *agger*, and where the access to the camp is weakest, by numerous pointed stones set upright and so thick as to render it inaccessible to cavalry and difficult to foot. I never yet have seen a similar mode of fortification.[11] But this eminence merits the attention of the non-antiquary from the very fine and extensive prospect which it commands. . . . NB. The area of this camp is uneven and near the *agger* has many cavities which in ancient times probably were made for huts and habitations.

Fortune favored us with regard to weather during our stay at Conwy, and we had an opportunity of viewing with minuteness and satisfaction the peninsula to the north-west of Conwy. It possesses many natural beauties, as well as objects of historical enquiry. The first is the site of the ancient town and fortress of Deganwy situated on a point of land up the river . . . two conical hills which were united by a strong wall most admirably joined to the native rock. On the west side of the largest hill there are considerable traces of a high wall, a round tower etc, etc. . . . Between Diganwy and the rocky promontory of Landudno is a dreary tract of sand and marsh.[12] A steep ascent led us near some copper mines to the Government signal house [*p. 240*] on the heights from whence we proceeded over a smooth and verdant turf, pastured by sheep, to the extreme point of the headland, enjoying a most extensive and delightful prospect both by sea and land. . . .

On such a retired and exalted spot we naturally expected to discover some curious British remains, such as *tumuli*, cromlechs, *kistvaens* and similar marks of ancient colonization but I could only see one mound that appeared sepulchral. The whole of the hill bore evident signs of a more extensive cultivation than it bears at present; the ridges of the furrows are very visible, and some scattered foundations of various buildings. A few patches of corn are still to be seen but few in comparison to what they must have been formerly. On the north east side of the promontory is the parish church of Llandudno, a solitary building in a very exposed situation, open to the winds and sea. On returning to the plain we deviated a little to the left and ascended a hill to see a rocking stone and fortress mentioned by Pennant (vol 2, page [*332*]) but found his account rather fanciful and exaggerated. . . . I cannot think that its moving qualities can be fairly attributed to any agent but chance . . . there are some very perfect models of the ancient huts and habitations of the Britons. They are slightly excavated and surrounded with rows of stones placed upright. . . .

This ride occupied one morning most pleasantly and the following *iter* was equally satisfactory on the succeding one. Bodscallen [*Bodysgallen*], a seat of Sir Thomas Mostyn, was the first object which arrested our progress and where we were most politely received by Mrs Mostyn who resides there with two unmarried sisters of Sir Thomas Mostyn. The mansion is surrounded by lofty forest trees, who dread not the approach of the merciless woodman and his axe. The immediate environs of it are enlivened by the gay parterre and sweet-scented flowers. The interior contains some interesting portraits mentioned by Pennant (vol 2, p. 337) and some curious old MSS. . . . From Bodscallen we proceeded to Gloddaeth, another seat of Sir Thomas Mostyn. It appears to great advantage from the fields through which we passed. . . . The library contains some objects of antiquity amongst the most remarkable of which I must place the wreath or torques of gold found in the neighborhood of Harlech Castle, the diameter of which is thirteen inches [*p. 240*]. We also saw the fine illuminated vellum MSS of Froissart in fine preservation, a fine collection of medals, brass celts etc, etc. The house commands a rich and varied view. Beneath it are warm and sheltered gardens. The interior of the mansion bespeaks the comfort and hospitality of ancient days. The chimneys are large bearing mottos over them. The hall is a respectable old building and the buttery and kitchen with their massive doors of heart of oak remind us strongly of days of yore. Hospitality seems still to be attached to these walls, if I may be allowed to judge by the hearty reception we met there from the present inhabitant of it, Mr Kenrick Lloyd.

From Gloddaeth we proceeded by a farm called Penrhyn, where an old chapel now serves the purpose of a stable, to the sea coast. . . . Open beach and sea. Immediately on it under a bank is a small building covering a spring of water, once probably held in high veneration for its miraculuous qualities and dedicated to the saint of this district, S. Trillo. It certainly was not a chapel, not being placed east west. . . .[12] We next visited the church of Lllandrillo . . . contains within it four of the best proportioned arches I ever remember to have seen of the architecture of Henry VII, when the arch began to lose its pointed form and to assume a broader curve. In the window are some fragments of old painted glass amongst which is the escutcheon born by Ednyfed Vychan. . . . At a short distance from this church are some extensive ruins rendered very conspicuous by a lofty chimney bearing the resemblance of a column. They are called Bryn Euryn which my fellow traveller says in Welsh means the hill of sloes . . . visited the church of Llancwstenin [*Llangwsteinin*] or church of Constantine. . . . Here I saw one of the handbells used formerly and even now at funerals and mentioned by Giraldus in his itinerary through Wales [*drawing*].

From this place we proceeded to the great road from Abergeley and from thence to our quarters at Conwy. In this morning's ride we saw two singular instances of strength of mind and strength of body: the former in a farmer who, though blind, beat down his own walnuts from the tree, and the bushes for a hare; the latter in a poor deranged woman who lived in a state of nature rambling over the country and had not for a long course of years slept under the cover of any habitation.

Friday 20th July. The whole of the day was spent at Caer Rhun [*Caerhun*] and neighborhood. . . . We filled up our morning in visiting the ruins of ancient *Canovium*. They are situated below the church which is enclosed within the square area of the camp, at least the only part of them which has been hitherto well explored, consisting of a villa with its several compartments. . . .[13] We could see evident traces of the causeway issuing from the station in its course westwards to the next station of *Segontium* (Caernarvon), and we were shown the spot where the Romans crossed the River Conwy in their course to the other station of *Varis* (near Bodfari) in Denbighshire. It was near a projecting rock on the Caer Rhun side where it descended in a slanting direction to meet the road on the Denbighshire side and is not so far down the river as the present ferry at Tal-y-cafn. . . .

Saturday 21st July. Some MSS notes collected *per* the papers of the late ingenious Mr Griffith of Caer Rhun induced us to visit the heights of Penmaen Bach. . . . We continued our ride towards Conwy along the ridge of hill and found a path which led us to the highest part of it. On this strong and rocky eminence is one of the finest *gaers* I ever beheld, of the most remote British antiquity, and commanding such a variety of views by sea and land as I never before witnessed. [Pennant, vol 2, p. 235 calls it Castell Caer Lleion but speaks of it too slightly. . .] The interior of this camp presents a striking picture of ancient British days, when our ancestors, disdaining the more luxurious and sheltered situation of the wooded vale resided in the bleak heights in huts cut in the native rock. Of these there are numerous examples within the area of this camp. They are excavated in the rock, of a circular form and surrounded with stones set up on end. Similar excavations and residences are to be found in all the old fortified camps in Wales, and may be looked up[on] as certain evidences of the most ancient population. They are generally known by the name of *Cyttiau Gwyddelid* [-od] or 'the huts of the woodmen'.

But before I quit this delightful *séjour* of Conwy, to me, after repeated visits, 'ever charming, ever new', I must give some account of its town and contents. Mr Pennant very justly remarks 'that a more ragged town within or a more beautiful town without is scarcely to be seen'. The best general idea of the town and castle may be collected from the plans which he has annexed to his tour of each of them.[14]

He tells you that the castle was oblong in its form, placed on all sides on the verge of a precipitous rock, composed of eight vast round towers, each with a slender one of amazing elegance issuing from its top within which was winding staircase [after minute examination of the eight large towers I cannot find traces of any smaller towers issuing from the four which are nearest the town. . . .] The ground floor seems to have consisted of a long court parallel with which was a hall irregular in its form and built according to the shape of the ground. . . . Beyond the first court is a smaller one nearly square, a small apartment beyond it and two others on the opposite side. Of the eight large round towers two only present any peculiarities worth

36. Conwy Castle, entry by the original ramp and rustic bridge at north-west corner.

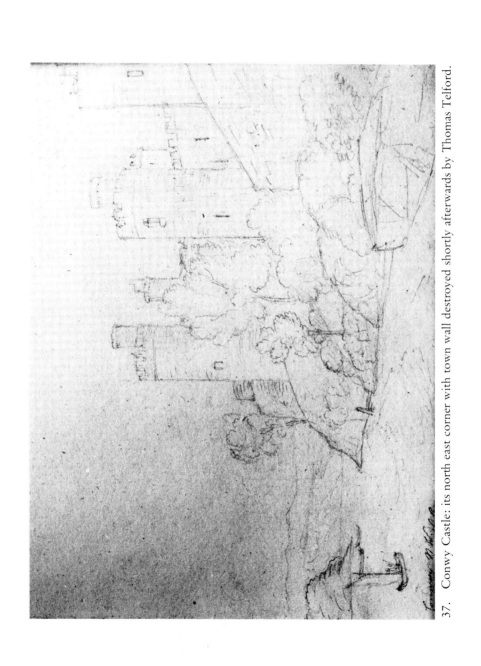

37. Conwy Castle: its north east corner with town wall destroyed shortly afterwards by Thomas Telford.

recording. The one at the extremity of the castle towards the north west [*east*] has an elegant recess cut within the thickness of its walls, richly ornamented with a groined roof, pointed arches and three lancet windows. . My friend Fenton exclaimed 'Why should not this be the chapel?' . . . The other peculiarity in these round towers is the one that is partly fallen and seems suspended in the air and which seems to strike everyone's attention and astonishment, particularly when looked up to from the shore beneath.

The whole circuit of the [*town*] walls can easily be traced and the several towers, gates etc remain in a very high state of preservation considering the aera in which they were built and the wanton depredations of people upon them. . . . It was surrounded by strong walls and intermediate towers which were not all completely circular but open on the side within the walls. . . . Within the town there are some objects worthy of notice, especially a very old fashioned house, curiously decorated with various devices mottos etc called Plas Mawr and built by Robert Wynn, 1585 (see Pennant vol 2, page 330). And in Castle Street there is a very singular window in a house now called the College. . . . In the eye of every artist this town and castle must convey unequalled beauties. I never saw one that could present itself in such varied and excellent points of view, and so fitted to the powers of the pencil. I now leave its walls for the fourth time but not yet satisfied with its picturesque beauties.

Saturday 21st.   In the evening rode over the Alpine pass of Penmaenmawr to Aber where we found comfortable accomodations, civil treatment and a quiet and charming retirement.

Sunday 22nd July.   Aber. The object of this morning's ride was the Roman road leading across the mountains from that station of *Canovium* (Caer Rhun) to that of *Segontium* (Caernarvon). . . . An abrupt turn in our road discloses a different view with a bridge and distant waterfall descending from the steep sides of a rocky mountain. This has been pointed out by tourist authors as one of the finest in N. Wales. It reminded me of the celebrated Pistyl Rhaiadr in Montgomeryshire. . . . May be admired for the height of its fall but will not afford a fine subject for the pencil [Much has been disputed about the word *picturesque* by Mr Price and Mr Knight etc. It appears to me that in its true meaning it ought only to be applied to such subjects in nature as will form a picture and not to those which from the great extent of prospect cannot be comprehended within the limits of the paper or canvas].

A steep ascent to the mountains where the eye accustomed to British remains soon finds food for reflection. The first object that attracted my attention was a *kistvaen* of rather a singular construction; it was of the usual circular form with the *kistvaen* or stone chest in the centre and surrounded by four circles of stones. . . . A little beyond it is a large circle, in diameter about 50 yards, of loose stones. . . . Dreary foreground of stone and mountain, Anglesey appearing like a map under your feet. Our eyes constantly on the alert in hopes of seeing the Roman road. Fancy often exclaimed: 'Here it certainly must be'. No certain *indicia* however appeared until we had passed the Bwlch y ddei fan [*ddeu faen*] or Pass of the Two Stones . . . we at last found the undoubted causeway of the Romans which ran to the left of the modern trackway . . . it approached the brow of the hill leading into the valley towards *Canovium*, where there is a *maen hirion* [*hir*], a large upright stone placed as it were for a direction post to those travelling in the valley. . . . We observed plainly Caer Rhun and a fine extensive view of the vale and distant country in Denbighshire . . . we returned towards Aber, and in our retrograde line followed the causeway most satisfactorily for several miles. [In tracing Roman roads much time and trouble may be saved by not attempting to trace the line until you have fairly got upon a part of them. The task will be then much easier and the straight line, which they almost invariably kept, will be less difficult to pursue] On drawing near towards Aber the vestiges of it became more doubtful and it is difficult to say positively through which of the many vallies it descended to the sea coast. . . .

Monday 23rd July.   We mounted our horses with impatience and anxiety to visit the heights of Penmaenmawr of which such various and interesting accounts have been given by writers.[15] None so much so as that by Gibson taken from the notes of that intelligent Welshman, Edward Lhuyd[16] . . . brought us to the foot of the mountain, where we dismounted, leaving our horses under the shelter of a high fence wall. This ascent to the summit was on the south west side and in a part between the two elevated points where there is an extensive plain . . . *Indicia* of ancient British population soon met our eyes. . . . By a rugged but gradual ascent we at length reached the summit of Penmaen [*mawr*] having passed through the dilapidated ramparts of its ancient fortress. On the top we observed a large *carnedd*, which had been opened, and discovered the pilfered *kistvaen* of the chieftain who claimed it as his sepulchral monument. To the north of this relict is an excavation in the rock called the well, and we were assured that it was a spring and never dry. If true what a singular phenomenon in nature to find water at such a considerable height. . . . Such an eminence must afford a most extensive view, of a sufficient height to satisfy the eye without confusing it; and although we found the accounts of authors rather exaggerated yet we cannot but consider it as well worth the attention of the tourist. It affords another instance of British castrame[*n*]tation and reminds us forcibly of the rude and uncivilised life and customs of days of yore. . . . We varied our route homewards by a less steep descent leaving the church of Llanvair [*Llanfairfechan*], prettily situated on an eminence, a little on our left hand.

Aber is a neat little village with a picturesque valley at the back of it. Our inn window commanded a pleasing view of Penmaen mawr, Priestholm Island and a part of the adjoining coast of Anglesey, and we left our inn highly satisfied with the accomodations and good treatment we met with.

Followed a narrow lane running nearer the hills than the turnpike in hopes of seeing some traces of the Roman road which I think took that line, but could find no traces of the *sarn*. On approaching to our halting place at Penrhyn the neat little church of Llandegai and the towers of Penrhyn rearing their castellated heads above a thick grove of trees attracted our attention. We stopt to see the former whose interior as well as exterior deserve the tourist's notice. It is castellated and varies in its architecture from the generality of country churches. Though the yellow wash and blacking have been profusely smeared over its walls giving it a very modern appearance yet I am inclined to think it a building of considerable antiquity. In it is a well sculptured tomb of Archbishop Williams kneeling before an altar. . . .

We were again fortunate in the choice of our resting place at the Penrhyn Arms and I believe few windows, and I doubt if any in England or Wales, can present such a scene as that we viewed from our rotunda at this place. In front was the little port of Penrhyn, well stored with vessels, and beyond it the ocean enlivened with trade. On a well-wooded bank in Anglesey the town of Beaumaris and castle etc. . . . Descend to the bowling green attached to a delightful coffee room and the landscape receives additional beauties from a richly cultivated and well-wooded country terminated by a most magnificent range of mountains. . . . During our abode at Penrhyn one morning was spent most satisfactorily on the banks of the River Ogwen. . . . At a distance of about [4] miles are the celebrated slate quarries belonging to the Penrhyn family and during the whole way you say [see] the useful appendages to them, *viz* railroads, windlasses etc etc. Note: saw 17 carts loaded with slate, drawn by three horses. . . . Lady Penrhyn's cottages. We visited first the one situated uppermost in the vale. This is the most simple and appropiated to the use of a dairy. . . . They are each placed near a waterfall of the Ogwen River.

Another morning was devoted to the house and grounds at Penrhyn where the same astonishing neatness pervades every department to a degree, I believe, unequalled.[17] The hall is a very handsome lofty room, the windows decorated with the armorial family arms in painted glass. . . . The architecture of the exterior is castellated; one of the towers which commands a most extensive view is ancient, the companion modern. The chapel once stood in front of the house but is now removed to a more commodious distance. The bath on the shores of the bay deserves notice, as well as the beautifully ornamented cottage near it which commands a delightful view of the bay. . . .

The town of Bangor is more to be admired for its pretty situation, the varied *emplacement* of its houses and the general neatness that pervades the whole town than for its history or antiquities. The cathedral church boasts only of two headless episcopal effigies. The general style of architecture is the broad Gothic, of that aera when the pointed arch began to take a wider curve, Henry Vll. The tower contrary to usual custom stands at the west end, not in the usual place over the transepts. . . . The remains of the castle mentioned by Pennant, p. 294, as having [*been*] built by Lupus [*Hugh, Earl of Chester*] on the hill opposite the school does not deserve notice, and can barely be recognised by a few shattered walls. The situation both of Bangor and Penrhyn is delightful. . . . No tourist should omit walking from Penrhyn along the seashore to the point where the Menai commences its more confined course. . . .

Saturday 28 July.   In our road to Caernarvon we took the old or upper one by Pentir in hopes of finding some traces of the Roman road leading to *Segontium* but during the whole ride we could not for certainty ascertain a single yard of it, though it undoubtedly took this line. At a short distance to the left of the common between two or three miles from Bangor is a farmhouse called Ty Coch where within these few years an interesting inscription has been found and was visible within these last ten days but has now unfortunately disappeared. I have however been favoured with an accurate copy of it [*Quoted*].[18] *Quere?* Might this not have been a Roman milliary, as the distance of nine miles corresponds very well with that of *Segontium* from this place. Some way further on we deviated to the left, passing by the church of Llandeinolen [*Llanddeiniolen*], remarkable for the extraordinary age and size of the yew trees in its cemetery. A little beyond it on a conspicuous eminence is an ancient and very curious fortification and unlike any I have yet met with in Wales. On the apex of the hill is a circular area surrounded by an *agger* of small stones supported by larger ones without placed upright. The diameter of this area is about 77 yards. In the centre of it are the remains of a *carnedd* with a large upright stone still standing in it, and in the N.E. corner there appears to have been another, the circular form of which is visible but the stones that composed it have been removed. The entrance about three yards wide faced the north-west. This certainly was the original work and a question now may arise whether it ws military or religious.[19] The thickness of the walls, about four yards, may plead in favor of the former supposition, but in situation it is very similar to the religious circles I have met with in my own county of Wilts. . . . Without this ancient enclosure we see the work of an after-age, and evidently military, composed of two well-raised ramparts of stone covered with turf and on the side where the approach is weakest a third outwork. There is a wider space than usual between the first and second rampart, viz 17 yards. The entrace is united with the more ancient one which was probably made a part of it in later times. Its true name is Dinas Dinorwig though the country people know it only by that of Pen y Gaer (see Pennant, vol. 2, p. 159). This was the only object of attraction which the ride afforded, for a more dreary and uninteresting tract was scarcely ever traversed.

We remained at Caernarvon till Tuesday evening, the 31st July. The chief object of attraction at this place is the castle built in the year 1282 immediately after his [*Edward I's*] complete subjection of the Welsh. The architect's name according to Mr Pennant was Ellerton or de Elvreton and it was said the whole line of fortifications with the castle was completed in less than two years[20] . . . at Conway all is round; here the angular prevails in the castle . . .

38. Caernarfon Castle: the Queen's Gate, and boats near southern face of castle.

39. Caernarfon Castle: inside looking west from Kings Gate towards the Eagle Tower showing vanished building.

we find towers with eight, nine and ten angles. The [*town*] walls, as at Conway, are formed by *round* projecting towers with intermediate high walls which appear to have been embattled with eyelet holes. A gallery or platform went round them. The gates also were round; of these there were four. The town stands nearly to the four cardinal points; the castle occupies the south end. . . . On the east side is the principal entrance into the town over a bridge from Bangor and it has five towers including the one at the angle and the two forming the gateway [*fig. 29*]. . . .

The entrance into the castle from the town is very striking over a bridge which loses much of its height and effect from being so much filled up in its ditch. The portal is of the pointed order and lofty, well guarded by portcullises. In the centre over it under a Gothic niche is the statue of the Royal Founder in the act of sheathing is sword, or as Mr Pennant says 'menacing his newly acquired unwilling servants'. . . .[21] The first *entrée* into the castle is very striking, as the area is open and not encumbered with intervening buildings. It was however formerly divided into two courts, which were separated by a gateway of which the vestiges still remain and was defended by two portcullises. In the western court were the state apartments and the Eagle Tower, which from its lofty and massive appearance must excite the admiration of every beholder. Its form is [*a*] decagon, the heavy appearance of which is rendered light by three angular towers that surmount it. On one of these is the rude figure of an eagle which can be recognised only by its beak and eye. It was lately thrown down from its perch by the local militia, but has since been replaced. Various other ornaments decked these battlements such as helmets, busts etc, some of which though much defaced by time bear the marks of good sculptures. This apartment [*tower*] had four rooms; all but the lower one (whose ceiling was supported by a pillar as in chapter houses) had chimneys, but it is somewhat singular that the two middle apartments had none but a borrowed light. The upper room had a window. Mr Pennant says, I know not on what authority, that Edward the Second was born in a little double room adjoining these apartments. The room shown for this scene of *accouchement* is not dark for it has a window in it, as well as a fireplace. True enough its dimensions are very small: not sufficient space for a bed and besides a thoroughfare. Is it then likely that the Prince should have [*been*] ushered into the world in so dismal a hole?

The state apartments adjoin the Eagle Tower on the south side of the court. They had only three stories with massive chimney pieces, varying from those on the Eagle Tower by projecting and are supported by rude pillars [*sketch*]. The windows in these apartments were long and square-headed. The lower room had had two windows; the middle one a large long window and a small narrow one; the upper one had three. So we see that no regularity prevailed in the plan. A long gallery connects these apartments with the tower at the entrance of this court. On the opposite side the ducts which conveyed the water to the castle and the cistern which held it are still visible. Some of the walls in the Eagle Tower are 9 feet thick. The buildings in the eastern court appear to have been of an inferior quality, but here was an entrance said to have been that through which Queen Eleanor made her *entrée* into the castle, and which in its present delapidated state is a great ornament to the outside front. It is of such an height from the ground that it could not be approached without the help of a drawbridge and the rising ground on the land side shows from whence it sprang. This gate, like the other, was protected by a portcullis. On the inside was a terrace elevated much above the level of the area. Quere: was it made so on purpose, or did it arise from fallen building? If the latter there must have been steps to descend from the gateway.[22]

The four fronts of this castle present very different views and vary in their architecture. That facing the north in which was the principal entrance presents a very grand and extended front of good masonry, and it is to be observed that this front being inclosed and protected by the city walls has the convenience of light to the apartments within, and the windows are handsome and well carved. The south front towards the river, nor any of the other fronts, have this convenience but only slits for the discharge of arrows. In short except in the north side defence more then ornament seems to have been chiefly considered. This side presents a grand line of massive fortification. The west side is truly picturesque and less monotonous in its outline. The Eagle Tower forms the chief object of attraction, and the port beneath it presents a lively bustling scene. From the east end the *tout ensemble* perhaps appears in a more advantageous point of view than from any other quarter, particularly if viewed a little way down the river. When the tide is full in the river it furnishes many good subjects for the pencil, but not so many as Conway. It is however a powerful rival in every point of view, either as an architectural record of ancient times, or a glorious study for the artist's portfolio. The interior also furnishes a very good view looking towards the Eagle Tower [*fig. 39*]. . . .

Tuesday 31st July. In the evening we continued our journey to Bethgelert [*Beddgelert*]. . . .

Thursday 2 August. We pursued our journey to Tre Madoc passing by Pont Aberglaslyn where copper mines are worked by a company of Cornish miners, and pursued our road over the new road lately cut under the rock by Mr Madocks[23] . . . the Traeth Mawr bore the appearance of a most beautiful and extensive lake. The sight of this tract of land caused sensations of pleasure and pain: pleasure in reflecting how many valuable lives will be saved by the abolition of the dangerous passage across the sands and how much land will in future times be brought into cultivation; pain in considering that I viewed this glorious scenery and expanse of water perhaps for the last time. . . . Pass under villa of Mr Madocks at Tan yr Allt, prettily situated on a little knoll and well embosomed in wood. I was much struck with the new creation I found at Tre Madoc on a spot which I remember to have been houseless: a neat little town, good inn, handsome town hall, shops, church and meeting house. All the work of an individual now engaged in the stupendous and arduous undertaking of excluding Neptune from his extensive dominion over the sands between this place and Pont Aberglaslyn and thereby reclaiming several thousand acres of cultivable land. The work is in great forwardness and another year will probably decide between Neptune and Ceres.

Friday 3 August. Proceeded to Pwlheli . . . a small seaport and apparently in a flourishing condition; many additional buildings since I last visited it. [*p. 189*]. . . .

Saturday 4 August. Passing through Bodvan [*Bodfuan*], a seat of Lord Newborough, proceeded to the seashore along a newly made road to Porth Dyn Lleyn [*Llaen*]. On our right is the lofty hill of Boduan on which we observed marks of an ancient fortification. I was much struck with the harbour of PDL and with its admirable position and good requisites for a marine bathing establishment . . . and I have no doubt but that the same spirit of improvement and accomodation which has shown itself so conspicuous on the shores of the Traeth Mawr within a few years will extend itself to this beautiful harbour and render it a place of great resort.[24] From hence we proceeded towards a lofty mountain called Carn Madryn [*Fadryn*] . . . the entrance of the stronghold on the south side of the hill. Both the area at the summit and the sides and base of this hill abound in British remains; numerous *cyttiau*, circles, *carneddau* etc etc ascertain its high antiquity. . . .[25]

Sunday 5 August. An interesting ride through an interesting country introduced us to some well preserved British antiquities. The first was a very fine *kistvaen* on a tenement called Kefn [*Cefn*] Issa [*in Llanystumdwy*] consisting of one large rude stone, mushroom-shaped supported [*by*] one long side stone and three others. . . .[26]

Monday 6 August. Under the guidance of Mr Ellis and Mr Williams, a neighboring clergyman etc we proceeded on a visit to Nant Gwitheyrn or Vortigern's Valley. . . .

Wednesday 8 August. Leaving the hospitable mansion of Gwynfryn we turned our horses' heads once more towards Caernarvon over a most dreary tract of badly cultivated land. Passed a tumulus adjoining our road on the left. We felt revived by the appearance of Clunnog Vawr [*Clynnog Fawr*], embosomed in wood and seated in a rich and well-cultivated vale. The church is the pride of N. Wales and now undergoing substantial repairs. Its architecture denotes the aera of Henry VII when the pointed arch began to assume a broader span. . . . A little out of town in a field opposite to Bachwen House is a cromlech in a high state of preservation with one impost of an irregular shape and four stones beneath it. . . .[27] Deviated on the right [*left*] to Dinas Dinlle,[28] an ancient fortress, which makes a very conspicuous figure on the sea coast . . . measuring 480 feet by 400, the vallum on an average is 60 feet . . . composed of gravel and sand. . . .

Thursday 9 August. Left Caernarvon, crossed the Menai. . . . We were now on Classical ground and could not but recall to our recollection the animated account recorded by Tacitus of the events that took place on this spot . . . visited Plas Newydd, the magnificent seat of Lord Uxbridge, magnificent as a building and magnificent in the views it commands over the Menai. Architecture Gothic, stone grey and remarkably fine; hall spacious with good portraits. . . . The antiquary will have a rich treat in viewing the fine British monuments behind the house. . . . From the ferry house on the Menai a new and beautiful road made at the expense of Lord Bulkeley conducted us to Beaumaris. Wales does not afford a better road or a finer ride. . . . The day was clear and the opposite coast distinct, the sea enlivened by the rival cutters etc, etc.

Friday 10 August. This day was devoted to the objects worthy of note in the neighborhood of Beaumaris. The first is Lhanvaes [*Llanfaes*] the seat of Sir Robert Williams, once the habitation of a fraternity of monks of whose residence a spacious barn still attests the former existence. . . . Of their church . . . three narrow lancet windows decorated the western front. . . .[29] Castell Aber Llienawg [*Lleiniog*] (see Pennant, 2, 258) . . . considerable remains of two of these round turrets exist but owing to the thick brambles etc with which the area is overgrown could not discover the square fortress in the middle. . . .[30]

Proceeded to Penmon, situated near the shore. Once a priory of which there are still some very interesting remains which Mr Pennant has over-looked, for his description of the place is contained *in two lines*. The mass of buildings, viz church, refectory, mansion house and dove house[31] form a picturesque *tout ensemble*. The detail of the church is truly interesting and of the highest antiquity. The church is surmounted by a square turret with a long and pointed roof of stone and has two of its original Saxon windows remaining in the east and north sides. On the south side is a Saxon doorway richly ornamented and with a *bas-relief* in rude sculpture of a winged dragon, but the interior presents one of the most perfect specimens of Saxon architecture I ever beheld and such as I little expected to have found in this remote corner of Anglesey. . . . Such examples of ancient architecture, and untouched by the fashionable hand of innovation are scarce even in England and much more so in Wales. . . . A magnificent dove house with a large stone roof proclaims the luxury of former ages. Penmon presents in different points of view many good subjects for the pencil.

Beaumaris. Adjoining the town is Baron's Hill, the seat of Lord Bulkeley, most advantageously placed on rising ground . . . but I cannot speak in favor of the appearance (exterior) of the mansion house [*p. 183*]; its yellow face and pea-green appendages by no means accord with the scenery around. At a short distance from the house under a neat Gothic building is the coffin

40. Penmon Priory, Anglesey, in 1810 looking east at nave and tower of church and adjoining house.

supposed to have once contained the remains of Princess Joan, daughter of King John and wife of Llewelyn, Prince of Wales. . . . Three inscriptions commemorate the history of this coffin in Welsh, Latin and English, one of which I here transcribe: 'This plain sarcophagus (once dignified as having contained the remains of Joan daughter of King John and consort of Llewelyn ap Iorwerth, Prince of North Wales who died in the year 1237) having been conveyed from the Friary of Llanfaes, and alas! used for many years as a horse watering trough was rescued from such indignity and placed here for preservation as well as to excite serious meditation on the transitory nature of all sublunary distinctions, by Thomas James Warren Bulkeley, Viscount Bulkeley, October 1808'.

Beaumaris Castle [*sketch plan*] is nearly square. . . . The principal entrance into the castle and its court is from the south [*p. 183*]. . . . It is much to be lamented that this perfect specimen of Edward's architecture should remain in so neglected a state; a trifling sum would restore it completely and a flight of steps from the court would add much to the facility of its approach. . . .

There is also a curious old house in the town once the residence of the Bulkeley family on the ground floor of which is a very singular and beautifully moulded ceiling.[32] A small fort (a miniature resemblance of Llandegai church) has been very injudiciously built on an eminence in sight of the royal castle.

Saturday 11 August.   Removed to Plas Gwyn, the seat of Mr Panton. . . .

Sunday 12 August.   Rode over the sands of Red Wharf Bay to the village of Llandona and ascended to a high point on which is an old fortification called Bwrdd Arthur[33] (Pennant, vol 2, p. 264) . . . adjoining the outward walls are the signs of *cyttiau* but other objects of discovery attracted my attention and recalled [*to*] me to our British villages in Wiltshire when Mr Lloyd remarked that coins had been found on this spot. My friend Fenton on that very instant exclaimed 'Here is one' and picked up a small Roman coin of —. Immediately afterwards I found a small fragment of red Samian pottery. . . . The area of this camp bears a very singular appearance having its surface bare to the very bone from the continual paring of the turf for fuel which has exposed the structure of limestone, and to this circumstance we are indebted for our Roman discoveries.

Note. It is truly interesting and satisfactory to me to find the system I had formed on our Wiltshire downs so corroborated in the Welsh mountains. *There* we find excavations in the smooth surface of the maiden down and religious circles surrounded with a neat *agger* of earth. Here we find the same excavations and the same circles surrounded with stones differing only in their materials; but telling the same story and marking the same aera and the exalted residence of the same early inhabitants. . . .

Monday 12 [13] August.   This morning was devoted to British antiquities on the banks of the Menai. Our place of *rendez-vous* was Plas Gwyn, the

residence of the Rev. Mr Rowlands, son of the author of *Mona Antiqua*.[34] In
our way thither we visited the church of Penymynydd in which is a rich and
finely sculptured tomb of alabaster. . . . Descended to the shores of the
Menai and rode along it to a little bay where it is supposed the Romans
under their leader, Suetonius, in the reign of the Emperor Claudius, crossed
the streights of Menai. This place still retains the name of Pant yr Yscraphicion,
the Valley of the Skiffs . . . between Porthamel House and the Menai and
nearly facing the Gaer or Dinas on the Caernarvon coast are the evident
signs of a British village, numerous *cyttiau* surrounded by an agger etc. . . .
on the left of the road is Caer Leb[35] which Rowland described as moated but
I think improperly. It is a square work with a double *agger* of earth, the
vestiges of some building at the angle and not of the remotest antiquity. . . .
Homewards to Bryn-celli where there is a most curious monument of
antiquity.[36] In a clover field are the vestiges of two large *carnedds*, one of
which I conclude, is that mentioned by Rowland, page 94, fig 3 as having
been mutilated. Of the other he says nothing. . . . It did not however escape
the attention of Mr Pennant who mentions it vol. 2 page 272. This *kistvaen*
is subterraneous and covered by a *carnedd* which is overgrown with
brushwood. A narrow and low adit through a narrow passage led us into the
centre which is a room of about 9 feet diameter, vaulted at top by two stones
. . . . [*Pennant*] says 'that along the sides of this room was a stone bench, on
which were found human bones which fell to dust almost at a touch'. We
did not notice this peculiarity. . . . This is evidently a *kistvaen*, and one of
very peculiar construction and magnificence. . . .

Tuesday 13 August.   The first place we visited this morning was Llanbedr
Goch church. . . .

Thursday 15 August.   Rode to Amlwch under the guidance of I. Williams
Prichard, a most intelligent farmer of this neighborhood. . . . In a field
behind the [*Llanallgo*] church some Roman urns and coins have been
found. . . . Lugwy: close to the road leading to the quondam mansion house
is a gigantic *kistvaen*, the largest I have yet seen. . . .[37] In a wood adjoining
the farmhouse are some fine British antiquities but so obscured by wood
that their extent and plan cannot be ascertained. . . .[38] Cross the sands of
Dulas Bay and then ascend; a fine extensive view. See on the right the seat of
Mr Hughes, the *Croesus of Cambria*. Small inclosure, furze hedges but little
wheat. Amlwch. Its port is distant a mile from the town . . . the color of the
rocks attracts the eye; a regular stratum to such a height is tinged with bright
orange and above it the rock assumes a pea-green color. These tinges (owing
to the copper) are extended to some distance on the shore [*p. 186*]. . . .

Friday 16 August.   On our return home visited the Paris mines [*p. 186*], a
detailed account of which will be found in Pennant, vol 2, page 276. The
first aspect of this mountain strikes you with horror, from its barren
appearance and the first look into the chasm of the mine must strike

everyone with astonishment. The artist and colorist will view this interior with rapture and his pencil will hardly know where to begin as where to end. Never saw more majestic scenery than the interior of these mines affords. The fantastic shapes of the rocks and caverns assume a peculiar character of beauty from the vivid tints of the stone, and heightened by the machinery and engines employed in these works. But the bustle which in my last visit prevailed here and the continued thunder of the blasts no longer pervade these caverns . . . fewer hands and engines are employed. This tract is divided into two mines, the Mona and the Parys. The whole of the former belongs to Lord Uxbridge and one half of the latter; the remainder is the property of Mr Hughes, the *Croesus of Cambria*. The Mona mine does not in general present so terrific or picturesque a view, except in one adit where the masses of rock are truly grand and the colors truly beautiful. The sulphureous vapors of these mines in former days infected the whole neighborhood and put a total check to vegetation, but since the smoke has been confined and converted into sulphur these impediments are removed. And the neighborhood of Amlwch yields the most luxuriant crops of wheat etc imaginable. . . .

Sunday 19th. August. Quitted the friendly mansion of Plas Gwyn and rested this day at Bangor Ferry.

Monday 20th August. In our way to Capel Curig we visited Lady Penrhyn's slate quarries where the *arcana* were ably explained to us by the Superintendent . . . and ascended to Idwal Pool at the foot of Llyn Ogwen. . . . The same unfavourable weather which had driven us away before from Capel Curig again received us and confined us for the first three days to our fireside, the more mortifying as we saw clear weather in the vale below. . . . The *iters* left for us led towards the mountains which are accessible only in fine weather. . . .

My last *iter* was the Vale of Llanberris, a precious morsel reserved for a *bonne bouche* and *finale*. And considering the trouble and danger of reaching it through its tremendous pass it ought to repay us . . . the winding steep hill which leads you through the pass into the Vale of Llanberris. Here all vegetation (I mean trees) ceases. The character of savage wildness pervades the whole scenery. Towering rocks, deep chasms like craters, huge disjointed fragments fallen from above and by far the largest I have ever seen, a rapid babbling brook etc, etc excite amazement and almost horror. But the powers of the pen must here give way to those of the pencil; nor can these pourtray the grandeur or communicate the effect which every feeling eye must experience on viewing these sublime works of the Creator. When in sight of the lakes of Llanberis and Dolbadarn Castle I halted, having visited them in a former tour from Caernarvon. But my friend prolonged his ride to them, and the pencil most fully employed my time.

We returned, men and horses, safe and sound to Capel Curig, and on *Sunday 26th* we parted company and I returned to Vachdeiliog.

[*There is no journal later than 1810 in either the quarto or folio volumes, and Hoare apparently did not go to Wales in 1811 or 1812 but he is recorded as being in Wales in 1813 and in 1816*[39]]

NOTES

The abbreviation SC *(State Care)* means the structure is now in the custody of either the Department of the Environment or Welsh Office and if followed by an asterisk it means there is an official guidebook or pamplet. The most useful guidebooks are Pevsner's *Buildings of England* and Howell and Beazley's *Companion Guides for Wales.* Watkin, 1982, was published after going to press.

Introduction

1   Greig, 1925, p. 229.
2   Woodbridge, 1970, p. 251.
3   Nichols, 1840.
4   *The Stourhead Heirlooms,* 1883 and 1887.
5   Nichols, 1840, pp. 447-8.
6   *Cardiff Free Library. . .,* 1888, p. 7.
7   Mr G.A.C. Dart, County Librarian, in a letter of 7th July, 1981 tells me that three purchases are recorded: 1887 (from Sotheby's), 1902 (direct or indirect from Maggs Bros), 1925 (from the National Museum of Wales). He thinks the quarto volumes were acquired in 1887 and the folios in 1925. When or where the folios were burnt is uncertain; the repairs are thought to have been done in the City Library. A puzzling point is that when Fisher was working on Fenton's manuscripts (published 1917) in the City Library he makes no reference to the Hoare journals, although Fenton of course refers to Hoare being in his company. Surely he would have compared the two if Hoare's MSS were available?
The following is a rough concordance between the quarto and folio volumes, bearing in mind that the leaves in some folio volumes are misplaced, particularly in volumes II and III.

Quarto/MS.3.127	Folio/MS.4.302
I 1801	1802
II 1802	1793, 1796, 1797, part 1810, Rivers and Lakes of Wales.
III 1793, 1803 (separate pagination)	1798, 1799, 1804 ?, 1808, part 1810
IV 1806 (Ireland)	1801
V 1800 (N. England)	1800 (N. England)
VI 1796, 1797, 1798, 1799 (continuous pagination); 1810 (separate pagination)	1793 (small folio, not by Hoare)

8   Hoare, 1818.
9   Woodbridge, 1970.
10   Nichols, 1840, pp. xii-iii.
11   Hoare, 1807, p. xvii. For tourists in general see Moir 1964; for Wilson and earlier artists in Wales see Solkin, 1982.
12   Gosse, 1884, I, p. 276.
13   Gilpin, 1973.
14   Gilpin, 1792.
15   Boswell, 1950, II pp. 195, 197.
16   Pennant, 1778 and 1784.
17   Hoare, 1806, I, footnote on pp. v-vi.
18   Wyndham, 1781; Coxe, 1801, p. iv.
19   Hoare, 1807, p. iv, footnote.

20   Powel, 1584.
21   Nichols, 1840, p. 478.
22   Fisher, 1922, p. 90.
23   Burke, 1958; for Gordale Scar see Nygren, 1982.
24   Marshall, 1795.
25   Price, 1810, I, p. 22; for modern accounts of the picturesque see Hussey, 1927; Nygren, 1982; Watkin 1982.
26   Price, 1810, I pp. 50-53.
27   Price, 1810, I, pp. 88-89.
28   Coxe, 1801, II, 227 *et seq.*
29   Woodbridge, 1970, p. 128.
30   Gosse, 1884, I, pp. 295-302.
31   Turner, 1974, p. 37.
32   Woodbridge, 1970, p. 104.
33   Woodbridge, 1970, pp. 172-75. Hoare was a patron of John Carter, the main opponent of restoration.
34   Wyndham, 1781, p. i.
35   Hoare, 1804.
36   Hoare, 1806.
37   Hoare, 1807.
38   MS. 4.302, vol. II, p. 102.
39   Hoare, 1807, pp. 314-16.

Chapter I — 1793

1   The Old Passage was near the present motorway suspension bridge; the New Passage was further south, roughly on the line of the railway tunnel.
2   General William Roy (1726-1790), founder of the Ordnance Survey.
3   The road is still very narrow, but one can hardly speak of precipices.
4   Can Giraldus have meant the winter sun? Llanthony Abbey, SC*.
5   Recent road-straightening has allowed full exposure of the mound and three chambers of this long barrow at Gwernvale; see *Antiquity*, LIII (1979), pp. 132-34.
6   SC*.
7   Nash-Williams, 1950, No. 68.
8   SC*.
9   SC*.
10   SC.
11   SC*.
12   SC*.
13   SC*.
14   Carreg Coetan, now on a housing estate. SC.
15   This point had been made by Wyndham (1781, pp. 130-32).
16   The first meeting with Richard Fenton, see p. 28. The handsome house built for himself at Fishguard still survives as the 'Glyn y Mel' guest house.
17   Hoare seems to be more influenced by Giraldus than his own observation.
18   St Davids was not a monastery in the high middle ages. See note 36 in Chapter VIII for Loretto.
19   SC*.
20   Hut circles within a promontory fort.
21   This supposed resemblance of a rock to a Druid's head is a fair indication of Sir Richard's state of mind!
22   The ruins of the Augustinian Priory by the river have recently been taken into care by the Welsh Office.
23   SC*.

24 SC.
25 Mr R. Kennedy, Curator of Haverfordwest Museum, has pointed out to me that the word *eligug* is derived from the Welsh word for guillemot, *heligog*, in spite of Camden's view that this was an English word (Gibson, 1695, *c* 640). Elegug Stacks are marked at SR.931944 by the Ordnance Survey. The south Pembrokeshire coast is famous for its sea birds, see Fenton, 1811, p. 411.
26 Both castles SC, and Llansteffan SC*.
27 SC*.
28 Nash-Williams, 1950, No. 212.
29 These and other crosses from the area are now assembled at the old school at Margam, SC*.

Chapter II—1796

1 'Cone wheat', perhaps spelt wheat.
2 SC*.
3 Cross and abbey SC*.
4 See Watkin, 1982, p. 112 and for Hafod pp. 99-101.
5 See note 4 above, and p. 200.

Chapter III — 1797

1 Sir John Leicester (see pp. 60, 77 etc) who lived at Tabley Hall, Cheshire; Hoare had met him in Italy and he was a particular friend with whom he often stayed and who was sometimes his travelling companion. Leicester like Hoare was a patron of Turner.
2 The figure is that of his son, Edward II. The castle SC*.
3 The Menai Strait; in Welsh it is usually referred to as a river, Afon Menai.
4 Recently acquired by the National Trust.
5 The present Penrhyn Castle, owned by the National Trust, also in the form of a castle, was not erected until 30 years after this.
6 John Williams (1582-1650), Archbishop of York, took a prominent part in Welsh affairs during the Civil War.
7 Polygonal rather than square. Conwy SC*.
8 The bridge possibly attributable to Jones but the lower chapel definitely not.
9 A castle mound.
10 SC*.
11 Laura's Tower on the mound, part of the 'modernising' by Telford; see Pevsner, Shropshire, 265.
12 Millraces rather than waterfalls.
13 Now removed to a park; see Pevsner, Herefordshire, p. 228.
14 See Woodridge, 1970, pp. 172-5.
15 Presumably Tuesday 1st August.
16 SC*.
17 The traditional boat trip from Ross to Chepstow, made by Wordsworth at about this time and prompting his famous poem. Hoare later wrote of this trip '. . . In my early youth I made the tour of the River Wye and the remembrance of its beauties had not faded from my recollection' (MS. 4/302/11.f. 58).
18 SC*.
19 SC*.
20 SC*.
21 The medieval castle is still largely intact.
22 SC*.

23   The bridge was built in 1756 and designed by William Edwards.
24   The Merthyr Canal had recently been constructed to carry the iron produced at Merthyr to the outport at Cardiff.
25   SC*.
26   ? '. . . range of ruined stables . . . of the Royalist Cavalry during the Civil War. . .' Howell and Beazley, 1977, p. 278.
27   Nash-Williams, 1970, pp. 139-44.
28   John Kyrle (1637-1724), benefactor of town; see Pope's *Moral Essays*, Epistle III.

Chapter IV — 1798

1   See note 1 of chapter III.
2   Now National Trust.
3   SC. Wrought iron gates made by Davies Brothers in 1711-20, now at the outer entry to the park.
4   Telford's Chirk aqueduct, masonry with an iron trough, on the Llangollen Canal. The second was Telford's major work, Pontcysyllte, nearer Llangollen, and contrary to Hoare's remark much longer.
5   SC*.
6   SC*.
7   The Roman legionary fortress has recently been explored by Professor W. Manning.
8   SC. Fig. 2.
9   SC*.
10   SC*.
11   SC*.
12   Hoare's drawing in Fig. 20.
13   SC*.
14   SC*.
15   Wyndham, 1781, pp. 15-16. Perhaps a vaulted sewer like that recently discovered near the Bull Inn.

Chapter V — 1799

1   A dining club that met at the Deptford Inn, Warminster.
2   For circumstances of the move see the guidebook to Llanthony Prima, Gwent.
3   Now in the church; see Howell and Beazley, 1977, pp. 193-4.
4   Sir Richard seems to have preferred to share a double room with his son or friend.
5   Howell and Beazley, 1977, p. 199.
6   Now owned by Newport Borough Council.
7   Howell and Beazley, 1977, p. 211.
8   The reason for Sir Richard's fleeting return to Stourhead is not explained; he had presumably been accompanied by Coxe in Monmouthshire.
9   Payne Knight and Price were the principal champions of the Picturesque, although interpreting or explaining it in very different ways. The catalogue associated with the exhibition mounted by Manchester University in 1982 gives details of Knight's life and views with a detailed account of Downton Castle in chapter 3; Clarke and Penny, 1982. He designed the house himself. Hoare's suggestion that the 'rotunda' was based on the Pantheon at Stourhead is of interest. Compare Hoare's visit to Price's property at Foxley where he was shown over by the owner, p. 200.
10   SC*, recently more fully revealed.
11   National Trust. Quarrying has altered, and is altering, the shape of the Breidden.
12   See note 4, chapter IV and Fig. 3.

13 SC*.
14 SC*.

Chapter VI — 1800

1   The figure on the three-way bridge has presumably come from the abbey after the Dissolution.
2   The famous 15th century inn is still in use, owned by Trust House/Forte Ltd.
3   Open fields have survived to the present day in this area in the famous example at Laxton.
4   Most of the Norman buildings in this graphic description still survive.
5   The Newport Arch, still in use, is here referred to.
6   SC*.
7   SC*.
8   Sir Richard's experiments and explanation of the natural origin of Brimham rocks are revealing of his attitude towards practical experiment.
9   Gosse, 1884, I, pp. 276-7. Hoare's version differs slightly; for Gordale Sear see Nygren, 1982.
10 See Pevsner, West Riding, p. 443. A church was built there in 1837-8.
11 Presumably Malham Tarn House.
12 The fifteenth century Devil's Bridge — Hoare apparently did not know the name.
13 Thomas West (1720-1779) published his guide to the Lakes in 1778. See Watkin, 1982 pp. 109-10. Richard Watson (1737-1816). Fellow of Trinity College, Cambridge. Chemist and tract writer.
14 By the edge of which the Wordsworths had taken up residence the year before. Gosse, 1889, I, p. 256.
15 The reference is to Sir James Radcliffe (1689-1716), third Earl of Derwentwater, who supported the Old Pretender in 1715 and was executed in the following year.
16 Lord Gordon's villa was no doubt the model for Fach Ddeiliog by Lake Bala.
17 This and Mayborough SC.
18 Lowther Castle was rebuilt by Smirke six years later.
19 See Pevsner, Westmorland, p. 288; some stones of the avenue and circle survive.
20 SC*.
21 SC*.
22 Pevsner, Westmorland, p. 220.
23 Appleby is not identified as a Roman station by OS map of Roman Britain.
24 SC.
25 The Roman fort of *Virosidum*.
26 SC.
27 SC*.
28 SC*.
29 SC*.
30 SC*.
31 SC*.
32 SC*.
33 Normally regarded as a place for the display of the saint's relics.
34 Now burnt down but stable block survives.
35 SC*.
36 The tower was erected by Marmaduke Huby, Abbot 1494-1526.
37 Known as the Devil's Arrows.
38 I have not traced the comparison but in the *Tour* Defoe regarded York as the finest medieval cathedral: Defoe, 1962, p. 230.
39 Milton, *Il Penseroso*, I, 161.
40 Apparently the 'multiangular tower', a Roman work, is referred to.

41 John Watson (1725-83), Fellow of Brasenose College, Oxford, published '*The History and Antiquities . . . Halifax*' 1775.
42 Knight had made a particular point about lake edges in his poem, *The Landscape*.
43 Kedleston was designed by Brettingham, Paine and Robert Adam.
44 See note 1 of Chapter III.

Chapter VII — 1801

1 William Cunnington (1754-1810) who in the remaining years of his life was to excavate barrows for Hoare; see Cunnington, 1975.
2 Thomas Leman (1751-1826) played a large part in the archeological researches in Wiltshire. He was at this time Chancellor of Cloyne (1796-1802) and was with William Bennet (1746-1820), Bishop of Cloyne (1794-1820). Both men were Fellows of Emmanuel College Cambridge and very active antiquaries.
3 Tsar Paul ll assassinated 11th March 1801.
4 Claude of Lorraine (1600-82) whose work was central to the theory of the picturesque. Jan Both (c. 1618-82), influenced by Claude.
5 The battle took place on 2nd April, 1801.
6 SC.
7 Just built by Thomas Telford.
8 The bridge SC, but the ironworks etc now an extensive museum.
9 Before the remedial works, when Hoare visited, it had only a single arch.
10 Wenlock Abbey SC*. Hoare is speaking of the chapter house.
11 The abbey SC*; the iron bridge, now demolished, was designed by Telford, and had been built five years before. Pevsner, Shropshire, p. 90.
12 SC*.
13 Attingham Hall, just built.
14 The medieval tower was retained when the church was rebuilt in 1793-5; Pevsner, Shropshire, p. 256.
15 The Welsh Bridge had been rebuilt by the same architects as rebuilt St Alkmunds Church.
16 The second aqueduct is Telford's major work of Pontcysyllte.
17 Possibly steps were taken to start the construction of Fach Ddeiliog during this fortnight when there is no record.
18 SC*.
19 SC*.
20 Chapel over well SC.
21 SC*.
22 The castle, the ruined church (Leicester's church) and the surviving tower of the 'modern' church now SC*.
23 Literally 'Helen's Causeway', Helen presumably being not the Emperor Constantine's mother but the wife of Magnus Maximus.
24 Richard Wilson (1714-82). See Solkin, 1982.
25 SC*.
26 The Roman fort at Caerhun excavated by P.K. Baillie Reynolds in 1926-30 and recorded in the volumes of *Archaeologia Cambrensis* of those years; the bath building between the fort and the river was what had been excavated at the time of Sir Richard's visit. See also pp. 250, 253.
27 SC*.
28 SC*.
29 Baron Hill, now derelict, built 1776-9 by Samuel Wyatt (1737-1807): Colvin, 1954, p. 735.
30 Hen Drefor; Daniel, 1950, p. 187.
31 Hoare is presumably describing an eletrolytic process.
32 Hen Walia, not SC but Segontium and the castle SC*.

33   SC*.
34   W.A. Madocks (1774-1828) had started his imbanking operations; his name is com-
     memorated in the Welsh place names Porthmadog and Tremadog.
35   Dinas Emrys, a native Welsh castle.
36   SC.
37   Now the Chepstow Racecourse. For Hawkstone see Watkin, 1982, pp. 73-5.
38   Knight, 1794, I, lines 79-82.
39   Knight, 1794, II, lines 1-6. Popes *Moral Essays, Ep. IV*, 117.
40   SC.
41   James Wyatt (1746-1813), who did the work at Lichfield in 1788-95.

Chapter VIII — 180?

1   For Avebury see Hoare, 1806, 11, pt. 1, pp. 55-96. Although Hoare had not yet replaced
     Coxe as the presumed author the decision to write an History of Wiltshire had by now
     been reached and hence the interest.
2   In 1797; Hoare, 1812, I, p. 148.
3   William Stukeley (1687-1765), the famous antiquary.
4   The current Ordnance Survey Map of Roman Britain is only unable to identify *Spinis*. Sir
     Richard dealt with the Roman roads in Wiltshire in Hoare, 1812, II, pt. 2.
5   See Note 2, Chapter VII.
6   *Magnis* is put at Kenchester by OS. Map of Roman Britain.
7   Mr (later Sir) Uvedale Price who, with Payne Knight, was the main protagonist of the
     Picturesque.
8   This year Hoare made a deliberate effort to follow the route of Giraldus who had hitherto
     been only a guide; now an edition of the translation was clearly in mind.
9   One of these on the west side of the river appears to be an earlier Norman motte.
10   Evidently Admiral John Gell, died 1806. Cf. Fisher, 1917, pp. 26-27.
11   See note 7 of chapter I.
12   Evidently one of his step brothers.
13   The incumbent at Newport, an antiquary who gave Hoare much help.
14   The first Marquess of Bute; the major alterations were made by the third Marquess in the
     second half of the 19th century.
15   SC*. Painted by Turner.
16   The town and castle of Kenfig were overwhelmed in the later Middle Ages by the sand
     dunes that are such a feature of the South Welsh coast.
17   The ancient crosses in this area have been collected in the old school by the church at
     Margam; SC*.
18   Altered shortly afterwards, see page 242.
19   The 'noble greenhouse' survives and is known as the Orangery, but the 'noble con-
     servatory', then used for the orange trees, no longer exists.
20   SC*. By 'ichonography' Hoare means ground plan.
21   Attributed to Bishop Henry of Gower.
22   Presumably the surviving Spwdwr Bridge, now out of use for traffic.
23   SC*.
24   Demolished in the 1930's after being weakened by flooding.
25   Hoare did not appreciate that the Roman town, Old Carmarthen, lay just to the east of
     the medieval town at the walls of which he was looking.
26   Sir Richard Steele (1672-1729) spent his last years on his wife's property at Llangunnor
     and died at Carmarthen 1st September 1729.
27   SC*.
28   SC.
29   SC*.
30   Salvator Rosa (1615-73), the Neapolitan painter whose work played a key part in the
     Picturesque.

31   Marine fish, John Dory, usually associated with Cornwall and Devon.
32   Hywel Dda, Prince of Deheubarth before 915; his code of laws belongs to the time between 943 when he established rule over most of Wales and his death in 950.
33   Now SC, since 1982.
34   For the creation of the town of Milford Haven see Howell and Beazley, South Wales, 1977, pp. 122-4.
35   This is legendary, attributable mainly to Geoffrey of Monmouth.
36   Loretto owes its existence to the legend of the Holy House and its main industry was pilgrimage; the city of Palmyra in Syria after immense prosperity was destroyed by the Emperor Aurelian in 273 AD.
37   The chapter house erected in 1791-3 was demolished in 1829 and similarly the west front of the cathdral was altered again by Gilbert Scott.
38   SC*. Bishop Henry of Gower rebuilt the Palace.
39   The French evidently thought the Welsh population would rise to support them.
40   Gibson, 1695, pp. 638-9.
41   SC*.
42   SC*.
43   The site of the earlier castle.
44   Gibson, 1695, pp. 643-4; Nash-Williams, 1959, Nos. 115-20.
45   OS Roman Britain identifies *Luentinum* with Dolaucothi and *Bremia* with Llanio. Could the parson of Llandewi Brefi have been mildly joking at Sir Richard's mispronunciation of the Welsh?
46   It was. SC*.
47   Nash-Williams, 1950, pp. 95-6, fig. 89.

Chapter IX — 1803-09

1   Happily very substantial remains still survive both at Llanthony and Margam. Both SC*.
2   Error in date continued until 31st May.
3   SC*.
4   Browne Willis (1682-1760), antiquary, who published accounts of cathedrals.
5   For full account of Barry Island, now occupied by a holiday camp, see J.K. Knight, Excavations at St Barruc's Chapel, Barry Island, Glamorganshire, *Reports and Transactions of the Cardiff Naturalists' Society*, XCIX (1976-8), pp. 28-76.
6   SC* Entirely rebuilt by William Burges 75 years later.
7   Theophilus Jones (1758-1812), author of the *History of Brecknock (1805-09)*.
8   Henry Wharton (1664-95), published *Anglia Sacra* (lives of English bishops up to 1540) in 1691.
9   See note 45 to Chapter VIII.
10   SC*.
11   The Roman fort at SO 169219, Pen y Gaer, is referred to.
12   Nash-Williams, 1954, No. 54. Now built into church wall at Llanfihangel Cwmdu.
13   Daniel, 1950, p. 214; see also *Archaeologia Cambrensis*, LXXX (1981), pp. 131-39.
14   *RCAHM*, Merionethshire, p. 65 (171E). A bar of twisted gold to fit round the neck. See note 26 in chapter VII.
15   SC. A small Roman coastal fort or harbour, now enclosing the churchyard.
16   The site has been acquired recently by the National Trust.
17   See note 45, chapter VIII.
18   Possibly the packhorse bridge at Pont Minllyn, SC, or the little vehicular bridge nearer Mallwyd, both said to have been erected by the Welsh lexicographer, John Davies, who was Rector of Mallwyd, 1604-08.
19   Mediolanum is located at Whitchurch, Shropsire, and *Mediomanum* at Caersws nr Llanidloes, by the Ordnance Survey.
20   Not the present Kinmel Hall built by Nesfield in the 1870's.

Chapter X — 1810

The restricted area covered this year was I have suggested (p. 29) intended to have been the basis for a 'historical journey'. It happens also to be the area that has been most thoroughly surveyed by the Royal Commission on Ancient and Historical Monuments, in Anglesey just before the war and in Caernarvonshire in the years following the war, so that there are detailed descriptions in their volumes of most of the structures mentioned by Hoare. There is a detailed journal of the same journey by Fenton in Fisher, 1917, pp. 158-268. I have reduced Hoare's descriptions very severely.

1   Ysbytty Ifan owes its name to the precentory of the Order of St John of Jerusalem founded in the twelth century; its church became parochial after the Dissolution but was demolished in 1860. *RCAHM*, Denbighshire, pp. 187-8.
2   SC*.
3   Paul Sandby (1725-1809), water-colour painter and engraver. He started his topographical drawing earlier than Hoare. Introduced the aquatint process into England.
4   See note 23 of chapter VII.
5   SC*.
6   Called Bryn-y-gefeiliau on the OS Roman Britain map.
7   Edward Lhuyd (1660-1709), Keeper of the Ashmolean 1690-1709.
8   Although a new church was built in the last century the old church happily survives and is still in use.
9   See note 26 on Caerhun in chapter VII.
10 To judge by drawing not a very close resemblance.
11 This type of *chevaus of frise* is known from some hill-forts in SW Wales.
12 The site of modern Llandudno which is a Victorian foundation. See Beazley and Howell, N. Wales, p. 167.
13 See note 9. Hoare seems to have been especially attracted by the Roman remains, no doubt because this was the only fort in Wales where excavations had taken place. The 'villa' was the garrison's bath house.
14 The modern student has both the descriptions in the Royal Commission's Inventory and the official guidebook to help him.
15 The top of the hill including the hill-fort was quarried away between the wars.
16 See note 7.
17 The present structure was put up later. See note 5, Chater III.
18 Fenton's reading (Fisher, 1917, pp. 214-15) quoted by the Royal Commission, of this lost milestone: *RCAHM*, Caernarvonshire, II, lxiii.
19 The Commission did not share Hoare's view that Dinas Dinorwig was a work of two distinct periods; *RCAHM*, Caernarvonshire, II, pp. 175-6.
20 Modern opinion attributes the design to Master James of St George, the Savoyard responsible for the principal Welsh castles of Edward I, but it took longer to build than the others and was not even complete in 1325! See official guidebook.
21 The figure is that of Edward II (its erection being recorded) presumably holding the sceptre and orb!
22 The mound is thought to be the remains of the Norman motte erected by Hugh Earl of Chester in the eleventh century.
23 See note 34, chapter VII.
24 The proposed development was not a success.
25 See *RCAHM*, Caernarvonshire, III. pp. 69-73 for details.
26 Daniel, 1950, p. 192, Nos. 9 and 7.
27 Ibid.
28 *RCAHM*, Caernarvonshire, 11, 189-190.
29 These remains have now vanished; *RCAHM*, Anglesey, 66-67.
30 Ibid., 123-24.
31 Dovecote and conventual buildings of Priory SC. *RCAHM*, Anglesey, pp. 119-25.

32   Henblas, since demolished.
33   *RCAHM*, Anglesey, pp. 82-83.
34   Henry Rowlands (1655-1723), cleric and antiquary of Anglesey.
35   SC. *RCAHM*, Anglesey, p. 103.
36   SC*.
37   SC. Daniel, 1950, p. 188.
38   SC. RCAHM, Anglesey, pp. 133-35.
39   Fisher, 1917, pp. 132-3 clearly indicates that the two men were together in North Wales
      in 1816. Hoare is not specifically mentioned in 1813 but Mr Woodbridge's notes from
      other sources shows that Sir Richard was in Wales in July and August, 1813. The two men
      were together in Wales in 1804, 1808, 1810 (both left large journals), 1813 and 1816.
      Fenton did not accompany Hoare to Ireland in 1806, and he travelled in Wales without
      Hoare in 1809. Prior to 1804, apart from his son, Coxe or occasionally Sir John Leicester
      were Hoare's travelling companions in Wales. There is no doubt about the closeness of
      the friendship ('Parted with Sir Richard Hoare and felt an awkward blank' — Fisher, p.
      149) but Fisher's remarks on page ix are a little exaggerated; one need only compare
      Hoare's remarks on his nostalgia for travelling with Coxe before he joined up with Fenton
      in 1808 (p. 242).

WORKS CITED

Boswell, J., *Life of Johnson* (Everyman's Edition) 2 vols. (London, 1950).
Burke, E., *A Philosophical Enquiry into the Origin of our Ideas of the Sublimbe and the Beautiful*. Edited with an introduction by J.T. Boulton (London, 1958).
The Cardiff Free Library, Museum and Science and Art Schools, 26th Annual Report of 1887–8 (Cardiff, 1888).
Clarke, M. and Penny, N. (ed.), *The Arrogant Connoisseur; Richard Payne Knight, 1751–1824* (Manchester, 1982).
Colvin, H.M., *A Biographical Dictionary of British Architects, 1660–1890* (London, 1954).
Coxe, W., *An Historical Tour in Monmouthshire* (London, 1801).
Cunnington, R.H., *From Antiquary to Archaeologist, a Biography of William Cunnington*, (Prince's Risborough, 1975).
Daniel, G.E., *The Prehistoric Chamber Tombs of England and Wales* (Cambridge, 1950).
Fenton, R., *An Historical Tour through Pembrokeshire* (London, 1811).
Fisher, J. (ed.), *Tours in Wales* (1804–13) by Richard Fenton, edited from his MS Journals in the Cardiff Free Library. Cambrian Arch. Ass., Sup. Vol. 1917.
Gibson, E. (ed.), *Camden's Britannia* (London, 1695).
Gilpin, W., *Observations on the River Wye*. Reprinted by S. Lyell (Richmond, 1973).
Gilpin, W., *Three Essays: on Picturesque Beauty; on Picturesque Travel; and on Sketching Landscape* . . . (London, 1792).
Gosse, E. (ed.), *The Works of Thomas Gray in Prose and Verse* 4 vols. (London, 1884).
Greig, J. (ed.), *The Farington Diary*, V (London, 1925).
Hoare, Sir R.C., *Recollections Abroad 1790, 1791* (Bath, 1818).
Hoare, Sir R.C., *Itinerarium Cambriae . . . Geraldo Cambrehse. Cum annotationibus Davidis Poweli* (London, 1804).
Hoare, Sir R.C., *The Itinerary of Archbishop Baldwin through Wales, AD MCLXXXVIII, by Giraldus de Barri*, translated into English and illustrated with views, annotations and a life of Giraldus (London, 1806).
Hoare, Sir R.C., *Journal of a Tour in Ireland AD 1806* (London and Dublin, 1807).
Hoare, Sir R.C., *The Ancient History of Wiltshire* 2 vols. (London, 1812–21).
Hoare, Sir R.C., *The History of Modern Wiltshire* (London, 1822–44).

Howell, P. and Beazley, E., *The Companion Guides to North and South Wales*, 2 vols. (London, 1977).

Hussey, C., *The Picturesque: Studies in a Point of View* (London, 1927).

Knight, R.P., *The Landscape, A Didactic Poem in Three Books Addressed to Uvedale Price* (London, 1794).

Knight, R.P., *An Analytical Inquiry into the Principles of Taste*, 3 vols. 3rd Ed. (London, 1806).

Marshall, W., *A Review of the Landscape . . . A Practical Treatise* (London, 1794).

Moir, E., *The Discovery of Britain: The English Tourists*, 1540–1840 (London, 1964).

Nash Williams, E., *The Early Christian Monuments of Wales* (Cardiff, 1950).

Nichols, J.B., *Catalogue of the Hoare Library at Stourhead, County Wilts.* (London, 1840).

Nygren, E.J., *James Ward's Gordale Scar: An Essay in the Sublime* (London, 1982).

Pennant, T., *A Tour in Scotland* (Chester, 1771).

Pennant, T., *A Tour in Wales, 1773*, 2 vols. (Chester, 1778–84).

Pevsner, Sir N., *Buildings of England*. County Series (Hamondsworth, 1951–74).

Powel, D., *The Historie of Cambria* (London, 1584) . . . A new edition (London, 1774).

Price, U., *Essays on the Picturesque, as compared with the Sublime and the Beautiful and on the Use of Studying Pictures for the Purpose of Improving the Real Landscape*. 2nd Edition. 3 vols. (London, 1810).

The Royal Commission on Ancient and Historical Monuments in Wales, Inventories of,

Solkin, D.H., *Richard Wilson: the Landscape of Reaction* (London, 1982).

The Stourhead Heirlooms: Catalogue of the Library Removed from Stourhead which will be sold by auction by Messr Sotheby, Wilkinson and Hodge . . . on Monday the 30th July 1883 and the Seven Following Days . . . .

The Stourhead Heirlooms: Catalogue of the Remaining Portion of the Library Removed from Stourhead including the Publications and Manuscripts of Sir Richard Colt Hoare, Bart. . . . which will be sold by auction on Friday 9th of December 1887. . . .

Turner, 1775–1851, Catalogue of the Exhibition at the Royal Academy, 1974–75 (London, 1974).

Watkin, D., *The English Vision: The Picturesque in Architecture, Landscape and Garden Design* (London, 1982).

Woodbridge, E., *Landscape and Antiquity, Aspects of English Culture at Stourhead, 1718–1838.* (Oxford, 1970).

Wyndham, H.P., *A Tour through Monmouthshire and Wales, made in the months of June and July 1774 and in the Months of June, July and August 1777*. 2nd Ed. (Salisbury, 1781).

INDEX

This index is primarily of proper and place-names with only a few subject entries; the Preface and Notes are not included. Page numbers of illustrations are shown in italic type. With geographical names a conventional rather than a purist Welsh or English version is used.